THE **COMPLETE**
IDIOT'S
GUIDE® TO

The Art of Songwriting

by Casey Kelly and David Hodge

ALPHA

A member of Penguin Group (USA) Inc.

ALPHA BOOKS

Published by the Penguin Group

Penguin Group (USA) Inc., 375 Hudson Street, New York, New York 10014, USA

Penguin Group (Canada), 90 Eglinton Avenue East, Suite 700, Toronto, Ontario M4P 2Y3, Canada (a division of Pearson Penguin Canada Inc.)

Penguin Books Ltd., 80 Strand, London WC2R 0RL, England

Penguin Ireland, 25 St. Stephen's Green, Dublin 2, Ireland (a division of Penguin Books Ltd.)

Penguin Group (Australia), 250 Camberwell Road, Camberwell, Victoria 3124, Australia (a division of Pearson Australia Group Pty. Ltd.)

Penguin Books India Pvt. Ltd., 11 Community Centre, Panchsheel Park, New Delhi—110 017, India

Penguin Group (NZ), 67 Apollo Drive, Rosedale, North Shore, Auckland 1311, New Zealand (a division of Pearson New Zealand Ltd.)

Penguin Books (South Africa) (Pty.) Ltd., 24 Sturdee Avenue, Rosebank, Johannesburg 2196, South Africa

Penguin Books Ltd., Registered Offices: 80 Strand, London WC2R 0RL, England

International Standard Book Number: 978-1-61564-1-031
Library of Congress Catalog Card Number: 2011901228

13   12   8   7   6   5

Interpretation of the printing code: The rightmost number of the first series of numbers is the year of the book's printing; the rightmost number of the second series of numbers is the number of the book's printing. For example, a printing code of 11-1 shows that the first printing occurred in 2011.

Printed in the United States of America

Note: This publication contains the opinions and ideas of its authors. It is intended to provide helpful and informative material on the subject matter covered. It is sold with the understanding that the authors and publisher are not engaged in rendering professional services in the book. If the reader requires personal assistance or advice, a competent professional should be consulted.

The authors and publisher specifically disclaim any responsibility for any liability, loss, or risk, personal or otherwise, which is incurred as a consequence, directly or indirectly, of the use and application of any of the contents of this book.

Most Alpha books are available at special quantity discounts for bulk purchases for sales promotions, premiums, fund-raising, or educational use. Special books, or book excerpts, can also be created to fit specific needs.

For details, write: Special Markets, Alpha Books, 375 Hudson Street, New York, NY 10014.

Publisher: *Marie Butler-Knight*
Associate Publisher: *Mike Sanders*
Executive Managing Editor: *Billy Fields*
Acquisitions Editor: *Tom Stevens*
Senior Development Editor: *Phil Kitchel*
Senior Production Editor: *Janette Lynn*
Copy Editor: *Andy Saff*
Cover Designer: *William Thomas*
Book Designers: *William Thomas, Rebecca Batchelor*
Indexer: *Julie Bess*
Layout: *Brian Massey*
Senior Proofreader: *Laura Caddell*

This book is dedicated to my good friend
Todd David Cerney,
writer of some of the
funniest, saddest, hardest-rocking and
most beautiful songs
ever.
—Casey Kelly

Contents

Introduction

Songs fill our world. Most often they float by without us giving them a second thought, lifting our moods, playing as a backdrop to our daily lives, and helping fill otherwise empty spaces of time when we're driving our cars, riding the elevator, or waiting on hold on the telephone. Even the songs we recognize and enjoy hearing go by without many listeners realizing that someone spent a lot of time composing the melodies and crafting the lyrics.

If songwriting's in your blood, however, the fact that someone wrote the song you're listening to is probably the first thing you think about. You notice the way the words go together, the way the story unfolds, the unusual rhymes and rhyme schemes, the chord changes, the unique musical touches, the overall sound, and many other things that other listeners take for granted.

Have you ever heard a song that was a big hit performed live by the songwriter who wrote it and experienced the obvious intimacy between the writer and the song, each word dripping with the truth of its intended meaning? It can be palpable. You feel it and perhaps it's moved you to want to make a statement that moves listeners the way that moment moved you.

You want to be a songwriter!

The Complete Idiot's Guide to the Art of Songwriting is a step-by-step guide designed to get you started writing your songs. Even if you've never written one before in your life, you should be able to follow along step by step and create a good song.

While trying to include everything you need to know, we've given the most weight to the aspects, concepts, and practices of songwriting that are, in our experience, the least understood and the hardest to discover on your own.

How This Book Is Organized

The Complete Idiot's Guide to the Art of Songwriting is set out in twenty-four chapters, which are arranged in five general parts. They are:

Part 1, Getting Yourself Ready, prepares you for your lifelong songwriting adventure. You will learn about the basic structures of songs, some helpful history, and observations about the many different musical genres songs can fall into. You'll also get help finding the inspiration to write terrific songs.

Part 2, Painting with Words, focuses on crafting great lyrics that are the heart and soul of most songs. You will learn how to turn your ideas into memorable lyrics that grab and hold your listeners' attention, and you'll discover the importance of making strong first impressions with your song's title and opening lines. You'll also read about how to make great choruses, verses, and bridges as well as get good tips on making sure you're getting the most songlike lyrics you can.

Part 3, Making Music, covers the music side of songs. Beginning with an incredibly easy introduction to the basics of music (notes and chords), you then get lessons in the three main musical components of songs: melody, harmony, and rhythm. Not only will you get a good overview of each component, but you'll also get to work on putting all the pieces together to make your songs sound great.

Part 4, Getting Better All the Time, helps you do just that by introducing you to the importance of rewriting and all the work you can do to improve your songs *after* you've written them. You also explore ways to constantly refresh and improve your songwriting abilities, both lyrically and musically; for example, you'll look at how co-writing and collaborating on music can help you improve as a songwriter. A discussion on making demos of your songs and a quick look at how songwriters use the Internet concludes this part.

Part 5, Going Pro, offers you invaluable knowledge if you should decide to try your hand at selling your songs in the musical marketplace. You'll learn how the music business works and how your songs earn money. You'll also get vital information on copyrights and some tips on the businesspeople whose experience you're likely to need.

At the end of the book, you will find two helpful appendixes: a glossary of various terms used throughout this book; and a list of books and other tutorial material, as well as online organizations and other songwriting communities where you will be able to meet with fellow writers.

Special Features

You'll also find even more advice and useful information in the numerous *sidebars* found throughout *The Complete Idiot's Guide to the Art of Songwriting*. There are four types of sidebars that appear in this book:

DEFINITION

These provide explanations and details of various musical and song-related terms.

TUNE TIPS

These offer you pointed/aimed pieces of advice or lore on various relevant topics, from finding inspiration to saving your song ideas to crafting great lyrics and music and more.

WRITER'S TALK

These are tips, guidance, and insight from some well-respected and successful songwriters in their own words.

SONG STORIES

These let you in on some interesting information about how specific songs were written.

In Part 3 of this book, you will find web icons that indicate that the example in question is available as an MP3 sound file on the "Book Extras" page at Alpha Books' website, which you can find here:

www.idiotsguides.com/artofsongwriting

If you right-click on any file and then select "save target as," you can download the audio file directly to your computer for later use. We hope that these music examples of chords, melodies, chord progressions, and ways of putting them together will be of help to you.

Acknowledgments

Books, like a lot of songs, are the result of collaboration. Both Casey and David want to thank their agent, Marilyn Allen, as well as all the staff of Alpha Books for making this book become a reality. Very special thanks especially go to Alpha's editors Tom Stevens and Phil Kitchel (who's also a great songwriter, by the way!) for all the time and energy, not to mention enthusiasm and patience, that they contributed to this project. And thanks to all the rest of the team at Alpha, including Marie Butler-Knight, Mike Sanders, Billy Fields, Janette Lynn, Andy Saff, William Thomas, Rebecca Batchelor, Julie Bess, Brian Massey, and Laura Caddell, we also express our gratitude.

Casey's Acknowledgments:

I'd also like to thank the many songwriters—Alex Call, Todd Cerney, Jeffrey Comanor, Paul Craft, Leslie Ellis, Ruthann Friedman, Sheldon Harnick, Liz Hengber, Larry Henley, Kenny Loggins, Pat and Pete Luboff, Ralph Murphy, Wood Newton, Don Schlitz, Sonny Throckmorton, and Doak Turner—who contributed to the writing of *The Complete Idiot's Guide to the Art of Songwriting*. I hope you enjoy their stories, ideas, and suggestions and find inspiration in them, just as we did.

I was fortunate enough to have parents who introduced me as a toddler to the joy of songs. Love and thanks to my mom, Lois Cohen, for the gift of music; my dad, Haskell Cohen, for the appreciation of well-crafted lyrics; and to Leslie Ellis and Dani Cohen, for their talents, wisdom, love, and unending support.

Additionally, I wish to thank, from the bottom of my schedule "A," all the writers with whom I've had the opportunity to write and commiserate through the years. I consider what I've learned from those encounters and in that environment to be by far the biggest and most useful part of my songwriting education. Oh, the stories we could tell.

David's Acknowledgments:

In addition to all the songwriters Casey has thanked, I'd like to thank the many songwriters I've met and enjoyed working with and without whose encouragement I wouldn't be writing in the first place: Jeff Brownstein, Alan Green, Vic Lewis, Todd Mack, John Matsuura, Paul McKenna, Marilyn Miller, Tony Nuccio, Lisa Parris, Kathy Richert, Mike Roberto, John Roche, Glen Russell, Fred Schane, Joel Schick, Rich Schroeder, Bill Supplitt, Nick Torres, and Darra Wheeler Happ. Additionally, to all the people who have taken part in the "Sunday Songwriter's Group" at Guitar Noise over the past 10 years now (and about whom I'd need another book just to list all of you!), I give my thanks for your participation and feedback in the craft of songwriting. I don't think there's a friendlier and more supportive group of people anywhere.

I'd also like to thank Paul Hackett, Tom Hodge, Greg Nease, and Laura Pager for all the friendship and support throughout the years.

Finally, I have to give a huge, special "thank you" to Karen Berger, my partner in life as well as in music. Not thanking Karen for everything she does would be like not thanking life for all it gives us.

Trademarks

All terms mentioned in this book that are known to be or are suspected of being trademarks or service marks have been appropriately capitalized. Alpha Books and Penguin Group (USA) Inc. cannot attest to the accuracy of this information. Use of a term in this book should not be regarded as affecting the validity of any trademark or service mark.

Getting Yourself Ready

Every craftsman needs to know his materials and tools, and songwriters are no exception! Writing a song can be a magical experience, but it also usually involves *work*.

Fortunately, you can find more help and guidance than you can imagine in the huge history of songs. Just by listening to and thinking about all the music you know, you'll be able to find certain "rules" that often apply to songs. But you'll also find that breaking, or just tweaking, those rules a bit can make songs even better.

Since it also helps to know something about songs and song structure, you'll get a rundown on how songs are pieced together and the forms they often take. A brief discussion of musical genres is included.

Plus, you'll also get some great advice on how to find inspiration for your songs, not to mention how not to lose any of the great ideas you come up with. You should find yourself in the perfect mindset to get started writing your own songs!

Magic and Myth

In This Chapter

- Introducing the magic of songs
- Getting prepared to craft a song
- Communicating with an audience
- Some songwriting "rules" that can help
- The importance of listening and critiquing

Songs are magic. They can introduce you to new characters and tell you incredible stories, usually in less than four minutes! Then they can hang around in your head for days at a time. They can bring words to emotions that you've never *personally* known how to describe. They can convince you that a total stranger has experienced the same feelings that you have. They can help you travel back through time to remember friends, faces, and places you haven't thought about for ages. They can make you feel that you're still 16, 22, or however old you want to be. Songs can teach you of events, both current and historical, of different cultures and lifestyles, of lands on the other side of the world, and of places created solely in one's imagination.

And the most magical thing of all is that songs can be created by anyone—even you!

Art and Craft

Writing a song may seem simple enough. You just come up with some words and sing them, right? How many times have you read or heard interviews where a songwriter relates how a tune came to him "in a dream" and that it only took 5 or 10 minutes to write it all down?

Truth be told, that may happen on occasion, and it certainly makes a great interview—almost myth-like, in fact—but most songs are *crafted* like any other piece of art is. The initial ideas, whether musical or lyrical, are worked and shaped into a finished song much like a piece of clay can become a beautiful sculpture.

Good songwriters, as you'll learn throughout this book, are always striving to improve their craft. Just as there are thousands of different types of songs, not to mention millions of reasons to write them, there are all sorts of ways to go about taking one's initial inspiration and crafting it into a song. A songwriter may have preferred methods when it comes to creating her art, but she is always aware that a song requires something special to make it truly stand out.

Sometimes finding that bit of uniqueness may require rewriting or even rethinking whole sections of a song. Melodies, lyrics, and harmonies get touched up or even tossed out. Quite often, a finished song bears little resemblance to the idea that it started from.

It Takes Two

Even then, a song might not be quite as good as it could be. Think about your favorite songs. What, exactly, makes them stand out from the hundreds of thousands of songs that you have heard in your lifetime?

The reasons a song appeals to you has a lot to do with who *you* are. Good songs are all about communication, and any true communication involves at least two people—one to send the message and one to receive it. Whatever your reasons for writing a song, at some point you have to consider your potential listeners, especially if you're looking to write for an audience outside your circle of family and friends.

Putting History to Use

Go to any open mic night or songwriters' circle where songsmiths display their skills and you might find that one person's songs immediately strike a chord with you—while another's might seem like he was reading a list of unrelated words and phrases to the accompaniment of ancient Chinese music played on a kazoo.

A songwriter who wants his songs to be heard (and listened to!) by a large audience usually has to work a bit harder on his art than the heard-it-in-a-dream mythology might lead you to believe. But that is both easy and fun, as there are, literally, several centuries' worth of songs and music history to draw from.

If you can figure out why any particular song is so appealing to you, it makes perfect sense to try to use some of that essence in your own music. The songs that you enjoy were almost certainly polished and reworked with you, the audience, in mind. Even if you have no desire to play your songs outside of your circle of friends, you certainly don't want them thinking your music is hard to listen to—or, worse yet, boring!

Casey's Story About Discovering "the Rules"

When I was a young rock-n-roller and still knew everything there was to know about playing music and writing songs, I had the good fortune to fall in with a group of players who were far more experienced in the music biz than I. They had played on hit records and written songs that were on local Baton Rouge radio. Better still, one of the guys had written a recent national Top 10 hit and, as a cover band, we would play it at our weekend gigs and everyone would sing along.

Through my association with these players, I was introduced to studio recording very early on and, more importantly, to writing songs with the goal of getting them on the radio and on the charts. I discovered quickly that the best songs were the first and surest to be recorded. Plus, whoever wrote the song got to be involved in the recording and, more often than not, got to sing it for the record.

The studio we had access to was woefully unsophisticated by today's standards—equipped with an Ampex quarter-inch tape recording deck and a handful of microphones and stands. Located in a corner of the warehouse of a local fruit and vegetable distributor, it was owned by S. J. Montalbano, whose successes included a #1 hit for two weeks on the national charts by Dale and Grace, "I'm Leaving It All Up to You," and its follow-up, "Stop and Think It Over" (which reached #8).

We would generally work late at night. Not only was that when there was the least amount of interfering noise from the surrounding building, but everybody *knew* that also was the coolest time to record. Our engineer was Junior Avants, a DJ from the local country music radio station who had spent some time in Nashville as a songwriter and guitar player and who also worked weekends with a country band. He was amiable and easy to work with, even though it was clear he merely tolerated our style of music. He would patiently push the "play" and "record" buttons and adjust the recording levels through the night as we'd perform take after take of our live performances of our next self-proclaimed smash hit.

One early morning after an especially long night of recording, as we were headed home through the control room, Mr. Avants stopped me and said, "You know, you almost write good songs."

I'm sure it was intended as a compliment, but it didn't feel like one. He continued, "Has anyone ever told you the rules for writing a hit song?"

I skeptically said something like, "The rules, huh? No, what are they?"

He said, "Well, they're mostly for country songs, but I think they apply pretty much to all kinds of songs."

I probably sighed, and he went on, "The first thing you have to do is put the title on the most musically emphasized part of the melody—usually that's the highest notes."

I said, "Okay, then what?"

He said, "Then make every line in the song point directly to the title."

I nodded and asked, "Anything else?"

He grinned and said, "Well, this is *really* for country music, but you can only write about three things: a three-way affair, drinkin', or truck drivin'."

We both laughed. He said, "If you just follow those rules—even based on no other inspiration—you'll be amazed how often that song will be the one they ask you to leave them a copy of."

Having never pitched a tune to anyone, I had no idea what he was talking about, but to be polite, I thanked him for his sage advice, said goodnight, and went on home.

Putting the Rules to the Test

I found what he'd suggested amusing and gave it no further thought as I went on writing songs as I always had. For several years thereafter, I had enough success to have songs cut by major-label recording artists, and several publishing and major-label recording deals in New York and Los Angeles. On the strength of my songwriting ability, I signed with one of the top management firms in Los Angeles to pursue another record deal, and they suggested we concentrate first on pitching my songs and becoming more recognized as a hit writer. Then they would parlay that into another major-label contract.

One weekend while I was reworking a couple of promising songs, I had one of those magic moments when a few interesting lines appeared in my mind. I worked with them for about a minute and came up with what sounded like the chorus for a country song. It was a bit hokey, I thought—and suddenly my mind went to that moment years before in Baton Rouge, when Junior Avants had given me the "song-writing rules" that I thought were so foolish. I decided to finish this song following those rules to the letter—to prove to myself how off base he was.

I launched into the verses, laughing out loud at the process I was engaged in. I soon had three verses with a melody that seemed appropriate and, most important, strictly followed the rules. As luck would have it, I was interrupted for a few minutes to help bring in some groceries from the car. When I returned to my humorous task, I couldn't remember the chorus that had been the original inspiration for the experiment. I tried and tried to get it to come back, but it was gone. So I finally decided that, since the whole project was a joke anyway, I'd just use the magic guidelines and construct a new chorus. I ginned up a title line that every other line in the song pointed to and put it on the highest notes in the melody, which happened to be the first and last lines of the chorus. The "song by the rules" was complete, and I was sure I'd proven my point.

"You'll Be Amazed ..."

The following Monday, I went to my managers' office on Sunset Boulevard and was greeted with the news that Roger Miller's "people" were going to come in and listen to tunes, and they hoped I had something they could play. Amazing, I thought, a hit writer like Roger Miller was looking for something to record and his people were going to listen to my songs! I named all the songs I considered my best, and we came up with a couple to try on them.

"You were going to work on some new tunes this weekend," they reminded me. I played them the cassette of what I had done with those two songs and at the end of each they said, "Cool, what else have you got?"

I said, "Well, there is one other song on here, 'A Good Love Is Like a Good Song,' But it's just a joke and there's no way you're going to play it for anybody." They wanted to hear it anyway, so after warning them again that it was just foolishness, I played the song for them.

They said, "That's the one we're going to pitch to Roger!"

I couldn't believe it. I begged them not to. They insisted it was a hit and they were going to pitch it. I finally gave up and left for my writing appointment. When I got home that night, there was a message to call the office. My managers had played the song for Roger's guys and they wanted it. I couldn't believe it, but it was fantastic news. A cut by him would mean a lot for my career!

As it turned out, my managers decided not to let Roger have the song, theorizing that it was a hit and I should record it for my record deal. I begged them to let him record it—he was a hit artist and could probably have a much bigger record with it than I could. But they insisted I keep it for my record, and that was that.

So I recorded "A Good Love Is Like a Good Song," and, as soon as my album was released, other artists started covering that song and some of the others. Roger Miller wasn't one of them, but B. W. Stevenson, who'd just had a hit with "My Maria," cut it, as did Johnny Rivers, Bob Luman, Skeeter Davis, Dottsy, Garland Frady, the Oak Ridge Boys .... (To date, there have been thirty-some cuts, and five or six of those were released as singles.)

Tweaking the Rules

So I have to admit that Junior Avants was exactly right, I was exactly wrong, and I proved it to myself. Over time, I've developed a better understanding of those "rules," or what I prefer to think of as a few basic characteristics that most successful songs share, and have added a few others to the list:

- The title is about something that a very large audience is interested in.
- The title falls on the most musically emphasized notes in the melody, usually the highest in pitch.
- The title is repeated *more* often—not *as* often, *more often*—than any other line or phrase in the song.
- The first line of the song captures the listener's attention.
- Every line in the song leads the listener clearly and directly to the title with no wasted words.
- The listener has an emotional response to the song.
- Some part of the song is memorable.

We'll cover many of these songwriting ideas throughout this book. Right now, it's enough to introduce you to these concepts so you'll have them in the back of your mind as you read the first part of this book. As Mr. Avants said, "you'll be amazed" at how often you'll think about them as you listen to music.

Learning by Listening

Listening, by the way, is one of the most vital talents for any musician to develop. And it's a skill that every songwriter wants to practice and hone as much as possible. Throughout *The Complete Idiot's Guide to the Art of Songwriting*, you'll get numerous suggestions for how to use your ears first to become a good songwriter, and then become a better one.

And the cool thing is that you can work on your listening skills each time you hear a song, whether it's one you know or not. Start with ones you know. Figure out specifically why you like them or don't like them, even if the specific reasons seem silly. The more you delve into analyzing a song, the more information you have to help yourself write better songs.

 WRITER'S TALK

If you're going to write a lot, you've got to read a lot! Stephen King, in his book *On Writing*, says, "If you want to be a writer, you must do two things above all others: read a lot and write a lot. There's no way around these two things that I'm aware of, no shortcut."

Go to open mics and songwriters' circles and do the same thing with songs you are most likely hearing for the first time. Understanding how a song makes a good first impression is vital for the songwriter. Mentally catalog what it specifically is about any single song that makes you like it, or not like it.

Delve into the Details

Then take the extra step and write all your observations down. Again, be as detailed and specific as you can. Instead of just saying, "I like this," think about *why* you do. Is a particular line of the song exceptionally clever? Do you like how the chords sound? What don't you like about the song? Does it start out promising but then ramble on endlessly?

This is all personal and subjective, of course, but you are someone who listens to music, so your credentials count. But be sure to compare notes with other listeners and take their observations as seriously as your own, whether you agree with them or not. As you analyze more and more songs, you will start to see that more people share your reactions than you might have thought.

Being able to objectively critique a song will help you understand why some songs just naturally appeal to a great many people and why some are simply "okay"—they're good, but don't become favorites. And this will help you create songs that will have the best chance to communicate your emotions and ideas to as many people as possible.

But you also need to understand that no strict set of rules can ever govern how you write. Writing songs is very personal, and writing them to communicate with others is actually even more personal. Sometimes, mystical moments really will happen, but you will also have songs that require a lot of work to get from initial inspiration to finished masterpiece. And it's a good bet that most of your songs will be a combination of both.

By the way, when I finally met Roger Miller and walked across the room to shake his hand, he began singing the chorus of my song to me. He said, "That's a hit song—we really wanted to record it!"

And I said, "I'm so sorry you didn't."

The Least You Need to Know

- Anyone can write a song.
- Songs are a means of communication. That means you need an audience to communicate with.
- There are no fixed formulas for songwriting, but many good songs share common qualities.
- Be sure to get opinions about songs from other listeners besides yourself, especially if their opinions are different from yours.
- Listening objectively to songs will help you both write and improve your own songs.

Defining Structure

In This Chapter

- The four basic song components
- The building blocks of song structure
- Combining verses, choruses, and bridges into songs
- Common song structures
- Allowing for variations

Songs have structure. Think of songs as being like houses or apartments. There's an entrance, a doorway where you come in and get a little preview of what the rest of the place may be like, maybe even a glimpse into a room or two. And there are rooms of some sort, usually defined by their function. There will be a kitchen, a bathroom, and a bedroom, possibly a living area, maybe even a dining room or a study/office.

The cool thing about songs, much like houses, is that, although you have an idea of what to expect, it's rare that any house is exactly the same on the inside. You might first go through the living room to get to the rest of the house, or the kitchen might be the first room you visit. Sometimes rooms share functions—a family room is also a study or a dining area might be part of the kitchen. And even if two houses have the same layout, it's rare for them to be exactly the same. There may be obvious differences—one may be built of wood and another of brick—and some differences can be as subtle as a different shade of green on one wall of a single room. Likewise, the parts that make up a song may be structured in any number of ways. And even songs that share the same structure are often different in other ways.

Ultimately, as the architect of your song, you choose the layout. When it comes to shaping the song as you see fit, you are limited only by what works or doesn't work.

Overall Components

When someone says the word "song," what comes to mind? This may seem like a silly question, but it actually will determine your expectations of songs. You have four basic materials with which to build a song:

- Lyrics
- Melody
- Harmony, or chord structure
- Rhythm

Generally, the first thing one thinks is that songs are sung. That means that there will be lyrics. It also means that there will be a melody, since you can't really *sing* a song without one!

You create harmony when you set chords (groups of individual notes) to your melody. Or you might have a chordal framework to start with and then create a melody to go with it. Either way, once you give your song some rhythm, you're set to go!

We'll cover each of these song components in detail later in the book. Part 2 deals with lyric writing and Part 3 explores the musical aspect of songs—the melody, harmony, and rhythm.

Song Parts

As a songwriter, you definitely want to know the basics of song structure, if only because it makes it easier to work on a section of a song if you know what section you're talking about! Over the course of history, songs have been organized into various parts that you're already familiar with, even if you don't yet know their names.

Chorus

Most dictionaries define *chorus* as a group of people singing as one, and that's precisely what you want to hear. The term is adopted from ancient Greek drama, where an ode (or musical refrain) that comments on or summarizes the main action of a drama (song) would be sung by a group of actors (singers).

The chorus, which is also called the *refrain*, is the part of the song that repeats the most times. Everyone usually knows it, so they're going to sing along when they hear it. Giving your chorus a strong, memorable melody is essential.

> **TUNE TIPS**
>
> Typically, the lyrics of a chorus are the same each time, but sometimes a single chorus (usually the last one) or even each chorus is slightly different. Think of Joni Mitchell's "Both Sides Now," where each chorus deals with either "clouds," "love," or "life," depending on the subject of the previous verse.

The chorus's lyrics often contain the song's title (sometimes that's *all* it is!) and usually sum up just what the song is meant to be about.

Verse

A song's story generally takes place during its verses. It often unfolds chronologically, but could also be told through a series of descriptions of events, recollections, or even emotions—like looking through the songwriter's photo album, if you will.

The verse usually sets up the melodic, harmonic, and rhythmic patterns of the song. It's rare for verses to differ much from each other in terms of melody. Sometimes there may be more or fewer notes owing to the number of words and syllables being used in the lyric. Occasionally, though, verses will be slightly longer, shorter, or even structurally different than previous ones. The last verse of "Cat's in the Cradle" (by Harry and Sandy Chapin), for example, has two more lines than the first two.

Bridge

Listening to a verse and chorus, followed by another verse and chorus, followed by yet another verse and chorus can get a little boring. So some songs use what's called a bridge section. Not all songs have a bridge, but when they do, it tends to come up between the second chorus and the final verse or chorus.

The bridge represents a musical detour that intensifies or at least varies dynamically with the rest of the song, allowing the listener to reapproach the final verse and chorus from a different point of view. Typically, a bridge is relatively short, not more than two to four lines of lyrics. Even when the same chords are used in the bridge, the melody will not sound at all like the melody used in either the chorus or verses. The lyrics of the bridge also are frequently different from those of the verses. Sometimes they will contain a twist of the story's plotline or a change in the narrative point of view.

Entrances, Exits, and Other Hallways

In addition to some combination of these three main parts, many songs will also have some sort of *intro* or introduction and/or *outro* or *coda* (from the Italian for tail, by the way). Intros are usually strictly instrumental—a short musical solo based on the melody of the song's chorus, verse, or even the bridge. Good intros immediately catch the listener's ear, drawing her in to hear the rest of the song.

Outros, also called "codas," are more varied in nature. They can be as simple as an instrumental reprise of the chorus (even just the final line of the chorus), the repeated singing of the final line of the song, or even a repeat of the first one or two lines or the full verse.

Some songs use a structural device called a *pre-chorus*, which is usually a short phrase that precedes the chorus. A good example would be from R.E.M.'s "Man on the Moon" (written by Bill Berry, Peter Buck, Mike Mills, and Michael Stipe), where the pre-chorus starts with the line, "Andy, have you heard about this one," and the chorus starts with the line, "If you believe they put a man on the moon ...."

A pre-chorus builds emotion or energy and brings the listener into the chorus. If musically (or informationally) we're not ready to hear the chorus, we throw in some stepping stones to take us there more smoothly.

> **DEFINITION**
>
> A **pre-chorus** is a short buildup, musically and lyrically, to the chorus. It's also a bit of a newcomer to the vocabulary of songwriters. Most songs do not have a pre-chorus and many songwriters will tell you that the pre-chorus is actually a part of either the chorus or verse.

A pre-chorus can be lyrically identical each time it appears, but often it might contain slight alterations. It can be as short as a single line or as long as four. It can also be purely instrumental, creating a dynamic musical buildup for the chorus.

Piecing Parts Together

Both musically and lyrically, some song parts can be further divided into what writers tend to call "A parts" and "B parts," particularly when it comes to verses that are fairly lengthy. We'll discuss this further when we look at how parts are put together.

Songs are assembled out of these various pieces, but, as you might imagine, there are all sorts of ways to combine them—assuming you want to use more than just verses for your song.

In this section, you'll get a rundown of the most common song structures, focusing on the three primary song parts—verses, choruses, and bridges. Of course, you'll probably want to toss in an intro and an outro, not to mention the occasional pre-chorus from time to time.

Don't get caught up in thinking that any one particular song format is better than another. If all songs were structured the same, life would get boring fairly quickly! Structure is often dictated by the timing of the story in the song. The manner in which the title "pays off" is also a factor.

Verses Only

The most basic song structure is simply to play one verse after another, with each verse following the same melodic, harmonic, and rhythmic patterns. There can be slight variations in the melody to accommodate more or fewer words (or syllables) in any given verse. Many folk songs and other traditional songs use this format, such as "House of the Rising Sun" or "Scarborough Fair."

Verses in this format often have their own subsections, called *stanzas*. For instance, the first two lines of a verse (which is often called the "A section" of the verse) may have the same basic structure in terms of melody and chords, then the second two lines (the "B section") may have a different melody and harmony. A good example of this would be Green Day's "Good Riddance (Time of Your Life)." You also have instances where the B section is then followed by another A section.

DEFINITION

The A A B A stanza form of a song is used so frequently that it's often referred to as the **standard** song structure.

Many songs that are in the verse-only format begin or end each verse with the same line (or two) of lyrics in order to give the song a sense of coherence. Again, Green Day's "Good Riddance" fits the bill here, as do songs like Bob Dylan's "Tangled Up in Blue" or most of the so-called *standards*, like "Blue Moon," "If I Didn't Care," and "Strangers in the Night."

Finally, a song may also be pieced together using a number of very different verses. "Stairway to Heaven," by Jimmy Page and Robert Plant of Led Zeppelin, uses three different sets of verses, each with its own structure.

Verses and Choruses

The verse-chorus format is one of the most familiar song structures in almost all musical genres. In a typical verse-chorus song, the verses are usually short to medium length, from 4 to 8 or 12 lines. The chorus will be about the same length or slightly shorter than the verse.

As we discussed, the chorus usually employs a different melody and harmony than the verse, but there are instances, such as "You Are My Sunshine" (by Jimmie Davis and Charles Mitchell), where the verse and chorus have identical melodies and harmonies.

Sometimes a song will go through a set of two verses before playing the first chorus, as in Lynyrd Skynyrd's "Sweet Home Alabama" (by Ed King, Gary Rossington, and Ronnie Van Zandt). The chorus doesn't always have to follow the first verses, either. Many songs start out with the chorus (like David Allan Coe's "Take This Job and Shove It") and then go into the first verse. This example again emphasizes how important a winning chorus is in popular music. If the audience is going to remember any part of the song, it's going to be the chorus and/or the first line or the last line they hear.

Adding Bridges

Adding a bridge to a song helps to break up the monotony of the verse-only structure and bring a bit of surprise and variety to the verse-chorus style of writing. Placing a bridge between the second and third verse of a verse-only song has been heard so much that it's part of the standard song format. A typical variation to this format would be to repeat the bridge before a repeat of the final verse. Roger Miller's "King of the Road" would be a good example. Another idea would be to have the bridge section repeat with different lyrics, as in the Beatles' "Nowhere Man" (by John Lennon and Paul McCartney).

In a verse-chorus format, the bridge usually comes between the second chorus and the third verse and chorus. Many songs, though, use it as a replacement for the third verse, following the bridge with either an instrumental verse or a final chorus. "Human," by the Killers (Brandon Flowers, Dave Keuning, Mark Stoermer, and Ronnie Vannucci, Jr.) follows this format.

Mixing Up a Bit of Everything

As you already know from listening to songs all your life, there is no single type of song structure. You'll run into many variations of the verse-only and verse-chorus structure in music. A song like Phil Everly's "When Will I Be Loved" uses two lines that rhyme and then the title line, like this:

A line

A line

Title line

B line

B line

Title line

C bridge line

C bridge line

D line

D line

Title line

Blues songs also tend to use standard structures, which could easily be considered verse-only, but could also be cataloged otherwise. The verse of a typical 12-bar blues, a "bar" being a measure of musical beats (usually four in the case of blues songs), would be like this:

> A line
>
> A line (often an exact repeat of the first line)
>
> B line

A typical "verse-chorus-bridge" song structure would be:

> Introduction
>
> First verse
>
> Chorus
>
> Second verse
>
> Chorus
>
> Bridge
>
> Third verse
>
> Chorus
>
> Outro

Some songwriters will add a chorus between the bridge and the third verse. Others might totally eliminate the third verse and go directly from the bridge to the chorus and then to the outro. Another variation would be to place the bridge between the first chorus and the second verse and forego using a third verse and chorus. As you can see, there are numerous ways to customize this single basic structure to your liking.

And you're not limited to beginning a song with an introduction or a verse. Songs like Bob Dylan's "Mr. Tambourine Man" start out with the chorus and have structures like this:

> Chorus
>
> Verse
>
> Chorus
>
> Verse
>
> Chorus
>
> Verse
>
> Chorus

Occasionally you will come across a song that uses this "chorus-verse" format that also incorporates a bridge.

Remember that a song's music is just as important as the lyrics and can help create an interesting take on a basic song structure. Using half of a verse for singing and half for an instrumental solo, for instance, can make for a nice change from a typical verse-chorus format. A bridge can be a short musical interlude, totally different from other parts of the song, as the simple but intense slide guitar solo that happens in R.E.M.'s "Man on the Moon." This song is also interesting in that it starts out with a verse of six lines, but the second and third verses have four lines. It also incorporates a "pre-chorus" in its structure and repeats the bridge after the third chorus:

Intro

First verse (six lines)

Pre-chorus

Chorus

Second verse

Pre-chorus

Chorus

Bridge (instrumental)

Third verse

Pre-chorus

Chorus

Bridge (instrumental)

Outro (two times through the chorus)

Keeping an Ear on the Clock

No matter what type of structure you decide on, keep the song's overall length in mind. Unless a song is incredibly compelling, there's little reason for it to be over four minutes in length. Most songs tend to be between three to five minutes long and that seems to work for almost all listeners. Some people argue this is because of the physical limits of the old 10" vinyl records, but I think it's a little of both. The early Beatles singles were around two minutes long, which also worked hand in hand with the popular radio "business model" of that time.

TUNE TIPS

Solos, regardless of what instrument is being played, are often considered part of a song structure. However, solos are usually played over a part of the song that has already been established in the listener's ear, such as the verse or the chorus.

The Benefits of Form

It might seem strange to study song structure when music itself (not to mention writing songs) is all about creativity. But a lot of the art of writing is in how one works within a structure and still manages to make a song sound fresh and exciting. You can come up with all sorts of structural variations.

Of course, we shouldn't forget how the freedom of writing for one's own enjoyment and/or performance differs from the limitations of writing songs to compete in the market. The sense of familiarity is part of what makes a song marketable. It's a song that almost everyone will want to sing, simply because they feel like they already know it. And that's important because you have to keep your audience in mind when it comes to structure. Structure gives a song a pattern for the ear to hold on to as a home base, and it's going away from and returning to the familiar that helps create tension and resolution within a song.

Again, think of your favorite songs. Part of the lasting appeal is that they do follow a familiar format where one part of the song leads unerringly to the next, building the joy and excitement of the music as it moves along.

That's not to say that you can't coax your audience into following you down different interesting paths. Songs like Queen's "Bohemian Rhapsody" (written by Freddy Mercury) may initially sound like they ramble all over the place, but they still have enough structure for listeners to catch on to and that helps them enjoy the song more. By giving your listeners a solid structural format to start with, you can give yourself more room to experiment and work out variations in subsequent parts of the song. As always, it really can be a matter of personal taste and adventure.

Learning by Listening

Song structure is not an exact science! Even among songwriters there are arguments as to what constitutes a pre-chorus or whether one person's bridge is another person's B section of a verse.

What matters is that you learn to see and hear songs in their parts as well as their wholes. And as with much about learning the art of songwriting, you can do this just by listening to songs you know. Take a moment and sketch out a song's structure on a piece of paper. Figure out whether the song is verse-only, verse-chorus, or another of the major song formats we covered in this chapter.

Then listen to how the different parts flow from one to the other. Does the bridge segue smoothly into the next part of the song, be it verse, solo, or chorus? What parts of the song are used as intros or outros?

When you next listen to a song, try to use your knowledge of song structure to anticipate where a song may be going next. Getting a feel for where you think a song should be heading can help you work out the flow for your own song should you ever find yourself stuck on a particular section. A lot of being a successful writer is about developing the ability to judge correctly how a word, a melodic interval, a chord, a storyline, the apparent length of your song, and so on, will be perceived by others. When is it too much or too different? When is it too similar to other songs? Listening to what's working for other writers and paying attention to the audience's reactions to your songs are paramount in acquiring that skill.

The Least You Need to Know

- Lyrics, melody, harmony (or harmonic structure), and rhythm are the four basic components of any song.
- The three main song parts are the verse, the chorus, and the bridge. There are also intros, pre-choruses, and outros, which are all part of a song's arrangement.
- There are many different ways to combine song parts into a whole structure.
- Many songs use similar structures such as the verse-only and the verse-chorus format.
- Sometimes it's the small variations made in structure that make a song memorable.

A Look at Musical Genres

In This Chapter

- The four major music genres
- Blues, jazz, folk, and more
- Music in the entertainment world
- Listening for genres and blends

Great songs transcend genres. When people think about their favorite songs, they don't usually think, "That's my favorite rock song, that's my favorite pop song, and this is my favorite blues song." Each listener just knows what he likes. A great song connects with the listener regardless of what type of song it is.

That being said, most songs can be categorized into some musical style. Songwriters tend to write in the genres they like or feel comfortable in, often the styles they've enjoyed most of their lives. As they say: Write what you know.

It's kind of funny when you think about it. Songs bring people together in their shared enjoyment of the music, whereas genres seem to serve little purpose outside of division or marketing. Many genres nowadays overlap so much that it's difficult to say just where "alternative country rock" ends and "pop" begins.

Still, while it's a great idea to think of songs first and genre second, it also doesn't hurt to have a good idea of the major musical genres and how they came to be. This is especially true if you're planning to sell your songs at some point down the road. And if you're going down that particular route, you also want to note that different genres often do business in different ways, from demoing to pitching songs to how copyrights are shared among writers. You'll read more on those topics in Part 5.

The Main Highways

Lyrically, most genres cover the same ground. Where they differ (when they differ) is often in the ways the same ideas and sentiments are expressed. Rock, metal, and rap have harder, edgier lyrics than pop or country, for example. Most often, though, if you were given a lyric sheet with no clue as to the melody or musical style of a song, you might not be able to place it in any particular genre.

The musical aspects of songs, from the choices of instrumentation to the arrangements, usually determine which genre a song will fall into. But not always. Many songs often cross over from one genre to another. This certainly makes sense, as many genres share common histories. Rock and jazz grew out of blues and country swing. Funk, disco, and rap evolved out of rhythm & blues (R&B).

The four major music genres these days are rock, country, R&B, and pop. Whenever you think about "mainstream music," chances are you're thinking about one of these four genres. Each can also be subdivided into an astonishing number of subgenres, many of which probably don't seem much different to the casual observer. In terms of commercial music, though, these four categories are where you'll find most professional songwriters working on their craft.

Rock

Rock and roll, like almost all the musical genres we have today, gained its identity by mixing and hybridizing bits and pieces of other genres. Rock traces its roots back to the country and blues music of the early twentieth century, and pulls in a good bit of jazz and gospel as well. The advent of the electric guitar, as well as (if not more so) the electric bass guitar, brought a dramatic change to the sound of everyday music in the 1950s, and rock is still riding this guitar-driven wave for all it's worth.

Just as important, rock (again like many musical genres) keeps evolving by adapting and absorbing characteristics of other musical styles, cultural trends, and technological advances. Early rock of the '50s and early '60s included rockabilly and surf music, both mixtures of other genres. Later in the 1960s, rock took on the social commentary of folk music and the rhythm and passion of soul music and funk, and also expanded into esoteric, electronic, and psychedelic sounds. The '70s and '80s saw rock co-opt the dance grooves of disco and R&B while embracing both the synthesizer and the crunching distortion of even louder guitars.

Rock continued to subdivide through the end of the twentieth century, adding blues rock, hard rock, progressive rock, acoustic rock, metal (a subgenre with several subgenres!), punk, post-punk, power pop, alternative rock, Christian rock, grunge, electronic and techno, garage rock, and many, many more subgenres.

Country

Traditional country music sprang from the old-time music of the southern Appalachian Mountains and its typical instrumentation of guitars, fiddles, mandolins, and banjos. Bluegrass music still keeps to the essential basics of old-time country, with the addition of the resonator guitar (a guitar that has a resonating cone in its body to amplify its sound, much as a five-string banjo does).

Slide guitar, often used in old blues, evolved into lap-steel and pedal-steel guitars, and the latter became a major, defining instrument in country music throughout the last half of the century. Believe it or not, it wasn't until the last 50 years that a drummer was a member of the typical country band!

Like rock, country has evolved quite a bit. Some country music, usually thought of as "traditional," still sounds much the same, but a look through the country charts will give you songs that sound very much like some more mellow genres of rock, differing only in lyrical content and certain traditional instrumental accents.

Rhythm & Blues & a Whole Lot More

Rhythm and blues, better known as R&B, also covers a lot of ground, especially these days. The term *rhythm and blues*, earlier called "race music," dates to the 1940s, when record companies marketed hot jazz and country blues to urban African Americans. In addition to incorporating urban, electric blues, R&B embraced gospel and developed into soul music, not to mention contributing a lot to the birth of rock and roll.

Like country music, what passes for R&B today can sound totally unlike the R&B music of not all that long ago. The heavy dance rhythms of disco and funk and stylistic nuances of rap and hip-hop can all be found in contemporary R&B, which sometimes goes by the name of *urban* or *urban contemporary*, just to make things more confusing.

Pop

Probably no genre of music is more maligned than pop music, and that's actually pretty sad, because no other genre is more inclusive or does more to bring divergent styles together. "Pop," of course, comes from "popular"—which you'd think every songwriter would want his or her songs to be! As you might imagine, pop music has undergone many, many changes. Many old songs you know were the pop songs of their day, from folk songs to children's songs and lullabies, from the beautiful melodies of Stephen Foster to the marches and ballads sung by soldiers of the American Civil War, from sailor's sea shanties to amusing honky-tonk pieces that might have been played in some Wild West saloon. These were the songs that families and friends would gather 'round the piano in the living room to sing together. Melodies and lyrics were usually simple enough to learn quickly (especially as there was no recorded music to learn from) and everyone could join along.

This simplicity   strong, memorable, and sing able melodies along with a fairly uncomplicated harmony—gives pop music its power. But it could also be sophisticated or topical. Before radio or recorded music, people got all their songs from either sheet music or live performances. People would leave the old fashioned music-hall reviews where they may have heard any number of singers (from solo performers to barbershop quartets to full choruses) or even a performance of the local band at the village square singing "Bicycle Built for Two" or whistling the melody of the latest John Sousa march.

It's easy to think of pop music as watered-down versions of the "real" music of its day (and to be fair, some of it probably is), but there were also very talented songwriters whose ambitions were to make music *everyone* would like. These are the people who created tunes like "There is a Tavern in the Town" or "Hold That Tiger." They are the songwriters who provided Frank Sinatra or Patti Page, or Celine Dion or Michael Bolton for that matter, with songs to sing. And these are the songs that early jazz musicians improvised over to create their new style of music.

Because pop music is meant to be popular, it also has a tendency to be polarizing. In some ways, pop music suffers from the same "you can either be an artist or a sell-out" mentality that other types of art constantly argue over. From the British Invasion of the 1960s onward, the term *pop* has been practically synonymous with "anti-rock," even though the genres have more in common than either side would admit.

Pop is a blend of many different nuances taken from rock, soul, rap, and other genres. Whether it's a power pop anthem or an adult contemporary ballad or even the latest dance-pop hit, you'll hear a lot of music genres wrapped up in one neat package, meant to be shared with as many people as possible.

Pop and country music may not be your personal favorites, but they are two genres where the song-writers are as important as the performers. Many artists write their own songs, but both country and pop music have more than a fair share of songs written by songwriters (and producers) rather than the artists who perform them.

Other Roads to Travel

There are, of course, many more genres than just these four. Some are old (and some are older!) and some are fairly new. All are worthy of your attention, if for no other reason than you might find some inspiration for your own songwriting.

Blues

The blues grew out of the African American work songs, chants, and spirituals of the American South. These unaccompanied vocal pieces evolved into songs in different regional styles that could be accompanied by anything from a single acoustic guitar to a big band. In the middle of the twentieth century, the blues moved from the countryside to the urban scene, especially Chicago, as well as from acoustic to electric instrumentation.

Early blues music has influenced virtually every musical genre since, from jazz to rock to country and more. And the song structures used in the blues are still used by songwriters today.

Jazz

Jazz dates back to the early 1900s, when it grew out of elements of the blues, military music, and early popular music, matched with swinging rhythms. Dixieland jazz, swing, and bebop of the first half of the twentieth century expanded into various fusions, such as Afro-Cuban jazz, Latin jazz, and even acid jazz with its funk influences.

That Old-Time (and Modern-Day) Religion

Music has a long, shared history with religion going back to the chants of Medieval Europe and far, far beyond. Almost every religion incorporates some sort of music into its rituals and services.

If you want an excellent crash course on both melody and harmony, you really can't do much better than to grab a church hymnal to study. These songs of praise are often little gems when it comes to melodic lines, and they offer inspiring ways of putting together memorable chord progressions.

Songs and religious chants from religious services developed into gospel music, which in turn helped launch the blues, soul music, rock, pop, and more. Here in the twenty-first century, we have urban contemporary gospel, Christian country music, and a host of other Christian subgenres that incorporate rock, metal, and even punk.

Folk and New "Old-Time" Stuff

The definition of "folk music" depends on whether or not you think of the term on a worldwide basis or a region or a specific time period. The "folk movement" of the '50s and '60s, which started out as a revival of old songs from the turn of the century (and older), re-created itself into new original music being performed with traditional folk instruments, such as the guitar, banjo, and autoharp.

But even while folk is creating new subgenres such as folk rock, electric folk, and even folk metal, those old roots keep poking through the surface. Folk gets its influence from songs that date back hundreds of years and come from places as diverse as Ireland, India, the Balkans, Iceland, and Turkey.

All Over the World

Technically, every culture has its own folk music. It's easy to forget that the music you've heard in your lifetime is an incredibly small fraction of all the music in the world. Songs from many different countries and cultures are always being "discovered" and brought to the attention of the rest of the planet.

From the reggae and ska of Jamaica to Indian raga, from the bossa novas of Brazil to the fado of Portugal to the koto music of Japan, people almost everywhere have grown up with music and songs ringing in their ears. And songwriters all around the world find inspiration just by listening to the many, many styles of music the world has to offer.

Stage and Screen

Virtually every aspect of entertainment involves songs. You've undoubtedly found yourself humming a song that you heard on some television show. You probably know at least one song from either a film or a musical.

TUNE TIPS

"I have the utmost admiration and respect for those with the talent (which I seem to lack) to write hit songs. My talent has led me, instead, to the musical theater. What whets my appetite is the challenge of writing a song for a character in a dramatic situation in a specific time and place. To me, there is great satisfaction in creating lyrics which help to bring that character to life onstage, expressing himself or herself in such a way that an audience is either absorbed, amused, or stirred by what that character is saying. (And if, on occasion, one of my show songs happens to coincide with popular taste and gets performed outside of the show, that's a lovely bonus!)"

—Sheldon Harnick (lyricist, "Fiddler on the Roof," "Rex," "The Madwoman of Central Park West," "The Umbrellas of Cherbourg," and many more)

Writing songs for the stage, as lyricist Sheldon Harnick says, requires a songwriter to also think like a playwright. The ability to tailor a song's message and lyrics to many different narrative voices is a skill in and of itself (and you'll be reading about the importance of your song's narrators in Chapter 6). Creating great lyrics for specific characters in specific situations is a rare talent.

On the other side of the coin, someone writing the musical score for a film or television show has to be adept at creating almost any type of mood or emotion using just music and no lyrics. These days a lot of scoring work can be done with computers and synthesizers, but the composer still needs to be able to conjure up the right sound, tone, tempo, and tension to give just the right musical touch to a visual moment.

Further Afield

Music and songs are found everywhere these days. You can hear music not only on CD players and radios, but on almost every electronic device you own, from your phone to your computer. But music starts with songs, and songs start with some songwriter who made the music you're hearing.

But that's just the tip of the iceberg. People write music and songs for video games and computer applications, as well as ringtones for cell phones. And while more and more advertisements are using more "real songs" instead of jingles these days, you can still hear a few of those short memorable melodies being sung. There are many ways of getting your music out to the world, should you decide that's what you want to do.

Playing with Songs and Genres

When you listen to any particular song, try to hear in your head what the melody and chords might sound like in a different style of music. Many songs have been remade in different genres, such as UB40's reggae version of Sonny and Cher's "I've Got You, Babe."

One great way to come up with a new song is to play a chord progression you know from one song in a totally different style and then come up with a new melody. The first part of "The Girl from Ipanema" has the same basic chord progression as Pink Floyd's "Brain Damage," but you certainly wouldn't think that on a casual listen.

If you listen to songs and genres with an ear toward learning, you will be more in tune with incorporating the best of all the music you hear into your own songs. Stephen Foster, claimed by many to be the "Father of American Music," blended the parlor music of his time with the music of the traveling minstrel shows and came up with a unique style that is still admired, sung, and played over 150 years later.

Learning by Listening

As you've read in the first two chapters, listening is one of the most important skills you can develop, especially when it comes to dealing with genres. It's very easy to dismiss a song that can teach you a lot about songwriting simply because you don't like it. You want to become an objective listener, so that every song you hear can teach you something.

Too many writers become almost addicted to listening for and identifying what they think is wrong with a song, especially hit songs on the radio. They'll proudly tell you why that song doesn't deserve to be a hit—some glaring error the writer or writers made in creating the song. This is the least productive thing you can do with your listening time, because you don't come away with any clearer understanding of how to create a good song. Listening in this way won't teach you anything about why that song *is* on the radio, and negative comments won't teach you anything at all. Try to figure out what it is about the songs you hear that gave them the appeal or success they have. Going at it the other way is a fool's errand.

Find at least one constructive, positive thing to say about any song you hear. And also try to find one thing that you think could be improved.

The Least You Need to Know

- Songs are usually categorized into different musical genres.
- The four major genres are rock, country, R&B, and pop.
- Most music genres share common roots as well as other stylistic characteristics.
- Songwriters create music for all sorts of entertainment, from CDs to cell phones.
- Try to learn something from every song you hear.

The Chicken *and* the Egg

In This Chapter

- Taking inspiration from everywhere
- Where to find lyrics and music
- Keeping ideas from slipping away
- Getting through your first song
- Practicing your art

If a songwriter were an electronic device, it would have no off switch. Songwriters are always on. When a songwriter isn't actually working on songs by writing down words or working through chord progressions, he is usually thinking about putting lines together or wondering whether a piano might sound better than a guitar for a certain song he's working on.

And if he's not doing either of those things, then he is actively listening to the world around him, gathering material for future songs. He's constantly either taking notes or making notes about something that catches his attention. And anything that catches his attention is likely to catch someone else's ear once he's shaped those ideas into a song. An overheard conversation here, a clever word there, a snippet of a killer melody that just comes out of the blue one day—it all gets stored in the warehouse in his head so that he can put it to use later when he is actively working on a song.

Right now, though, you're probably more worried about just flipping on that switch and getting started on your first song! You may be wondering whether you should be writing some lyrics, coming up with music, or simply gathering ideas. Just what do you do to make that first step?

It's like that age-old question: Which came first, the chicken or the egg? Fortunately for songwriters, both answers are acceptable. It's not about which comes first—it's about coming up with a finished song! Before moving on with the next two parts of this book, which will give you a detailed look at both the lyric and the music aspects of songs, let's get an overview so that you can remember to focus on the goal—to write the best possible songs you can.

Using Your Heart

It's almost impossible to be totally original when it comes to a song topic. After all, over the past two thousand years or so, songs have been written about almost every subject you can think of. Well, maybe no one's written about a cat who lost his purr but got it back by lying by a window on a Tuesday in July when a hummingbird came by to say hello. But somebody will, just wait!

But the cool thing about songwriting is that even when you're writing about something other people have written about, it's *you* doing the writing. And the world has yet to hear from you.

Songs are about communication, so it's a good idea to have something you'd like to communicate, whether it's a simple story or a complicated emotion. Recalling our "rules" from Chapter 1, you want your listener to have an emotional response to your song, and the best way to do that is to have some emotional connection to your topic yourself. If your heart isn't in it, your song will reflect that, and you won't intrigue or engage your listeners, let alone get an emotional response out of them.

Finding Inspiration

Song ideas are everywhere. If you're tuned in, you'll hear and see ideas for songs all around you all the time. In conversations, someone, maybe even you, will say something that just has that ring to it, and all you have to do is recognize what you're hearing and save it for when you can work on it.

TUNE TIPS

Get into the habit of always carrying around something to write down or record song ideas. It's a lot easier nowadays when just about everyone totes a cell phone or a personal electronic device, but even if you opt for the lo-tech approach of a pocket-size spiral notebook, you'll always have something close at hand in which to jot your ideas.

It's best to make a mental note of your discovery nonchalantly, and perhaps either write it down or sing or say it into the recording device you always carry with you. It's also a good idea to elaborate on how you could use the idea and capture the feeling you had while it's still fresh. Otherwise, you may look later at the phrase or word and find it hard to recall the context that seemed so special when you first heard it.

Many hit song titles and ideas have come from movies, television shows, newspapers and magazines, advertisements and billboards, greeting cards … they're just about everywhere. The trick is to recognize them when you see or hear them. Books, both fiction and nonfiction, can make you aware of a situation or concept that will start your creative wheels turning. With any luck, a suggestion will lead to an idea of your own, so that you're not taking someone else's idea and writing your own version of it.

Interacting with the world will bring you even more ideas than you could ever come up with by yourself. Simply talking with your friends and family will often give you more potential material than you can imagine. Many songs start out as reactions to everyday events, whether they are newsworthy, like Gordon Lightfoot's "The Wreck of the Edmund Fitzgerald," or simply a reaction to (or reflection on) a normal life, as in "Boulevard of Broken Dreams," by Green Day.

SONG STORIES

"In songwriting little things can mean a lot. There was a girl I used to date who had a small KLH radio in a wooden box. Even if you tried to turn it off, you'd always hear a little music coming out of it—it was a constant background.

"I had spent some time dating her close friend Molly, who I was very fond of. One night after Molly had to go back to Seattle from San Francisco, where I lived at the time, I was thinking about our last night together a few weeks earlier and how I hated that night to end. That radio came to mind, with the picture of us together with that radio always playing way down low—and that began the hit song 'We'll Never Have to Say Goodbye Again:'"

> *Turn on the radio*
> *We'll play it way down low*
> *There's a tear in your eye*
> *That's reflecting the fire's glow*
> *And I wish that this night would never end*
> *The sun ain't gonna' be my friend*
> *Lying here waiting*
> *And wishing I knew when…*
> *We'll never have to say goodbye again.*
> *We'll never have to say goodbye again.*

—Dr. Jeffrey Comanor, writer of "We'll Never Have to Say Goodbye Again" (recorded by England Dan and John Ford Coley), "Making It Natural" (recorded by Dr. Hook and the Medicine Show), and many other songs.

Paul Craft is the writer of many award-winning hit songs including, "Dropkick Me, Jesus, Through the Goal Posts of Life," by Bobby Bare; "Brother Jukebox," by Mark Chestnut; "Midnight Flyer," by the Eagles; "Keep Me From Blowing Away," by Linda Ronstadt; "Hank Williams, You Wrote My Life," by Moe Bandy; "Come as You Were," by T. Graham Brown; and "It's Me Again, Margaret," which was a hit for Paul and later again for Ray Stevens.

Paul's an outstanding and witty performer, with an encyclopedic knowledge of artists, writers, and popular music. He claims one of his greatest gifts is an ability to recognize talent and hit songs, which has served him well as a publisher. Along with some of his own hit songs, he published Don Schlitz's huge first hit, "The Gambler," a career record for Kenny Rogers. Here's his enlightening story about how he wrote two of his well-known country hit songs:

"I'd just broken up with my girlfriend. I was living in Memphis at the time, getting ready to move to Nashville. So I set about packing my stuff in boxes and, for background music for the task, I started playing Hank Williams records. I'd bought the complete, re-issued vinyl LP collection during my previous trip to Nashville.

"The music and the lyrics seemed to mirror my life at that time and touch on what I was feeling so exactly, and I'd stop every so often and actually write out the lyrics of the song Hank had just sung. That went on for days, and eventually I'd made lyric sheets for every song in the entire collection. That exercise resulted in me writing two hit songs based exactly on what I was going through: 'Take Another Swing at Me,' which was cut by Randy Travis, and 'Hank Williams, You Wrote My Life,' for Moe Bandy. Try picking out a writer you admire, and writing out or typing the lyrics of a bunch of their songs and see what ideas you get."

Treat every day as an opportunity to find and gather song ideas. Be open and aware of what's going on around you.

Using Your Eyes and Ears

This awareness will pay off in many ways. Your powers of observation will help you write better as well as separate great material from the merely good. It's all in the details you see when you look at something. Where one writer might see a "truck," you might see an "old, beat-up, red Chevy pick-up" (that almost rhymes!). Which description gives the listener a better picture?

As you look at the world through the eyes of the songwriter, you will develop the knack of finding these little details that bring a song home to your audience.

You want part of yourself to be like a satellite, collecting ideas and bits of information that can later be used in songs. At first you want to take in everything, from big general themes like love and loss to the small details that evoke emotions or memories. It's like going to a parade and getting caught up in the excitement and anticipation of the marching bands and floats and then being totally absorbed by a single bit of purple confetti that happens to blow by in the wind. The little details bring the big picture to life.

The more consciously you work at this, especially in the initial stages of your songwriting, gathering material will just turn into something you do subconsciously. Some people are great at remembering just about every little thing that happens during the day, but most of us need to write things down, so be sure to do so.

Listening for Ideas

Collecting musical ideas is just as important as collecting lyrical ones. This can be tricky because you obviously don't want to copy someone else's music. But many great songs have been written using someone else's song as a starting point.

As you'll learn in Chapter 12, there are only so many chord progressions that sound good together—it's creating a different melody for them that makes a song yours.

Listening to how other songwriters approach melody—and harmony, for that matter—will open your ears to more possibilities for your own melodies and harmonies. And don't limit yourself to listening only to songs with lyrics. Instrumental songs and jazz pieces are full of melodic and harmonic ideas for you to keep in your head.

Whistle While You Walk

One of the easiest ways to work out ideas for melodies is to simply take a walk. Go at a steady pace, letting the sound of your footsteps act as your drummer. If you're working on a line or two of lyrics, try singing them to the beat of your steps. If you don't have any lyrics yet, just hum or whistle as you go.

If you come up with a melodic phrase you like, keep repeating it to yourself the rest of the walk. The idea is not to come up with a million different ideas but to find one memorable enough to stick with you until you get home, or wherever your destination happens to be. Getting one great melody is a huge cause for celebration!

For any lyric-less melody you create, try singing some words with it. Any words will do—you want to hear how different sounds work with the tune. In turn, this may give you some inspiration for lyrics. Not too bad an accomplishment for just a stroll around the neighborhood!

Trust Your Instinct but Write Things Down!

As you go through your normal day, you will find yourself discovering more and more ideas for potential songs. There are so many stories of great songs that the world will never hear because the songwriter didn't write down a lyric, a melody, or a chord. When you happen across a great potential song line, stop everything and write it down! Don't trust yourself to remember it because, more often than not, you won't.

You have to help yourself remember as much as you possibly can. It's a great idea to always carry around a small notebook. A small spiral-bound will fit into your pocket or bag. And be sure to have a pen or something to write with as well!

In these digital days, setting ideas down is a lot easier for the fledgling songwriter. Most cell phones are able to serve double duty by being your personal recording device. Whenever you have a lyric or a melody you don't want to lose, take a moment and record it for later when you have the time to set it down and work on it.

You can also find apps for your phone, such as Musix, Chord Play, Chordmaster, or Chord Alchemy, that will give you chords so you can hear harmonies. And there are lots of places online where you can find cool rhythm tracks to give you some ideas for your songs.

Getting the First One Done

For many songwriters, the hardest part of getting started is simply finishing a single song. You want your first song to be special. Truth be told, you want your first song to be so good that it blows everyone away and goes on to be #1 on the charts for 587 straight weeks!

The odds may not be in your favor on this one, but nothing is going to happen with your first song unless you finish it. It will always be on your "to do" list with all the other song ideas that you'll never get to.

Avoiding Pre-Editing

When you write, it's important that you do write. Put words down on paper or on a computer screen. Record some music and write down the melody line or the chords that go along with it. You have to get past the editor in your head that tells you "this isn't good enough" and go ahead and put something down; then you can work on it and improve it to the point where it is not only good, but decidedly impressive.

TUNE TIPS

Don't hold back when writing. Put down whatever you can think of without judging it. Get as much of it as you can on the paper and/or recorded. You can edit it later.

Most of what you write down probably won't make it to the final draft, but it will help guide you along the way to shaping and crafting your tune, ultimately giving you the satisfaction of completing a whole song of your own.

Singles Are as Important as Home Runs

Few artists hold their first songs up as examples of professional songwriting skill and technique. And no artist would say that *every* song he or she wrote is a masterpiece. Don't worry about your first song being anything other than your first song.

Every song you write is going to be a learning experience. Every song you write is going to make your next song even better. That's why it's important to get the first one done. There are hundreds of songs, maybe even more, inside your mind waiting to be written. Some will be fun and entertaining. Some will be poignant and move your listeners to tears. Some will tell incredibly inspiring stories, while some will simply make people get up and dance and have a great time.

And they all will be your songs. So don't let them get held up in limbo while you're waiting to make your first song your "masterpiece." Let your listeners do that for you!

Songwriting as a Craft

Songwriting is a craft. You may have been born with a natural talent for it, but having talent is only part of the songwriting process. Talent has to be developed and eventually guided by experience to become a skill. And that requires work, trial and error, practice, and a lot of learning on your part.

If you're like most people, the words "work" and "practice" immediately put you off and you start thinking, "No way!" As a songwriter, you will become a master of words, choosing one over another precisely because of the connotations and emotional power it will have for your audience. That also means you'll understand that there's nothing good or bad about "work" or "practice." It's simply part of getting better at your craft.

The Importance of Practice

As it is with any musician, practice is an important part of developing and maintaining your skill. Pianists practice every day to become better piano players. Songwriters need to practice regularly to become better at their craft. Take a cue from Richard Thompson, who still tries to set aside time each day *just* for working on his songwriting. And he's been writing songs for over 40 years!

WRITER'S TALK

"Carole King once told me she would sit down at the piano first thing every morning and just play whatever melodies came to her for as much time as she could reasonably devote each day. I took this advice to heart and tried it, and after a couple mornings I found I was waking up with melodies and lyric ideas. Apparently, our minds and bodies get ready for what we expect them to do."

—Casey Kelly

Try to get into a regular routine. Schedule your practice for the same time each day if you can. The more seriously you treat your songwriting, the better songwriter you will eventually become.

And be patient. Some songs will seemingly write themselves, taking next to no time, but others will need a bit of coaxing. You may get a great idea that sits around for days, weeks, or even months before you find some lyrics that best fit the song. Remember that songwriting is not a race—the song that gets written fastest is not necessarily (or even usually) the best possible song you can write.

Even someone like Ruthann Friedman, who is famously known for writing the hit song "Windy" for the Association and who's been writing songs for well over 40 years, knows that some songs just can't be rushed.

WRITER'S TALK

"Writing a new song used to take no time at all; I could knock out a tune like 'Windy' in an afternoon. Now it may take a couple of years to get to the finished work.

"Music comes first for me. I play my guitar until I find a combination of chords and riffs that move me, then find a direction toward the storyline. A song I am working on right now has three sets of lyrics and none has been settled on. I know they will come to me; they always do. Putting a piece of work aside gives my unconscious a chance to put flesh on the bones…."

—Ruthann Friedman

Being Flexible

When you sit down to assemble a huge jigsaw puzzle, you may have a plan for working through it, but chances are you end up doing something totally different. You may decide to just assemble the border, but, when you come across some pieces that obviously fit together, you don't just ignore them and leave them until later. A section may spring out from one of the borders, or a lot of independent sections may come together while you're sorting through pieces. Either way, you eventually find yourself with a finished puzzle. And if you take that puzzle apart and do it again, the odds of you piecing it together in exactly the same manner are pretty slim.

Songs can be very much like puzzles. You have inspiration, maybe some ideas for lyrics, and perhaps even a great chord progression and melody to get you started. But it will often take some playing around with the pieces of your song, not to mention probably adding some new pieces or discarding old ones, to make your song complete.

Every song you write will be different, and you'll probably start out with different pieces of songs each time. You can see it's important to be flexible when it comes to your songwriting process. It's rare for every song you write to go exactly from step 1 to step 2, and so on.

Songwriting is seldom linear. Books, on the other hand, are very linear. So as you go through the next two parts of this book, remember that each chapter is designed to help you with a specific part of songwriting—lyrics in Part 2 and music in Part 3. Feel free to bounce around from chapter to chapter (or from section to section within any chapter) as you work on your own songs.

The Least You Need to Know

- Ideas and inspiration for songs are everywhere around you.
- Have a means and a method to immediately capture and keep track of your ideas, both musical and lyrical.
- Don't pre-edit yourself and write everything down. Save your editing for later in the writing process.
- Get your first song finished!
- Learn by doing. You have to practice songwriting to get better at it.

Painting with Words

There's a famous songwriting story and, whether it's accurate or not, it feels like a fitting way to introduce the lyrical part of this book. Allegedly there was a cocktail party in New York City in the 1940s at which the wife of the brilliant composer Jerome Kern and Dorothy Hammerstein, the wife of the genius lyricist Oscar Hammerstein, were attendees. The hostess is said to have been introducing Eva Kern to the other guests and explained, "Her husband is the famous Broadway composer who wrote 'Ol' Man River.'" Legend has it that Mrs. Hammerstein spoke up quickly, correcting their hostess: "Actually, *my* husband wrote 'Ol' Man River'! Mrs. Kern's husband wrote, 'Duuum-duuum-dee-duh.'"

Here in Part 2, we'll talk about all the basics of crafting great lyrics to support and sell your song's "hit" title. You'll get tips on making your lyrics sing-able, memorable, and musical, and on keeping them focused on your song's message, from the opening line to your final phrase—which hopefully will be much better than "Duuum-duuum-dee-duh!"

What Have You Got to Say?

In This Chapter

- Finding something to sing about
- Getting details out of a general topic
- Setting your song as a story
- Framing the picture of your song
- Stocking up on lines and images

It may sound ridiculous to say it, but it sure helps to know what you're trying to say *before* you start speaking or writing. How do you feel when you're listening to someone who doesn't really know what he or she wants to say? It's easy to get lost, frustrated, or simply bored in a conversation like that.

The same holds true with songs. Think about it—in a universe full of words, you've got maybe 15 seconds to catch the listener's attention, and a little more than 3 minutes to tell your whole story or to convey an intricate emotional message. And when you add the idea of repeating phrases (as in a chorus) to help make a lyric memorable, you can see that a songwriter has to get the most out of each word!

The "Moment" of Your Song

Songs often start from close to nothing. Sometimes you'll start off with a musical idea. Perhaps a little melody line comes out of nowhere, or a chord progression sounds promising, and you begin singing it and playing it on an instrument to see what the rest of the melody wants to sound like. You might begin with a title or even a couple of lines you like, with no melody in mind. Maybe you've heard a catchy phrase that you can't get out of your head, or maybe you have a great story you'd like to tell.

However you start out writing it, whether with a title or an opening line or a germ of a chorus, your song is *about* something. Some theme or story or idea is inspiring you to write. Simply put, you've got something to say! But if you don't know what that something is when you start writing, it helps to stop and spend some time figuring out just what you're trying to convey.

Think of this message as the "moment" of your song. It's the moment in which all the action of your song's "one expressed idea" takes place. Most hit songs describe the feelings of a moment—exploring what the singer is experiencing in the moment being described. You only get to say one thing in an effective song, and, allowing for sufficient repetition to "weight" your title (a synopsis of your song's statement), there's only so much time, so your words have to be concise and effective. To paraphrase one of the theories of popular songwriting: The total length of time passing in the scenes depicted in a song should not exceed, to any great degree, the time it takes to sing the song.

What's It All About?

Songs can be about anything. They can shout the giddiness of being in love for the first time; they can convince you that no one in the entire world can understand the way you feel when you first break up. They can relive stories from history and they can tell you to have a good time and party down right here, right now.

You should be able to say what your song is about in one declarative sentence: it's a song about a woman dating a married man, or it's a song in which the singer has just realized he is in love with someone he thought was just a friend. Even when your song is a story, that story usually has a broader overview that a listener can easily relate to—like it's a song about someone who, while growing up, realizes how much he misses his father, or a song about someone who, while growing older, realizes that his child has picked up all the same mistakes he made himself.

Broad emotions, written simply on their own, can seem a little mundane and obvious. Your job as a songwriter is to describe common feelings and situations in a way that will make listeners identify with what the singer is saying and bring their own experiences into your song.

TUNE TIPS

Most songs tend to be love songs of some sort. Falling in love, falling out of love, falling in love with the wrong person, getting the blues because the one you love doesn't love you back—you've undoubtedly heard them all at some point. Love songs also include love of family and friends, love of country, and love of God. And let's not forget simple love of life and wonder. When it comes down to it, people love "love songs." Exploring your unique take on love can create many great songs.

Song as Story

Most people think of songs as stories. You're introduced to a major character, perhaps the song's narrator, and then you get to follow the story for as long as the song goes. Sometimes the timeline of the story is as long as the song itself, maybe a few minutes. But the story could also span much greater lengths of time—hours, days, years, even generations. For example, "Ob-La-Di, Ob-La-Da," by the Beatles (written by John Lennon and Paul McCartney) tracks the courtship and early family years of its protagonists.

Thinking about songs as stories has advantages: Stories have beginnings, middles, and endings, which can give you an instant song structure in terms of verses or stanzas. Stories also have underlying themes the writer wants to put across, as you do, although you want to focus your song on a single idea, since you've only got three minutes to work with instead of a few hundred pages!

A song's limited length may seem like a restriction, but it can actually turn you into a much better writer. You can present only so much of the whole story to your listener, so you want to be both creative and precise with the details you fill your song with.

How Much Story?

The moment of your song shouldn't be much longer than the actual length of the song, so you have some details to consider before you know where to start. The subjects of your song have some history or backstory—what brought them to this point—that we may need to know to understand the action or mood of the song. Some of that can be obvious or implied obliquely, but sometimes you need to spell it out.

As the writer, you should already know everything about the people in the song—where they've been, what they've done, what's happened between them. Make sure anybody listening also knows who, what, when, and where—and *why* you're talking about it. It's too easy to lose your audience's attention. You've got to give them enough knowledge of the situation to be able to easily understand and relate to what's going on.

 WRITER'S TALK

Remember that backstory is all about what a listener *may* need to know to understand what's going on and where the characters are coming from. I've often critiqued songs in which the writer assumed the listener knew necessary details that actually weren't obvious. But limit the backstory to what is necessary to understand the story. You also want to consider how timing in the story affects what the listener learns, and when.

How Much Scene Setting?

In addition to providing your listener with some backstory, you may also decide to set the stage a little with some physical description. Providing a bit of scenery for your audience can put them right in the story, as in Bobbie Gentry's "Ode to Billie Joe," which sets you smack down in "the third of June, another sleepy dusty Delta day."

Like citing a specific date or giving a mini–weather report, evoking places draws your listener into the story. You can place them in the familiar landmarks or streets of specific cities or towns, or give them the bang-clang of a generic factory or the smell of a diesel truck rolling down a highway.

Song as Snapshot

Songs that "show" what's happening, when, and where draw listeners in much more powerfully than those that "tell" them. If you set the stage and depict a circumstance the listeners recognize, they will project their own feelings and thoughts into your story. If you tell them every detail about what's being thought and felt in the story, you don't leave for them to become involved. Describing, rather than dictating, allows your listener to be an active participant in the story, free to develop her own thoughts and interpretation.

Accordingly, it might help to think of your song not so much as a story but as a snapshot of one specific instant of that story. That's the "moment" we've been talking about. It's like you've clipped out one particular part or parts of the story so your audience can examine it under a magnifying glass.

But while they are wrapped up in the details you're showing them, you still are the framer of the snapshot. More important, you're the one who knows the context of the snapshot, whether these are all small bits of a single larger picture or part of a montage.

Going back to "Ob-La-Di, Ob-La-Da," each verse is a 20-second snapshot/description of the family's situation, starting where we meet them and checking in on what they're doing at sequential intervals. You can almost hear the repeated sound of a loud camera shutter. Then we have a bridge that tells us, "In a couple of years they have built a home-sweet-home," and have two kids. And finally the last verse is the fairytale ending. By the end, we've seen many years in about three minutes.

Inside the Frame

A song, no matter how rich in detail, can't possibly describe every part of a story or emotion. You know what your song is about, but you don't necessarily want to give your audience all the information right at the start. Instead, you may have them consider just the snapshot you've given them. This can be a bit of backstory or even a touch of scenery, as we've discussed, or you can put your listener right inside the first frame of the story.

As your song progresses, you are continually giving them either new snapshots (like looking through your relatives' photo albums on a rainy Sunday afternoon) or expanding the range or the perspective of the original snapshot. Again, let your audience get involved in the story or the message, giving them the freedom to interpret what they hear in their own way.

Remembering the Big Picture

Of course, what's inside the frame is just part of your whole story. You are the one who decides just how much of the big picture your song actually reveals. Your song may stay within one small frame, or you may gradually widen the borders of the frame, allowing more of the picture to be seen by your audience.

For example, you may open your song with a glimpse of a man's face. He is a mixture of tangible emotions—loss, fear, regret, and resignation. It's a powerful picture in and of itself. In your second verse, you may pull back a bit and show that this person is not alone. Beside him stands a young woman whose face is a mirror of his. Finally, in your third verse, you pull the camera back further and show these two people staring at a house on fire.

There are still a lot of questions for which only you, the storyteller, know the answers. Is it their house? Is someone still inside? *Who are they?* This is why you need to know from the start what your song is about. You may decide that some of this information is totally unrelated to the point you want to make, to the emotions that you want your audience to carry home with them.

As a songwriter, you ultimately direct the focus of your listeners' attention. To do that effectively, you have to know exactly what you want to say in your song.

Learning by Doing

Let's say you have a phrase, perhaps something like, "How do you know?" Many scenarios come to mind immediately: a boy or girl asking a parent about love, religion, what he or she want to be in life; one lover asking another if she can believe what she's feeling. Maybe it's someone asking a friend for advice, even "how do you know" when a relationship is really over … we could go on forever.

Or it may be an image that's in your head. Maybe you are thinking of "a city street" or "a dark December day." Write out your phrase at the top of a page. Next, list underneath it as many scenarios as you can that relate directly to your initial phrase. Don't worry about how good or how bad you think the ideas are, just get them onto the page.

When you've got a page or so of scenarios listed, stop and read them over. Your task is to determine what, exactly, each scene is about. You want to write this main focus down so that it becomes the center of your writing when you further develop these ideas into songs.

Once you have a theme or main idea that you're excited to write about, reshape your theme into a story or scenario that will work as a song. One of the best ways to do that is to write down your major point at the top of a page and then write out what brought you to this message, whether it was a catchy phrase or idea for a title or even a story.

Now draw a heavy line beneath those ideas and start to write out *anything* that comes to mind when you think of what you wrote at the top of the page. It may be a line, a short phrase, or even a bit of description. Try to fill at least a page, then set it down and take a break to clear your head.

TUNE TIPS

A larger than usual page, like a sketch pad, works especially well for writing song ideas. The large, blank paper tends to free you psychologically from limiting or editing what or how much you write. Using a computer or a recorder offers some people the freedom to pour out everything that comes to mind onto a screen or into a microphone.

Later, when you read what you've written down, see which lines and phrases immediately link up to the main theme. These are keepers, at least for this stage of the process. You might even find a title and an opening line in what you've written down.

It's easy for songwriters to lose track of their story or their main theme in the early stages of writing a song. If you don't keep what you want to say directly in front of you, your writing can end up wandering off on all sorts of tangents, away from the "moment" of the song.

As you'll read in Chapter 8, every line of each verse should lead listeners to the chorus, where they'll hear your main point. Doing this little exercise beforehand will help you keep your song on target and will also give you a step ahead on writing your chorus and verses (and bridge, should you decide to have one).

The Least You Need to Know

- You have to have a clear idea of what you want to say in a song in order to say it effectively.
- Songs can be about any specific subject; your take on that subject will make it unique.
- Your song will have a story, but only a small part of that story becomes the actual song.
- Your lyrics should give your listeners as much background information as they need to understand the story.
- At this early stage of the songwriting process, write out every idea that comes to mind. Save trimming things down for later.

Who Is Singing Your Song?

In This Chapter

- Finding the right narrator for your song
- Four possible points of view
- First-, second-, and third-person points of view
- Advantages and disadvantages to each point of view

Once you know what you want to say, you want to address who's going to say it for you. You may think that's silly—obviously, whoever sings the song will be delivering your message to the audience.

But who does the singer's voice represent? Is it the voice of an anonymous storyteller who's not in the story, or someone in the story telling you what he or she saw or heard or did? Or is the singer's voice that of someone telling his or her own story?

In songwriting, whose voice the singer represents can make a big difference in how effectively the message and feeling connects with the listener. The storyteller's point of view can make all the difference in whether the listener vaguely "gets" the song or truly identifies with the person in the song and feels what that person is feeling.

Why "Who" Is So Important

The point of view you choose for the singer's voice determines how the story is related to the audience. It can be a one-on-one conversation, with the singer constantly referring to himself in the first person. It can be more of a typical story where a narrator simply describes the story in the third person as it unfolds.

Suppose you wanted to write a song about how terrible the Civil War was. You could have an anonymous narrator explain how there were a lot of horrendous battles and the soldiers were afraid and they shot each other and they died. Your song lyric might very well read like a history text book. And if it reads like that, it's probably going to sound that way when sung, too.

But what if you wrote the song from the viewpoint of the main character, a battle-weary soldier, writing a letter home, his voice describing what he sees around him? Your audience would overhear his words to his loved one:

> *I'm writing to say I love you, though my hand is shaking.... Everybody just flinched when a bullet ricocheted off the side of our wagon as we bounce along as if bombs were exploding under us.... I can close my eyes and see you there at home, but here all I can see is fear and craziness in my buddies' eyes looking back at me!*

Which approach makes you feel something? Which type of narrative would best hold your attention?

WRITER'S TALK

As Sheridan Baker says of effective writing in *The Complete Stylist and Handbook*, "It should not be altogether unworthy to place you in the company of those who have written well in your native tongue. But it should nevertheless retain the tone of intelligent and agreeable conversation. It should be alive with human personality—yours—which is probably the most persuasive rhetorical force on earth. Good writing should have a voice, and the voice should unmistakably be your own."

The Evolution from Personal Musical Journal

It's easy for songwriters to fall into the habit of using their songs as "personal musical journals." Almost every songwriter starts out from this viewpoint with his or her first songs about love. It's a strong emotion that you want to share. The songs are invariably in the first person and negative, and you make it clear that this song is all about how you feel.

But as songwriters grow and evolve, they hopefully realize that constantly using their own voice as a song's narrator eventually limits their writing. It's not that the individual songwriter doesn't have a wealth of emotions or experience to draw from, but rather that it gives all of his or her songs the same overall feeling. The songwriter's music runs a grave risk of sounding like the same song, only slightly different, sung over and over.

"Who," Indeed?

As a songwriter, you have an unlimited supply of narrators to sing your stories. Going back to the example of the Civil War song, you could "voice" your lyrics from many points of view: as a soldier for either side, the parent of a soldier, a doctor or nurse in the field, or a survivor telling the story to his grandchildren. Each narrator will give your song a different perspective and will touch your audience in a different way.

Beginning songwriters may think that any narrator other than the main character is getting away from the pure emotion of writing, but a third-person narrator sometimes allows the writer to introduce details the first-person approach would find awkward, and to gain greater room for expression. The voice of another character can say things the main character might not say himself. By looking at a story or an emotion through another set of eyes, you can often gain perspective and understanding you might not otherwise have.

Ultimately, it's up to you to choose the narrator that best suits your song. The "I" of your lyric may be someone entirely fictional, even though it's still technically you!

Choices of Person

When someone sings your song, three things must be obvious: who he's speaking for, who he's speaking to, and who or what he's speaking about.

The point of view from which your singer's voice will speak determines the pronouns you will use—first person ("I"), second person ("you"), or third person ("he," "she," "they")—and whether your narrator is speaking directly to the audience or indirectly. The listeners will know whose eyes they're seeing through and what their relationship is to the main character without any extra words.

> **TUNE TIPS**
>
> "Ask yourself: What is the moment of this song? Who is singing? To whom is she or he singing? Why is the singer saying this right now? Where is the song taking place? What is the turning point in the singer's life?
>
> "The answers to these questions will help you create a real person who has something real to say to another real person (or to the world). Once you have the situation and the characters of the song defined in your mind, you can put words in the singer's mouth that she or he would really use, in the order that she or he would really use them. A Texas cowboy would not use words that a New York lawyer would use. And a lyric that sounds like real speech uses words in normal conversational order, that is, the words are not re-arranged just to make them rhyme."
>
> —Pat and Pete Luboff, songwriters of "Trust Me" (recorded by Snoop Dogg), "Body Language" (recorded by Patti LaBelle), "I Wish He Didn't Trust Me So Much" (recorded by Bobby Womack), and more. Pat and Pete have been teaching songwriting workshops for over 30 years.

First Person

Most songs are written in the first person, which is generally the most intimate voice and identifies the singer as the person "speaking" in the song. In this voice, your narrator is usually singing about a story or an emotion that he or she has personally experienced or witnessed. First-person songs are full of the words "I," "me," "my," "we," and "us."

Remember that your first-person narrator may not know all the details of your song's story. Your Civil War soldier probably knows next to nothing about the intricate planning behind the battle he's about to fight. He simply knows where he is right now and what he's feeling, and that's what he'll relate to the listener.

Make It Clear Who "I" Is

Listeners tend to think the word "I" in a lyric literally refers to the singer. They assume the singer's telling a story about himself instead of just being a storyteller. So when writing in the first person, a skilled writer should always make sure that anyone who hears the song knows exactly the relationship of the singer and the "I" in the lyric.

For example, John Prine wrote "Angel from Montgomery" in the first person, but when he sings, "I am an old woman," as the opening line, no one thinks he's speaking of himself. Rather, he's subtly leading the audience to accept that he's channeling the old woman, whose voice is actually telling us the story. On the other hand, there's no mistaking that John Lennon is and always will be the Walrus.

Second Person

Second person, the "you" voice, can be confusing in songs because it's hard to tell whether the speaker is talking to someone else or using the "editorial you" for speaking to the audience. Listeners tend to assume they are the ones being spoken "of" or "to," which isn't always the case.

Publishers and tune pluggers often warn writers about second-person lyrics that tell someone what to do. They claim, "Audiences don't want to be preached to!" But you can say the same thing in the third person ("My Daddy told me not to drink …" for example), and as the singer you're not scolding the listener.

Still, there are times when the second person is the best choice, as in Bo Diddley's "You Can't Judge a Book" and Sting's "Every Breath You Take." Graham Nash's "Teach Your Children" is another great example of how the second person can work well as a choice of point of view.

In "The Gambler," by Don Schlitz, the audience could listen to Kenny Rogers singing about what "you" must do and what "you" must never do without being offended and without feeling like they'd been lectured to. The singer was "in" the song, so Don cleverly had the singer ("I") *quote* the gambler: "He said, 'You got to know when to hold 'em …,'" so the singer, not the audience, was the "you" being told what to do.

Third Person

Third person allows the singer to be the narrator, which means that whatever is happening in the song isn't necessarily about the singer.

Third-person narrators can come in many assortments. They may not know all the details of a story, or divulge them all if they do. They may keep themselves totally out of the song or occasionally be a participant at various points in the tale. "Seven Spanish Angels," sung by Ray Charles and Willie Nelson, is third person all the way and the singers/narrators do not appear in the story of the song. Some skilled writers get away with writing third-person narrative songs that occasionally jump to first person or second person. Townes Van Zandt's "Pancho and Lefty" comes to mind. As he wrote and sang it, it begins with a verse in the second person—almost like an intro, the singer singing to an individual. I always picture a saloon, a bunch of cowboys doing what they do in a saloon and Townes sing-talking directly to an acquaintance sitting with him at a table but loud enough to be overheard. As the second verse starts, Townes stands and begins addressing the crowd in general and the lyric switches to the third person and becomes a "ballad" of Pancho and Lefty for the rest of the song. As I said, the first verse is essentially an intro that sets the tone for the actual tale.

Bob Dylan's song "A Simple Twist of Fate" takes liberties with point of view. It's a third-person narrative, but the singer shows up in the first person in the second line of the second verse and in the last verse, which makes the song a little more mysterious than it would otherwise be. He uses it to bring emphasis to what appear to be statements he considers important and to make sure we know he's talking about himself.

Both of these songs did well *in spite* of these inconsistencies rather than because of them. The hit version of Townes song was recorded by Willie Nelson at his most popular, and he changed the lyrics slightly so that it addressed "everyone" from the beginning. Bob Dylan purposely breaks the rules. Both of these songs are the product of extremely gifted veteran craftsmen and they should not encourage you to ignore the principles of good writing until you've mastered them all.

It's Not What You Know—It's What You Feel

"Write what you know" is a bit of advice that new writers and songwriters get all the time. And although it is definitely good advice, it's also slightly misleading.

Imagination is a vital component of songwriting. Whenever you write a song, you're creating a little world with its own characters and emotions based on what you know. You'll probably pattern most of the characters after yourself or people you've known. Most of the stories will probably mirror things that you've experienced or read about.

So you might also want to explore other ideas and stories, to create tales that you can't possibly have had any experience with. That's where your imagination comes into play. Not to beat our Civil War example into the ground, but how do you write a song about being a soldier 150 years ago, or about anything else you've had no direct experience with?

TUNE TIPS

Basing your narrator's emotions and responses on real human beings, whether yourself or someone you know, is especially important when your song's character is supposed to be someone who can only exist in the imagination or when that character experiences something that can only be sheer fantasy. This sense of everyday human-ness enabled Bernie Taupin to pen the lyrics to "Rocket Man," and Randy Brooks to successfully fabulate "Grandma Got Run Over by a Reindeer."

You do this through imagination and, even more importantly, through emotion. Remember that songs are emotional messages that pass from singer to listener. As a person, you have experienced all sorts of emotions—love, loss, joy, sadness, anger, playfulness, etc.—and have experienced them all from mildly to incredibly intensely. You may not know what it's like to be shot at, but you certainly know what it's like to be cold, scared, and tired to the point where you don't know which way is up anymore.

WRITER'S TALK

"Even if the song is about a real experience of yours, the song has its own separate reality. The art of songwriting is to use your real emotions and experiences to create a focused message that makes sense within the song's world. For instance, you may personally be willing to take back a lover who cheats on you constantly, but most listeners would have trouble believing a song that said, 'I don't trust you. You hurt me again and again. I want you back.' In Nashville, we have a saying, 'Don't let reality get in the way of a good song.'"

—Pat and Pete Luboff

When you write a song using a narrator you've created, you want the emotions to be as real as possible. Project your own feelings and experiences, the "what you know," onto your fictional narrator. If you make those emotions authentic, both you and your audience will strongly connect with the song's singer.

Staying True to Character

Finding the right narrator can certainly give your song more power and depth. Simply searching for possible narrators can also open the door to a lot of other possibilities when it comes to your songwriting. Using the Civil War song once more as an example, you may ultimately decide that the private in the Union army best fits the song you're working on, but also discover that the other possible narrators (the parent, the Confederate soldier, the field doctor, and so on) each have an incredible song to sing. Don't hesitate to write one for each of them, too!

Do the necessary research to know where you're going and keep everything authentic. It's relatively easy with the aid of your favorite Internet search engine, and you're likely to discover other great ideas for your lyric while you're in the process of creating a narrator.

Try to really put yourself in your narrator's shoes. What would you be apt to say and do in his or her circumstance? The more you can understand and empathize with your storyteller, the more your song will breathe with true life. The more authentic the narrator, the more believable your song will be. If you can trust your characters, your audience will most likely accept them.

WRITER'S TALK

Another reality check has to do with the timeline in a song. If you leave the singer in a certain place and time at the end of verse one, you need to pick up right from that spot in verse two, *or* introduce the next section with a clear indication that some time has passed. You can't just jump 20 years forward without letting your listener know! Likewise, a real person does not leap to a completely different point on the planet from one line or one section of the song to the next, unless your song is about Superman!

—Pat and Pete Luboff

Using John Prine as an example again, another song from his debut album, "Hello in There," might be a typical song about growing older. To make it both engaging and powerfully moving, Prine sings in the first person as a retiree, living in an apartment with his wife and not doing much of anything. It's just a narrative of a typical day—listening to the news, meeting up with a former co-worker—with seemingly small details dropped in here and there ("… we worked together at the factory …") and the listener never for a moment considers that Prine wasn't even 25 when he wrote this lyric.

Paying attention to the little details is important when you write a song about something that happened in the past. Weaving these details into your lyrics can make a song come alive to the listener in the present day. Instead of just "firing a gun," it is better that your Civil War soldier "aim his Springfield" or "Enfield." Your audience may not know very much about "makes" of guns, but they will certainly infer the connection and assume the authenticity. And it will make your characters ring true and bring them right into the action.

It's important that you, as the songwriter, know exactly who your first-person narrator is. If it's you (that is, yourself as the songwriter), then you want the lyric to speak as you'd say it. If it's someone else—your Civil War soldier, for example—then you want the language to sound the way that specific person would communicate it as he spoke or sang.

Write out a few lines of your song's story, just as you might tell it in the first person. Once you have it in black and white, you can read it aloud and see how that approach would sound and work in your song. If it doesn't feel like that's who should be telling the story, you can rewrite or just say the lines as you imagine they would be spoken by a narrator who is directly involved in the story. For instance, in addition to the obvious change in point of view, if your Civil War soldier is a ranking officer, he might have had more formal education and that would certainly show in his speech. If your soldier is a private on the line, then his words might be more likely to carry a regional, working-class dialect of some sort. Usually one of the possible points of view will clearly show itself to be the one that will most effectively connect the listeners to your song/story.

Learning by Doing

Go back to the lists that you made in Chapter 5 and pick any one topic to work with. Reread what you've written, especially the phrases and details that you came up with to flesh out your initial main idea.

What's happening in your story/song? Who and from what point of view can you imagine telling your story? That narrator is going to deliver your title line. Will that have the effect you're going for?

Now imagine your story or major point being described by someone other than you. Pick a different character in your story to start with. Who is this person and what is his or her relationship to the story? How many of the original phrases and details would this new storyteller use? Or would your new narrator come up with other phrases, lines, or descriptions that you didn't see before?

Take a separate sheet of paper, label it appropriately, and start rewriting and adding new material as your new narrator. Compare the new narrator's sheet to your initial one and see which has more interesting (and attention-grabbing) material to work with.

Don't stop with just one possible new narrator! Repeat this process a few times with other choices of narrator. If nothing else, you may find yourself with some great material for a new song!

TUNE TIPS

If you're writing songs for other artists to sing, write a few songs from the viewpoint of each sex. Plenty of hit songs by female artists were written by men, and vice versa. "The Night the Lights Went Out in Georgia" was written by Bobby Russell and was a big hit for Vicki Lawrence, his wife at the time. "Killing Me Softly" by Charles Fox and Norman Ginmbel was recorded by Roberta Flack, Cleo Lane, Eva Cassidy, Susan Boyle, and many others. Diane Warren wrote "I Don't Want to Miss a Thing" for all-male Aerosmith, Dolly Parton wrote "Kentucky Gambler" for Merle Haggard, and Carole King's "You've Got a Friend" was a hit for James Taylor.

A song that is non–gender specific is twice as likely to get recorded as one that can only be sung by a man or woman.

While you're experimenting with potential narrators, be thinking about which voice seems to work best for each one. If you're working in the first person, try to write in the manner that your narrator would speak so that you can get the best feel for what your song lines are going to sound like. You don't have to use the whole song lyric. Just use the "write out a few lines" process you read about in the last section to decide whether you might be better off with a different narrator.

Remember that songs are intense and moving experiences. Choosing the right narrator for your song can make it even more dramatic and personal even though you are personally stepping aside to let someone else tell it.

The Least You Need to Know

- You don't have to be the "I" of your song.
- There are many possible "point of view" choices in songwriting, each of which has occasional advantages and disadvantages.
- Be sure to stay true to the knowledge and character of your song's narrator.
- Try out different narrators as part of your songwriting process.

First Impressions

In This Chapter

* Enticing the listener with a title
* Understanding the importance of repetition
* Finding song titles in everyday life
* Setting the scene with your opening line
* Using good questions to make good opening lines

You know the old cliché: You get one chance to make a first impression. You may also know of its twin: First impressions are lasting impressions.

It's absolutely important that your song makes the best possible first impression. Your audience of friends, family, and (you hope someday) people at the local bar, publishers, A&R people, other artists, and even folks listening to the radio won't listen very carefully to anything that doesn't immediately catch their attention and promise to pay off. If your song doesn't make sense from the beginning, you'll probably lose your listeners.

Fortunately, in songwriting, you often get two shots at a first impression: the song's title and its opening line. Playing live songs are sometimes introduced by title. If your title is catchy or intriguing, you have already enticed your audience to listen. The time you spend crafting a top-notch title and opening line will make the process of writing all the rest of the song's parts, especially the chorus and first verse, a whole lot more productive. If the song's opening line is compelling, then you've hooked them!

A Title Is Much More Than a Title

As songwriters, we all tend to become idea hunters and our senses become heightened when prey is around. Someone will say something in conversation that immediately rings a bell and you instantly realize that what you've just heard would be a great idea for a song. It may be a short phrase that rolls easily off the tongue, an unusual description or characterization of something that you haven't heard before, or some alliteration or lines that rhyme in a way that catches your ear. Just like a joke, which is invariably referred to by its punchline, the entire joke is constructed to set up the punchline. When you recognize a great title, it's because it's a payoff you know you can build a whole song to lead up to.

Sometimes the seed idea is the title. Then you have to figure out the story it sums up. Sometimes that's obvious as well and life is certainly easier when it happens that way. But when title and story don't present themselves together as a neatly wrapped package, the process of gaining that perspective begins. Depending on what the initial idea was, it may not be clear what song-worthy theme is suggested by that piece of the puzzle. But no matter how a song idea presents itself, the next step, as you read in Chapter 5, should be to figure out what story or situation that idea is going to be part of and come up with a title that embodies it. Some trial and error may sort it out.

Which brings us to another thing to consider: titles and concepts for songs are not protected by copyright. The song you write and copyright, your *expression* of your idea, is all that you can protect. If someone takes your written words or melody, you may have recourse, but if he or she writes a song about the same thing and/or uses your title, that person is within his or her rights.

So if you want to protect your title or ideas, you better write the best song that can be written with that title or idea. That's the best chance you have to be identified with and benefit from your work. If you don't write a song that achieves success with your title or ideas, someone else will. There are people who hear lots of songs who make a habit of writing the hit songs that should have been written with hit ideas but weren't.

Making the Title Matter

It's best to start with a title. You want to pick one that means something important to your audience. Your inspiration might be an idea of what the story's going to be, or a few lines that sound song-worthy, or perhaps even a winning melody. But the next step should be to figure out the title of the song before trying to develop any other part of it further.

This is especially true if you're writing songs you want someone else to stand on stage and sing. Most successful singers have a good idea of what their audience wants to hear. As the songwriter, you're putting words in the singer's mouth, so you're trying to say something meaningful to people in such a remarkable way that every singer will want to sing it. If your title doesn't convey this subject or message, or at least pique people's interest in some way, then your song may never be heard.

Repeat as Necessary (and Then Some More)!

Repeat the title more often than any other line in the song—not *as* often, *more* often! Listeners tend to identify the main point and then relate the rest of the lyric to that. If you present two equally emphasized points, listeners will either be confused as to what you're presenting or they'll pick the wrong one. You only get to entertain and make one point in an effective song lyric. Anything that doesn't do that dilutes or muddies the meaning.

What's In a Name?

A good title can do a lot of work for you. It can set up your audience, giving them a head start on the song's story, where or when it takes place, and who it's about. On the other hand, it can be mysterious and pique the listeners' curiosity. Titles may also provide interesting twists by creating an idea or image in your listeners' minds that eventually gets turned upside down by the song.

Titles and good ideas for songs are everywhere. You'll hear them in conversations you're having or hearing around you. The dialogue in movies and TV shows are full of them, as are books, magazine articles, and newspapers. If you're listening for them, you'll hear plenty, and you should write them down right away so you don't forget any gems.

Titles must be distinctive and catchy enough to make a lasting impression. You'll learn to recognize when a title has that quality. And you'll undoubtedly discover ways to make titles more memorable.

People

There are no set rules as to what makes a great title, but there are certainly more than enough examples to guide you. The name of a main character of a song, whether the narrator or not, can make a good title because people readily identify with names, whether it's "Gloria" (written by Van Morrison) or "Godzilla" (written by Donald Roesser of Blue Oyster Cult).

Likewise, you can use a specific image or characteristic of a person in the song for your title, such as the old folk tune "House Carpenter" or "Green-Eyed Lady" (by Jerry Corbetta, J. C. Phillips, and David Riordan).

Places and Things

Places, like people, can create images in your audience's mind before you even sing a word. You don't think of "New York, New York" when someone announces the next song will be "Istanbul (Not Constantinople)."

TUNE TIPS

Alliterative titles are popular. The repeated consonants and/or vowel sounds seem to stick in people's minds. Songs like: "Be My Baby," "Baby Got Back," "Free-falling," "All Apologies," "Wonderwall," "Barely Breathing," "Heartbreak Hotel," "Disco Inferno," "Speed of Sound," and "Viva la Vida" are good examples of alliterative titles. Others you might know are "We Three Kings," "(Ballad of a) Teenage Queen," "Blue Suede Shoes," "Dizzy Miss Lizzie," "Meet Me in St. Louis," "Paparazzi," "Russian Roulette," "Saturday Night's All Right for Fighting," "Okie from Muskogee," and "Kiss on My List."

Combining places with events or with people can also give you more ideas for your song's story, as with "Wichita Lineman" (by Jimmy Webb) or "Okie from Muskogee" (by Merle Haggard and Eddie Burris).

TUNE TIPS

One-word titles are hard to forget and have produced many a hit song. Just the Beatles' records alone offer many examples, such as "Help," "Yesterday," "Wait," "Taxman," "Flying," "Michelle," "Rain," "Revolution," "Because," "Something," "Misery," "Girl," "Blackbird," "Piggies," and several more songs they recorded but didn't write: "Money," "Shout," "Matchbox," "Boys," and "Chains." There are probably more, but the point should be clear.

If your song's story is about some object or idea, that might be your potential title, whether the subject is a general emotion ("Hurt," by Trent Reznor) or a very specific thing ("Itsy Bitsy Teenie Weenie Yellow Polka Dot Bikini," by Paul Vance and Lee Pockriss).

Phrases and Stories in a Nutshell

Good titles essentially come down to short phrases (sometimes single words) that easily describe the essence of your song. They tell the story, set the mood, and can sometimes write most of the song for you.

Old sayings and vernacular have already proven themselves to be unforgettable. "You Never Can Tell" did well for Chuck Berry, and "One Day at a Time," helped Kris Kristofferson along his way. Buddy Holly's "Oh Boy!" and "That'll Be the Day" are examples of utilizing common vernacular for titles that, in turn, create hits. They make good titles as they are or you can use their familiar structure and slightly alter them, as in "You Could've Heard a Heartbreak" or "Stop in the Name of Love."

Things you say every day can become really special when they find their way into a song title. Listen constantly for song title ideas in your everyday life. They are all around you, from the books you read to the conversations you have to the billboards you pass. Some writers keep a spare notebook just for title ideas, and, once you start writing them down, you might find yourself with hundreds of titles!

Opening Statements

You don't always get to introduce your song with its title. Then it's up to your opening line to grab your audience's attention and lead them through the first verse and chorus of your song.

Think about your own favorite songs and examine the effectiveness of their first lines. You may find the very thing that drew you to those songs, even if you never consciously noticed it before. Having a great opening line is essential for songs in general, but (just as with song titles) it's especially important if you're trying to sell your songs to publishers or get another artist to sing it. *A&R people* rarely listen to more than the first 30 seconds to a minute of any given song, and if you don't catch their ear immediately, they'll never hear the rest of the song, no matter how great it may be.

DEFINITION

A&R, which stands for "artists and repertoire," is the person or department at a record label in charge of making creative decisions. The people who work in that department help decide which artists to sign and work with, and what songs the artists should record. When you go to a record label to pitch a song, the A&R people are the ones you play it for. You'll read more about these folks in Chapter 17.

A strong opening line catches the listener's ear and sets the mood for the rest of the song. Whether listeners are specifically listening to your song or just happen to be within earshot, you are competing for their attention. Some of my favorite examples of effective opening lines are:

"It's the third hardest thing I'll ever do …" Hearing this for the first time, you immediately wonder what that thing could be! Then you wonder what the first and second hardest things could be. The writers of that song went on to let everyone know as the song progressed. It's from "Holding Her and Loving You," by Walt Aldridge and Tom Brasfield.

"Do you believe in magic?" This swings a door open so wide that almost anything could walk through. John Sebastian, who wrote this, had luck with another first line that was a question, "Did you ever have to make up your mind?" It instantly engages listeners, making them think about their answer.

Other examples of this technique include, "What's it all about Alfie?", or "Do you know where you're going to?" ("Alfie," Burt Bacharach and Hal David; "Theme From *Mahogany*," Gerald Goffin and Michael Masser).

Other proven types of opening lines are introducing the main character or dropping the listener right into the action of the story and then giving him or her just enough information to catch up on what's going on.

WRITER'S TALK

"I was on my way recently to teach at a couple of universities and do a master class at the by:Larm Festival in Oslo, Norway. At the end of every teaching session I always do song critiques. The students are always amazed at how quickly I hone in on the problems in a song, and I always tell them that it's easy.

"Just look at the opening couple of lines and if they don't lead you as a listener directly to the hook (title), then the song doesn't work! To illustrate that, I took all the #1 Pop songs and all the #1 Country songs in the United States in 2010 and connected the first two lines to the hook and read them out to the class.

"One hundred percent of the students felt like the lines were practically the same sentence! Make it easy for the listener to get into the song, invite them in!"

—Ralph Murphy, songwriter of "I'le Got You" (Ronnie Milsap), "Good Enough to Be Your Wife" (Jeanine C. Riley), "Half the Way" (Crystal Gayle), "21st Century Christmas" (Cliff Richard), and more.

Learning by Doing

It's time to go back to your songs in progress and to work up potential titles and opening lines. If you didn't start with a title in mind, you may find you already have one, as well as a first line, somewhere among the lines and phrases and ideas you've written down so far.

If a title or first line doesn't jump out at you immediately, don't worry. Read through what you've written and think about how it all connects to your main theme. Try singing or speaking a few of the lines out loud and listen to how they sound. Chances are you've already got something that will work as a terrific title.

Stockpiling

You never want to lose a good idea, especially if it's a possible title or opening line. As mentioned earlier, it's a great idea to keep a notebook or computer file specifically for titles and opening lines. Always write down ideas whenever and wherever you get them, but make the extra effort to put your titles in a separate place, along with the context in which you heard it and the date; such notes can make it easier for you to work with your ideas later.

You'll also find that going through your dedicated lists of titles and opening lines will often lead to more ideas for other songs. A title consisting of a person or a place, for instance, can conjure up multiple storylines. Instead of trying to cram all your good ideas into one song, set some aside to be seeds for songs you'll write in the future. Never be afraid to scrap something that isn't working in one song, and never be afraid to recycle it in another song. Never let an idea go to waste!

Getting Hooked

You've probably noticed by now that each step in the songwriting process has (we hope!) made each following step easier. A good title often gets repeated in the chorus, and sometimes the chorus is nothing but the title repeated several times. Come up with a great title, and you just might get two birds with one stone.

Above all, remember that your title is about making a memorable impression and characterizing the point of the song. If your audience is initially put off by your song's title, your song's going to have to work a lot harder to keep them listening.

The Least You Need to Know

- A song's title and/or its opening line is often the first impression you'll make on your audience.
- Choose titles that are going to mean something to your listener.
- You'll find ideas for song titles almost everywhere.
- Strong opening lines command attention.
- Keep a stockpile of ideas for song titles and opening lines. They can help you in many ways.

Choruses, Verses, and Bridges

In This Chapter

- Putting the focus on the chorus
- Getting the verse to take you to the chorus
- Adding additional verses
- Building bridges
- Piecing a song together

Songs tend to be very concise and there's usually no room for unnecessary words. You only get to make one point or major statement in a song (and as you learned in Chapter 7, that point better be what your title suggests). Anything extra will weaken the effect of the lyric and song. Every line, if not every word, must lead the listener to the one thought being expressed by the song—which, as we've already said, better be the title.

This mindset is necessary when putting together the body of your song—namely, the verses, chorus, and a bridge, if you decide your song needs one. When you're writing, it's easy to get caught up with every line you write, and new songwriters especially tend to think that every clever, catchy, or poetic line they come up with is essential. But if that line is not contributing or necessary to guiding the listener to your point, to the "moment" of the song, then it can't be essential.

In Chapter 4, you read how important it is not to pre-edit, to be so sure that a line isn't good that you end up not writing at all. Here you will learn that, after you have written everything, you also have to be willing to cut lines, even great lines, if they do not serve your song's major statement.

"All Together Now!"

When you're pretty sure of where you're going with your idea or title, start trying to create the most definitive section of the song: the chorus, if it's a song of that type, or perhaps a first or last stanza if there's no chorus.

Let's assume we're talking about a song with a chorus. The chorus, as you read in Chapter 2, is the focal point of your song. It's the part that everyone knows, or knows well enough to be able to sing part of it. There's almost nothing more pleasing than playing a song of yours and having the audience join in on the chorus.

Typically choruses repeat the same lyrics each time they are sung. This repetition helps to plant your chorus in the ears and minds of your audience so they keep singing it long after they've heard you sing it.

It's advisable to have the title at least once in the chorus. So examine the melody you're working with to decide where the title's going to fall. Quite often it's the first or last line of the chorus, and sometimes it ends up in both of those places. It's just a matter of what seems and sounds right. There are choruses that repeat the title twice, then have one line or a couplet, and then close with the title a third time. And let's not forget songs whose choruses are nothing but the title repeated several times.

There's no right way or wrong way, as long as it works. What works most often is having the title appear multiple times; what seldom works is not having the title in the chorus at all.

Chorus as Overview

The chorus states what your song is about. It clearly sums up your major point and delivers it directly, paying off your verses with a handful of well-chosen lines.

Think about the songs you've heard throughout your life. Chances are you can't immediately remember all the words to a particular song, but it's a safe bet that you remember the chorus—and once you've got the chorus in your head, the rest of the song's lyrics will usually start coming back to you.

SONG STORIES

Because the chorus is often the part of a song people remember most, it can sometimes unintentionally *redefine* a song. The verses of "You Are My Sunshine" or Bruce Springsteen's "Born in the USA," for example, are bitter and depressing. Many people think of these as happy songs (or even patriotic in Springsteen's case) when they are, in fact, very much the opposite.

A good chorus can stand on its own. You can sing it without knowing any of the rest of the song and know generally what you're singing about. You'll notice that effective choruses can be sung without the benefit of a preceding verse and are still understandable.

Titles and Single-Line Choruses

Some choruses are simply the title of the song repeated over and over again. This style of chorus usually has an adamant quality, declaring over and over such sentiments as "You're No Good," sung by both Betty Everett and Linda Ronstadt (written by Clint Ballard, Jr.) or "She's in Love with the Boy" by Trisha Yearwood (written by Jon Ims). Other examples are songs like Bob Dylan's "Knocking on Heaven's Door" and Paul McCartney's "Band on the Run."

Choruses That Change

In some songs, choruses change lyrically over the course of the song. Usually each consecutive verse of those songs changes some key factor leading to the chorus and in doing so necessitates changing words in the chorus to match the terms introduced in the verse right before it. Joni Mitchell is famous for using this advanced principle. In "Both Sides Now," she approaches the main point of the song—looking at things from both sides—in different ways in each verse. She looks at "clouds" in the first verse, "love" in the second, and "life" in the third. The chorus that follows each verse changes slightly in each occurrence to make use of and match the images carried over from the preceding verse.

Using slight variations on choruses can be very effective, and it's definitely something to try after you've written a few songs. For now, go with a more typical chorus so that you can focus on writing strong, concise choruses that capture the main point of your song and get that point across to your listeners.

Verses

The details of your song's story or situation are told in its verses. Verses tend to be slightly less dynamic musically than the chorus, but they serve the important function of walking us up to the climax of each chorus. When written correctly, the chorus seems to follow each verse as naturally as the stars come out after the sun sets. Each verse gives the audience details that make them want to hear the main point of the song, which is then presented in the chorus. It's important not to give away all the details at once and lose their interest.

First Verse

Right from your opening line (which you read about in Chapter 7), the first verse entices the listener with a bit of information designed to make him or her interested in what else will be said. The first verse obviously leads us up to the chorus, but it also has to give us enough information to fully comprehend the meaning or see the relevance of what's being said in the chorus.

Some songs need two verses to provide enough information to lead up to the first chorus. A good example of this is "Pancho and Lefty," written by Townes Van Zandt. This song form is easier to get away with when the verses are short (usually four lines or less), but you probably won't want to try it with your first few songs.

Second Verse

Your second verse should give your audience more information and details concerning the statement of the song, which again is the heart of your chorus. If your song is the narrative of a story, the second verse will simply pick up where the first verse left off.

TUNE TIPS

Effective lyric writing depends on your ability to make your point without straying into either of two deadly extremes. On the one hand, since you know the whole story and intent of your song, it's easy to assume something's obvious, but you're assuming the audience knows things you haven't said yet. On the other hand, it's just as mistaken to over-explain every nuance and detail of a song. A songwriter always has to work to have perspective on what his or her song has made clear to the audience.

Be sure not to write a second verse that essentially says the same thing the first verse did. If there's nothing new to say, don't say it.

Third Verse

The third verse usually brings your story to a conclusion. Often, especially after a bridge, there may be a bit of an ironic twist in the narrative, like in Jim Stafford's "My Girl Bill" or "You Don't Mess Around with Jim" by Jim Croce. This added twist is very common when a song has three or more verses. A good example of this would be the fourth and fifth verses of "Where Have All the Flowers Gone," which were added by Joe Hickerson to Pete Seeger's original three verses.

But, just as with the second verse, don't write a third verse simply for the sake of filling space. A good many verse-chorus songs don't need a third verse, or simply repeat the first verse as a final verse in order to keep the lyrics as strong and focused as possible.

Bridges

The bridge tends to be an alternate explanation of the main point of the song, or a contrasting way of approaching it or emphasizing it. If you're speaking to someone and you've tried repeating what you're trying to say and you're still not sure he understands, you might say, "Let me say it this way …," or show him a different set of circumstances that leads to the same point, and give him another way to look at it.

If you've ever done this, you'll notice that your voice changes in volume and expression, which tends to command more attention. In a song, the bridge usually gets a different musical treatment, and maybe a different dynamic intensity, to reflect this new approach.

More often than not, the explainer listener will then repeat the original expression of the idea, indicating or reinforcing the newly arrived-at understanding. Most of the time, that's what's happening when one uses a bridge: there's still time left in the song before the last chorus, and, "… if you haven't got it by now, here's what I've been saying …," followed shortly by the last chorus.

Structural Integrity

Using a variation of our "song as a house" metaphor from Chapter 2 may help you see how the parts of a song work together:

- **Chorus:** From the road, as you look at your song, the chorus is the house where your song's statement lives.

- **Verse:** From the street, the verse is something like a sidewalk that takes you right up to the front door of the chorus.

- **First verse:** This is the road that takes us to park in front of the house *or* the sidewalk to the front door.

- **Second and third verses:** This is the sidewalk that takes us to the front door from the road *or* the sidewalk to the back door.

- **Pre-chorus (also called the climb or lift):** These are stairs up to the door of the house (front and back).

- **Bridge:** This is another person's description/assessment of the house.

Case Study: "Soon"

We've covered a lot of ground in these last three chapters. Now let's look at how the writing process can work. Remember, once you have your title, the next order of business should be to establish what story or context that title suggests. If your original idea was a story, then you should choose a title that sums up the context of your story idea. Once you know where you're going (and what point you're trying to make), it's easier to monitor your progress. Identify the target and then choose the words that take you there.

Getting the Idea

For example, the song "Soon," which became the title track of Tanya Tucker's 1993 album, began with a couplet I had that I thought would be the basis for a good song:

> *Christmas finds her all alone with no call for rejoice*
> *So she calls his Codaphone just to hear his voice…*

So I started looking for a title. The two lines I had sounded to me like they were about a woman dating a married man. "Woman Dating a Married Man"? "The Other Woman"? Those and several other possibilities didn't seem to be very catchy or have any magic, and they seemed cumbersome.

 SONG STORIES

One of the first answering machines was called the Codaphone. It was so popular that for a long time the brand name was used generically for any device of that nature.

Well, I searched for a title off and on for 11 years. Then one day I saw a TV show that essentially portrayed the very situation I wanted my song to be about. The woman in question kept asking the married man she was seeing when he was going to leave his wife, and he would answer, "Soon." That seemed like the perfect title for the story I was trying to tell.

From Idea and Title to Chorus and Verse

Armed with a title, I approached a co-writer, Bob Regan, and presented what I had: the couplet, the title, and what I thought the song was about. Bob started playing a chord progression that sounded to me like something Paul Simon might use, and we began fitting the lyrics we had onto a melody against what he was playing:

> *Christmas finds her all alone with no call for rejoice,*
> *So she calls his Codaphone just to hear his voice…*

Here's what we came up with:

> *She knows that it's useless but she does it anyway*
> *She knows how he'll answer before she hears him say*

We had what sounded like a verse and we needed to construct a chorus. Usually I recommend writing the chorus first and then constructing the verses so they'll lead to the chorus. In this case, we felt we knew what the chorus was going to say, and we took the chance of writing the verse first, since we knew we wanted to use that couplet exactly as it was. The only way we could see to approach the chorus was to show the married man in the story answering "soon" to her questions. How do we get that out of an answering machine? What if the outgoing message she hears is his voice saying, "Soon, soon, soon…"? We said,

> *(I'll be back) <u>Soon</u>, I can't talk to you right now,*
> *But <u>soon</u> you'll hear a beep, and you know how*
> *To play this game, leave your number and your name*
> *And I promise I'll call back, <u>soon</u>.*

We wanted to give emphasis to the word "soon," and make sure we sold it. So we tried dropping the "I'll be back …," and even though the first "soon" sort of comes out of nowhere, it seemed to work. I'm not aware of anyone having questioned what's happening there or the meaning. I think we thought it might come back to haunt us and made a note that we might have to come up with something better later.

We were also worried that we had clearly created a chorus that was going to have to change after each verse. This is not easy to do effectively and not usually a good idea. The chorus should be easy to remember and, if it changes each time, listeners have a harder time learning and remembering it. We wondered if the singers (and producers) we'd pitch it to would view it as too complex—and therefore not commercial. After several cups of coffee and much second-guessing, hand-wringing, and refiguring, we decided to go ahead and see what happened when we got to the next chorus. We really liked what we had just come up with.

Change of Plans: First Verse Becomes Second Verse

So we pressed on to the second verse, since we needed to know where that went before we could attack the second chorus. We were stumped. It's pretty clear this relationship isn't working for our female character and that it's been going on for some time. What do we show next? There's not really much more we can say at this point in the story, and if we do find something, how on earth can we fashion a chorus around it?

After what seemed like forever, I started thinking about the specific words we used in our first verse and the situation our character had found herself in. Why did we say Christmas? How long has this been going on? What happened before? I asked, "Bob, do you think we've actually written the *second* verse and chorus? Could we go back and give some of the backstory in a first verse and chorus?"

It felt like our woman was experiencing something right then—a moment of realization. We decided to use a flashback to say what had brought her to this moment:

> *Looking back she thinks about that moment in the sand*
> *When what was just a summer fling got so far out of hand*
> *She knew that he was taken, but she gave in anyway*
> *Cause she believed it when she heard him say…*

That answered a lot of questions about how she'd arrived at the unhappy situation she was in. We liked having her get drawn—sort of, but not completely, innocently—into something she wouldn't normally consider, but we needed to paint the guy as having convinced her it was all right. We wanted the listener to still feel sorry for her.

> _Soon_, I'll be free to be with you
> _Soon_ I'll be telling you-know-who
> _The facts of life. That I want you to be my wife_
> _And our dreams will all come true... soon._

Now the story seemed really solid and the second verse and chorus seemed to follow the first naturally. She'd allowed herself to believe his promises that it wouldn't be long, but now it was Christmas and she still couldn't be with him.

Bridge and Resolution Make a Wonderful Twist

We had created a progressing time structure, with our female character looking back to summer, when it all began, and then being alone at Christmas. It felt like a turning point was inevitable, and we wondered if New Year's Eve might not be the perfect time. We wanted her to make a New Year's resolution, and though we didn't know yet what she would actually resolve, we came up with another couplet we really liked for a bridge at that spot in the song:

> _Someday slowly turns to never; tears and champagne offer no solution._
> _He'll say, "Soon..." to her forever, so she makes her New Year's resolution._

We marveled at what we had, but now we had to figure out what she was going to do about it. It was time for the story to end to the listeners' satisfaction, having made some worthwhile point, and we didn't have anything immediately in mind.

After thinking about it awhile, I said, "Well, if we were making a current movie, we'd have her go see his wife." Bob said he didn't want to go that way.

I said, "Well, the other ending that comes to mind is she knocks on his door and when he answers she whips out a gun and ...." Bob held up his hands and said, "I was hoping we could find a way to offer anyone who's in this sort of situation a way to feel better about themselves."

So I thought, "How can she turn this around?" We looked at where we were in the song's melodic structure and realized we were back at the chorus, the "Soon, soon, soon" section. If we have him say that again, there's no change in the story. But what if she turns the tables and says it to him? Wouldn't that be poetic justice? Within a few minutes, we had our closing:

> _Soon she won't call him anymore_
> _And soon when he shows up at her door,_
> _And asks her, "When can I be with you again?"_
> _It will be her turn to say, "Soon."_

As I mentioned earlier, Tanya Tucker ended up recording "Soon," which was the title cut of her 1993 CD—and a #1 single for which we received a Grammy nomination.

There are many ways to go about assembling the lyrics of your song, but remember that it's all about focus. Every line, every word should keep your listener tuned in to the message of your song. You don't want to toss in any lines that will break that hold over your audience. Keep them interested!

This mantra of keeping the listener interested is stressed by songwriter Kenny Loggins, who's written and co-written many hit songs, such as "Danny's Song," "Whenever I Call You Friend," "I'm Alright," and "This Is It." Kenny gave us the following advice to share with you.

Some Advice from Kenny Loggins

First off, as I suspect has already been mentioned, all rules are made to be broken, especially when it comes to art, and specifically songwriting. That said: I come from the "melody first" school. It's okay to let your song melodically ramble a little now and then, but for the most part, I try to stay on point, that is, keep the listener interested: first with a strong melody, especially during the chorus, but even during that more nebulous section we call the verse.

The verse's role is too often somewhat like the role bread plays in a sandwich: something to put the peanut butter in between. But a good verse relies more heavily on the lyrics, and its primary job is to suck the listener into your story, to catch his or her attention and make him or her want to stay involved. Therefore, even if the melody is just a piece of bread, those words become even more important.

So what's the story? Set it up like you might a novel, a little at a time. Be a little less specific and lean on poetry, imagery, and "illusion" to make the listener fascinated. Make him want to find out where you're headed. I like to start off a bit vague, setting a scene, with clues as to time and place. Then move slowly to the emotional setting if that's appropriate. Again, it's best to let the poetry or imagery do this job for you. An action by your protagonist will usually do the trick, as in this song I wrote with Gary Burr and Georgia Middleman, called "Little Victories." We set the scene in verse 1, then expand it emotionally in verse 2.

Verse 1:

> *Friday nights alone*
> *And callin' everyone you know*
> *Reachin' for the cigarettes you gave up long ago…*

In this example, the opening lines are mysterious enough to make the listener wonder just what might be going on. Within three lines, we've established time, place, and a clue to an emotional state.

Verse 2:

> *Photographs you tore in half and scattered on the floor*
> *Letters where she swore her love*
> *Mean nothing anymore…*

Now we're getting to the actual situation. Clearly the protagonist is dealing with the fallout of a broken heart. Common themes like this are a bit trickier to write, because it's more challenging to find a new, yet honest way to approach them. Luckily, all three of us have had plenty of experience living this scenario. Now, all this focus on lyric might seem to contradict my "melody first" axiom, but truth be told, we knew every note *before* the words started to fall into our jigsaw puzzle.

When melody is paramount, which I need to state here is *not* how all writers work, the *feeling* of the melody usually dictates the direction of the words. The two should be married so that all elements point to one emotional moment. And that's the central point I'm sharing with you: *All elements of your song should stay focused on that one, central emotion.*

Too many young writers try to bite off too much topic in their songs, too many emotional changes. Stay on point. Imagine a bull's-eye at the center of a circle of poetry, like wagons circled around your hero. *That's* your emotional center. *That's* the point of your song. Everything in your song should aim at that bull's-eye. Ideally, your title hits that bull's-eye dead-on. Not necessarily literally, but certainly poetically, emotionally.

Like I said at the start, there are some wonderful exceptions to that rule, where, for example, the speaker himself is rambling because he's upset and confused, but even his rambling, disjointed poetry might be leading you to the overarching reality that he's messed up and desperate and wants you to know exactly that.

So stick to the point, stay focused on the hook idea or line, and keep me interested.

Learning by Doing

Now it's time to totally flesh out the song idea you've been working on these past four chapters. Take any one of the themes, titles, or opening lines that you've compiled and try to come up with a compelling chorus. Then use your opening line to begin a first verse and see how things go. Don't make your verses too long, and don't write more than three at this point. Concentrate more on the quality of your lines, making all of them lead the listener to your chorus.

Test out your song by reading or singing it aloud, preferably to someone you trust to give you an honest opinion. See whether the chorus is catchy and whether the verses keep the listener's attention.

Above all, don't be afraid to cut out or replace material that isn't working—no matter how much you may like it. Remember, you can always use the great lines you trim out of one song in a future song. If a line's that good, it will create a new song for itself.

A great exercise you can use to make certain you stayed on track with your song's message is to say the title after each line in the verse. Look at the Lennon/McCartney song "She Loves You" as an example:

> *You think you've lost your love (she loves you)*
> *Well I saw her yesterday (she loves you)*
> *It's you she's thinking of (she loves you)*
> *She told me what to say (she loves you)*

Obviously, not every song is going to work this well! But it does give you a good idea of how to test the overall focus of each line of your song. If you have too many consecutive lines that do not direct the listener to your song's message, then you want to refocus those lines back to the main point of the song.

In addition, you might want to try this interesting songwriting exercise: Pick a classic song, one that's been popular for years, and examine it line by line to see whether you could change a line or even a single word without diminishing the quality of that song. It's surprisingly rare that you'll be able to substitute anything better or even as good as the lyrics as they were written.

The Least You Need to Know

- The chorus should concisely emphasize the major point of your song.
- Verses are meant to lead the listener to the chorus. You want this to happen as naturally as possible.
- Don't write extra verses if they don't add anything new or important to the song.
- Use the bridge to approach your main theme from a different perspective.
- When piecing a song together, you may sometimes have to rearrange the verses to make the best lyrical fit.

Lyrical Lyrics

In This Chapter

- Making sure your words are understood
- Using meter
- Applying rhyme schemes in songs
- Showing what's happening in your song—not just telling it!
- Using poetic devices to strengthen your lyrics
- Making your audience part of the songwriting process

Ever read an interview with or heard a hit songwriter talking about how he or she wrote an award-winning song in 15 minutes?

There are times when it happens almost that quickly, as if by magic or divine intervention. But most of the time, it's like the successful songwriter said about writing his biggest hit: "It took me 15 years to learn to write that song in 15 minutes."

The real story is that, after however long a period of training it takes you to learn the craft of songwriting, you automatically incorporate an array of proven principles, instantly reviewing and editing your thoughts and work, knowing what to strive for and watch out for, and judging your creations from the perspective of others. And when something's not quite right, you know what it is and how to fix it!

Making a List

You reach that level of competence by routinely checking your work against a checklist, mental or otherwise, of qualities a viable song must have. A common mistake you can easily avoid is becoming what we used to call an "early settler," declaring a song "finished" without making sure it does what it has to in order to be taken seriously. The amount of time you've been working on a song is, unfortunately, no way to tell whether it's done. When the song is right, it will sound so natural that singing and listening to it feels effortless. Judge your finished work by the effect it has on the listeners, not by the time it's taken to write it.

So let's review the basics: You've picked a worthy title and one main point to write about. You've effectively developed your point—your song's "moment"—by showing the story instead of just telling it, beginning with an engaging opening line and with verses that set up the chorus or the title line. The title falls on the most musically emphasized part of the melody and is repeated more times than any other line. You've added new information as the song progresses, leading to a conclusion that satisfies the listener.

Assuming you've done all that, here are a few other things you should watch out for and make sure you've taken care of before you release your song to the world.

First and foremost, are the lyrics easy to sing? This may seem obvious, but it's easy to get so involved in choosing words that rhyme and say what you want to say that you forget to make sure they're singer-friendly. Avoid words that are hard to pronounce or sing. Watch out for pairs or groups of words that are just plain hard to get your mouth around. No tongue-twisters, no words that aren't pleasant to the ear. Unless you need to jar the listener, don't use a word that does.

Are there any words or phrases that draw so much attention to themselves that the listener misses the next few words? If you include a funny word or punchline in your lyric, there better not be any important info in the lyric immediately following it, because the listener will be stuck on that line or too busy laughing to hear anything else. Artists who routinely sing songs that make people laugh will often pause or vamp momentarily, just like an actor in a live sitcom, until the audience is ready to listen. To a lesser degree, any line that stands out too much can be more trouble than it's worth.

Have you used words that have homonyms? Words that sound the same but have different meanings (brake/break, male/mail, seen/scene, feet/feat, patients/patience) open the door for misinterpretation and confusion. Avoid this possible distraction by using another word, or make absolutely sure that the context leaves no room for even a momentary misunderstanding.

Have you used a word in your lyric that has a slang meaning different from its dictionary meaning? Slang changes over time, but, once again, even if your intended meaning is obvious, even a momentary distraction will take the listener away from the meaning and emotion of your song. Don't let that happen.

Avoiding Tongue Twisters

One way to check for trouble spots is to read your lyrics aloud. Some songwriters write lyrics without having a specific melody in mind, and if that's you, it's even more imperative to test drive each line. When you read or sing your lines out loud (record them if you can and play them back), listen to yourself and double-check that each word is audible and that the intended meaning is easily understood. If you have a hard time saying a line or understanding what you're reading, you need to change it.

There are countless other errors you may make in your lyrics, but if you proof your work carefully, you'll usually catch most of them.

Bringing in Outside Help

It's also helpful to cultivate relationships with a few people you can count on as "test listeners" for your new songs, friends and co-writers for whom you routinely play your new songs. These should be people you know well enough that by observing them as they listen, you can accurately judge their reaction to each part of the song. Do they understand the words? Can they picture what's "happening" in your song? What meaning or point did they get?

If there's any question, you can also develop the art of getting the information you want without having to ask pointed questions. Putting people on the spot tends to color their answers. Fortunately, they'll often spontaneously comment positively or negatively on something they heard, felt, or didn't understand.

When these listeners bring up questions or issues, you might be tempted to explain your lyrics further (or, even worse, argue with your listeners about them). *Don't do it!* You're looking for their opinion, not yours. Take note of their reactions and remarks, and make sense of them later. Figure out whether your song has problems, and then do whatever is needed to remedy them.

The Meter's Running

Most songwriters begin crafting their lyrics to fit an early basic melody they've created for that song. The stressed and unstressed syllables are mostly predetermined by the music, though it's common to have the developing lyric force a restructure of the melodic line when it doesn't quite fit. Obviously if you write the lyrics before you have a melody, you'll write the "pulse" of the music to follow the *meter* (natural rise and fall) of the words. In either case, there is usually a regular rhythmic pattern that's consistent in like parts of the song.

DEFINITION

Meter refers to the pulse or pattern created by the stressed and unstressed syllables of words used in song lyrics or poetry.

Your choice of pulse or rhythmic pattern of a lyric can be just as catchy as the other elements, such as melodic motif, alliteration, and internal rhymes. Applying a strong rhythm pattern to lyrics makes them more memorable, unlike strong or elaborate melodies, which tend to compete with the comprehension of the lyrics. The words of the Beatles' "Eleanor Rigby," for example, tend to stick in your mind. The words of "Penny Lane," other than the title line, might be a little harder to recall.

The regular, rhythmic pattern of lyrics is a major element of what makes them memorable. This is easily seen in "Eleanor Rigby." Ear-catchingly, the first five syllables of each half of each verse repeat exactly the same rhythm and meter:

El-ean-or Rig-by…

Waits at the win-dow…

Fa-ther Mc-Ken-zie…

Look at him work-ing…

As a matter of fact, every syllable in the entire song is stressed and unstressed identically to the others in the corresponding parts of the song.

Remember, though, that you can still take liberties with the meter, because musical syllables can be held for different lengths of time (beats). For example, the verses of Bruce Springsteen's "Blinded by the Light" have a distinct rhythmic feel because the stressed syllables fall roughly in the same place in regard to the musical beats (the first and third beat in this case) even though the actual number of syllables between the stressed ones changes.

WRITER'S TALK

"The marriage of the lyrics and melody ('prosody' in songwriter-speak) is another opportunity to make your songs real. Tune yourself into the emotion of the singer and make the melody express that feeling. At the same time, make sure that the melody rises up out of the natural cadence of the words. That is the emphasis on a syllable in a word or a word in a line is natural, the way we really speak. Don't put the em-PHA-sis on the wrong syl-LA-ble!"

—Pat and Pete Luboff

Rhyme Time

Songwriters—and listeners—have lots of opinions about rhyming. Some feel strongly that only "exact" or "perfect" rhymes are suitable, while others don't mind so-called "near" rhymes, and others don't have a problem with either—type! This only proves that songwriting is an art, not a science, and probably the truest path to perfection is to use whatever *works*. As long as the listener doesn't say, "Hey wait a minute—that wasn't supposed to go like that!" you've fulfilled your basic rhyming duty.

Songs are built on patterns, and having words rhyme in the same places in similar sections of your lyrics helps create and define those patterns. Listeners quickly and instinctively identify the structural elements of a song and expect the same pattern, rhythm, and rhyme scheme. Songwriters create an expectation and then either pay it off or use the expectation to slightly tease or create suspense in the listener … and then pay it off. Rhyme is an important part of that game.

Rhyme Schemes

Your head is a warehouse full of rhyme schemes, collected from the thousands of songs you've heard throughout your lifetime. Some songs use the same rhyme in every line, which is called an "*a-a-a-a*" pattern. Some rhyme every other line (*a-b-a-b*) and some rhyme on the second and fourth lines (*a-b-c-b*). Depending on how many lines you're using, you have many possible choices for patterns. A typical six-line pattern, for example, would be *a-a-b-c-c-b*.

Everyone is a critic, and the person writing the song is often the worst, wanting everything to rhyme in a certain way. Clearly some rhymes are more clever, exact, unique, or consistent than others, but as long as they create a pattern that helps keep the lyric memorable and fulfills the listeners' expectations, it's fine.

You *do* want to use the same rhyme scheme in similar sections of your song. If you've come up with a verse with a rhyme pattern of *a-b-a-b*, for example, you want your other verses to follow suit. And you'll probably want a different rhyme scheme in differing sections (for example, verse: *a-b-a-b*; chorus: *c-c-d-c*; and perhaps bridge: *e-e*).

Rhyming Within Lines

Rhyming words that are not the same parts of speech is supposed to be more powerful than, say, rhyming two or three verbs or nouns. The Beatles again come to mind, this time in "Can't Buy Me Love":

> *I may not have a lot to give*
> *But what I've got I'll give to you.*

This demonstrates internal rhymes as well. Internal rhymes and couplets occurring in the text when there's been either no rhyming or an alternating pattern of rhymes can emphasize that text in the lyric. John Lennon's lyric shows us another use of a short couplet in "Norwegian Wood," "marking" the end of a particular part of a song, in this case, each verse:

> *I once had a girl*
> *Or should I say she once had me*
> *She showed me her room*
> <u>*Isn't it good Norwegian Wood*</u>

Be careful not to use the same vowel sound too much as it can be annoying or distract from your lyric unless you're trying to make a point of that repetition. Your goal is to create a lyric that says exactly what it's supposed to without sounding contrived and subtly rhymes where the listener subconsciously expects it.

SONG STORIES

There is a remarkable song on Jackson Browne's first album called "A Child in These Hills," the lyrics of which are instantly memorable. The most extraordinary thing about it is he wrote it without using any rhyming lines.

Poetic Devices

Songwriting borrows a lot of tools from poetry and other writing styles. After all, anything that can make a lyric or line stand out can only help make your song better. Meter and rhyme both fall into this category and, in studying titles and choruses, you've already learned about the importance of repetition as a songwriting tool.

Here are some other tricks of the trade to incorporate into your songwriting:

imagery   The use of symbolism, figurative language, or description to suggest pictures or feelings in the mind of the listener: "the sky was dark" (something bad was about to happen), "the night crashed with thunder and lightning" (evil is afoot), or "it was a sunny morning and the birds were singing" (all is right with the world). Colors tend to suggest certain emotions. For instance, we routinely talk about someone feeling "blue" or seeing "red."

metaphor   Describing or referring to something by saying it *is* something else in order to suggest both objects have the same characteristics: your anger is a time bomb, being in her arms is heaven, he is a rock.

simile   Another form of comparison, this one using the words "like" or "as": "Your kiss is like a dream," and, "it feels as right as rain," are common examples.

alliteration   A succession of words whose first sounds or first accented syllables are the same: pretty Polly, a little lost lion.

apostrophe   Speaking in apostrophe, talking directly to someone who isn't present or doesn't exist.

assonance   Matching middle vowel sounds: glove, love; school, fool.

feminine rhymes   Two or more syllable rhymes in which only the first syllable is stressed: table, able; actual, factual.

dramatic irony   An outcome of events contrary to what seems likely, what would normally be expected, or what would follow from the audience's understanding of a situation, which is not clear to the characters in the story.

onomatopoeia   A word that imitates an actual sound, like "boom" or "clang."

personification   Speaking of animals, objects, or concepts as if they were human.

repetition   Repeating the same word or phrase for emphasis or to make it memorable.

   WRITER'S TALK

Joni Mitchell uses color imagery metaphorically with breathtaking effect throughout her song "Marcie" to tie seemingly unrelated things together:

> *Red is sweet and green is sour* (candy)
>
> *Red is autumn; green is summer* (changing seasons)
>
> *Red is stop and green's for going* (traffic light)
>
> *Red is angry; green is jealous* (feelings)

Creating Vivid, Memorable Lyrics

Imagery plays right into the idea of songs as a story or snapshot. Good imagery often employs metaphors and similes, and this combination of poetic devices can make a line linger in a listener's mind long after hearing the song. Placing specific details in your song lyrics helps create memorable images. "Raven hair" makes a more lasting impression than "dark hair" or "black hair."

Another way of creating interesting images is to take a phrase that most people know and give it a little twist. For example, in "Champaign, Illinois," by Bob Dylan and Carl Perkins, the saying "gainfully employed" is changed to "painfully employed," which undoubtedly strikes a chord with just about everyone. It also adds an emotional element and, as we know, memories are tied to emotions.

Alliteration

Alliteration and assonance are a bit like internal rhymes in that they help a listener remember whole lines and phrases. And they're pleasant to listen to. One of the best examples of alliteration in a song lyric would be "Helplessly Hoping" by Stephen Stills of Crosby, Stills, and Nash. Almost every line of its two verses is chock full of them.

It's important to be careful with alliteration, though. Used in moderation, a bit of alliteration can make a mundane phrase memorable. But running together a string of similar sounds can make a song lyric harder to hear and understand. Be sure to give your alliterations the "speak or sing aloud" test, preferably using someone else as judge.

Nonsense!

Not every song has to have a great, profound meaning. And even those songs that do can stand to have a little levity tossed in. Most people can't recite all the lyrics of Gordon Lightfoot's "The Wreck of the Edmund Fitzgerald," but everyone knows the one where the cook says, "Fellas, it's been good to know ya," just as well as the line that asks, "Does anyone know where the love of God goes …?"

Sometimes songs are just about having fun and being silly. "One-Eyed, One-Horned Flying Purple People-Eater," "Itsy Bitsy Teenie Weenie Yellow Polka Dot Bikini," "Rocky Raccoon," and "Bungalow Bill" come to mind. No instruction (or serious thinking) needed.

TUNE TIPS

Songwriters seem to have a knack for using opposites to create an interesting lyric. From Stephen Foster's "Oh! Susanna," with lines like, "It rained all night the day I left the weather was so dry," to the Beatles' "Hello Goodbye," you will find putting two opposite ideas together often creates a great line that catches the listener's attention and makes it memorable.

Having a sense of humor, as well as a good feeling for when to use it, helps your lyric connect with the audience. Likewise, the use of nonsense phrases and syllables can add a lot to a song. Who doesn't sing along with the "sha la la la" of the Counting Crows' "Mr. Jones" or Van Morrison's "Brown Eyed Girl"? And Gene Vincent and Donald Graves got a lot of mileage out of "Be-Bop-a-Lula."

Making the Personal Universal

Good songs are magical. They take a very personal emotion and allow each listener to experience that emotion in his or her own way. If your song is about a friend of yours, your audience should feel that they either know your friend as well as you do or that they have a friend just like him or her. We're all the same, and we're all different. If something in your song authentically captures what you feel about that situation, almost everyone else in the world will identify with it.

Picture the situation you're showing in your song and imagine the characters in it saying the lyrics you're putting in their mouths. Is that what they would actually say? Can you hear yourself using those words in that situation? Or, even better, are they saying something you *wish* you'd said in a similar situation? Is this a positive or empowering message song, one that will help listeners feel good about themselves? Is it a message that a large part of your audience would like to hear? These questions can lead to a winning song lyric and eliminate a lot of unproductive work.

Your goal as a songwriter is to come up with a concise way to *show* your listener the situation or story you're conveying. You want to paint a picture your audience will apply their own feelings to. How can you draw that scene so they will recognize it, react to it, and apply it to their own experience? The audience will have to *want* to have that involvement—but they don't have to know it's happening. It may be something they'll do unconsciously.

The Other Side of the Stage

It's not easy, but listen constantly to your lyrics as if you're hearing them for the first time. Even though every line and word is clear to you (we hope!), you have to listen with perspective and think about whether or not the lines and phrases would be equally clear to you if you hadn't written them. Are they discernable as words? Is the meaning you intended to convey coming through clearly? And is the message something your audience can relate to?

If you find that you have to explain too much about your song before or after someone hears it, then your lyrics aren't doing their job. And you also need to trust your listener to make connections. As a songwriter, you can do a lot to guide your audience, but your songs will be more effective if they encourage each listener to experience the song as it relates to his or her sensibilities.

Three Minutes—One Listen

Your listeners don't usually have a lyric sheet to read while they are hearing your song. Plus, they also get only about three to four minutes to take everything in. And then their attention will be taken by another song for about the same length of time, and then another. Not only do they not get the time to let your song sink in, they often have to distinguish it from the string of songs they heard that day.

This is one reason that repetition is so important to your lyrics, especially when it comes to a good, strong chorus. The more times you can drive your song's point home, the more chances it has to get stuck in the listener's mind.

Don't worry that your audience won't catch every line the first time around. Instead, create a reason for them to want to hear your song again. And the best way to do that is to have them take something home with them—an opening line or a chorus or just a short phrase that they can't get out of their head.

Striving for Clarity

Everything you've been learning in this chapter serves one purpose: to make your lyrics as strong as possible so that your listener understands your message and can share in the emotional experience of your song. Refining your work is all about delivering your song's message as clearly and effectively as you can.

It's not impossible to write an effective song that is intentionally vague—or ironic or sarcastic, for that matter—but you do have to take into account that these styles don't always translate successfully into song lyrics. As you know, song lyrics have to be economical and self-explanatory, because there isn't room in a lyric to show or restate concepts in different ways until it's unmistakably clear. When you're talking with someone, you can usually tell when he or she is being sarcastic, which, as you know, is to say something that is the opposite of what you mean or believe in an exaggerated fashion so that the listener knows not to believe you. We use body language and an exaggerated tone of voice, volume, and emphasis.

But when a person is singing, these extra hints are not as easy to detect because the melody controls the pitch, emphasis, and so on. You most certainly can't count on your audience to pick up on whether or not you're being sarcastic with your song lyric. Even when you are singing in front of an audience, it's difficult to ensure that they pick up on your cues, and it's even more difficult when the listener is only hearing a recorded audio version of the song.

Sometimes the intention of the songwriter is difficult to discern from what the narrator says. When Randy Newman's "Short People" was a hit, he received a lot of criticism for what some listeners perceived as prejudice and mean-spiritedness. They took what Newman the narrator was saying literally, and were unable to understand that Newman the writer was in fact sarcastically commenting against prejudice. Even though his message of everyone being the same was clearly spelled out later in the bridge, it was too late for listeners who were confused to understand the true meaning.

As skillful as Randy Newman is, his sophisticated, indirect method of communicating made his message unclear to a large percentage of the audience. His song was a hit not so much *because* of this device, but *in spite* of the confusion it caused. The singer can't always convey the light in which a statement should be taken the way a speaker can. It's best for all but the best and already successful songwriters to avoid saying anything lyrically except exactly what you mean as literally as you can.

Learning by Doing

You obviously want to apply all the various ideas described in this chapter to the lyrics you've been writing up to this point, but we can't stress enough the importance of reading or singing your lyrics aloud, both to yourself and to someone else whose opinion you trust.

Check your lyrics for spots where a bit of imagery might help make a line or phrase shape up. For instance, if you've written, "I took a walk downtown," you could put your listener right into the scene by saying something like, "Walking through traffic and the downtown crowd." Anything that puts your audience right into the story will get them more involved with your song. Verbally show the listener the familiar storefronts … waiting at the "Don't Walk" sign … dodging the parking meters … cutting through the shoppers on the sidewalks. Share the sounds, smells, and feelings.

Above all, don't be shy about cutting out any line or phrase that is unclear or isn't getting your song's point across. A particular line may have something in it that you think is great, but that doesn't mean it's great for this specific song. Don't be so attached to what you've written that you can't make it better.

Finally, remember to keep your lyrics as conversational as possible. It may be tempting to create a poetic bit of phrasing, but you will be the only one who appreciates it if your listeners can't follow it.

When working with rhymes in poetry, for instance, you might get away with reordering the sequence of words in a line to make it rhyme, but if that changes the line to something most people would never say, it probably won't fly in a song, even though it would in a poem:

> *To think of what I would've missed*
> *If I'd've never kissed your lips*

That's a far better lyric, even though the rhyme isn't perfect, than changing the second line to a poetically preferable exact rhyme, such as

> *If your lips I'd've never kissed*

or

> *If your lips never I'd've kissed*

People don't talk like that, at least not these days, and frankly, they don't listen twice to songs that speak that way.

Whenever you come across an awkward-sounding line or phrase, ask yourself whether you would ever say it in conversation, or whether you've ever heard someone else say it. If the answer is no, revise the line.

Once again, when judging your "finished" lyric, make sure you've picked a worthy title and one main point to write about. You've effectively developed your point—your song's "moment"—by showing the story instead of just telling it, beginning with an engaging opening line and with verses that set up the chorus or the title line. You have the title falling on the most musically emphasized part of the melody and repeated more times than any other line. You've added new information as the song progresses, leading to a conclusion that satisfies the listener.

The Least You Need to Know

- You only get to say one thing or make one point in a song.
- You suggest, hint, ask a question, and set up where the song is going; then you pay it off, resolve it, or answer the question.
- Read your lyrics aloud to catch any questionable, clumsy, or potentially weak lines or phrases.
- Meter and rhyme help listeners remember your lyrics.
- Make use of imagery and other poetic devices to create more powerful lyrics.
- Remember to maintain your perspective and put yourself in your listener's place while you write, review, and revise.
- Make your lyric as clear as possible. You want your audience to understand your message.

Making Music

You can't have songs without music. And the more you know about music, the more interesting and exciting your songs will be. After a quick introduction to the very basics of music, you'll learn about the three essential building blocks of every song: melody, harmony, and rhythm.

You will discover how easy it is to create a memorable melody and how certain chords and chord progressions work together to create harmony for your melodies. You will also get some hands-on experience at assembling melodies and chords and gain some knowledge of how rhythm holds all the parts of a song together.

With an understanding of both the lyrical and musical aspects of songwriting, you can focus on creating hooks for your songs to make them even more interesting to your listeners.

Chapter 10

Notes, Chords, and Keys

In This Chapter

- The makeup of music
- Twelve notes to work with
- Building the major scale
- How chords are created
- Why certain chords sound good together

It goes without saying that music is a vital part of any song. Music makes up the melody, so without it you've only got spoken words for your lyrics. Music also makes up the harmonies and rhythms of songs.

Even if you are a songwriter who focuses only on the lyrics of songs, you still should know a little bit about music and how it works. The word *lyric* itself is defined as "having a musical quality," so it's pretty obvious that lyricists have to know something about music.

Fortunately, the basics of music are as easy to learn as counting to 12. We'll give you a quick overview of the fundamentals of music that any songwriter should know. Don't worry if some of this doesn't initially sink in; the more you run across these aspects of music in your own writing, the more you'll make the connections between notes and chords, melodies and harmonies. We do recommend that, if you're interested in studying music theory more in depth, you check out Michael Miller's *The Complete Idiot's Guide to Music Theory, Second Edition*, as well as *The Complete Idiot's Guide to Music Composition*.

The DNA of Music

You learned in Chapter 2 that the musical component of any song can be broken down into three parts: melody, harmony, and rhythm. Let's focus on melody and harmony first.

Melodies are made up of single notes strung together. You can't sing, whistle, or hum more than one note at a time. But you can have someone else sing with you, singing different notes, or have a musical instrument playing notes or chords to back you up. These additional notes, pieced together like building blocks, create chords, which are the harmony of your songs.

Harmonies are often grouped together in sets of chords that focus on a tonal center, which we call the key of a song. To give you an idea of what we're talking about, sing the song "Happy Birthday" aloud. Don't worry about sounding silly—it's always someone's birthday! Now try singing it again, but this time, end by singing a different note than the actual final one. Any note will do. It sounds totally wrong, doesn't it? You're out of key! You've lost the tonal center of the song.

The notes of your melody often help define both the key and the accompanying harmony. Likewise, knowing what key you want to write a song in will usually predetermine many of the melody notes and harmony chords. It's all intricately connected.

Notes

Musical notes are named after the first seven letters of the alphabet, from A to G. They are endlessly cycled, so, for instance, if you are starting on A and ascending through these notes, the note after G is A again, which is then followed by B, and so on:

A   B   C   D   E   F   G   A   B   C   D   etc.

Obviously you can start at any note you'd like as long as you remember to stay in order and that A follows G. Starting on C, for example, would be like this:

C   D   E   F   G   A   B   C   D   E   F   etc.

In Western music, notes are spaced in intervals of steps and half steps. Think about how the keys of a piano are spaced. The note of each key, whether it is black or white, is a half step away from its next-door neighbor.

There are a total of 12 different notes, each one a musical half step from the other. This is accomplished through the use of *accidentals*, which are indicated by the use of a *sharp* symbol (♯) or a *flat* symbol (♭). You make a note sharp by raising it a half step. Flatting a note means you've lowered it a half step.

> **DEFINITION**
>
> To make any note **sharp** is to raise that note a half step in tone. When you lower any given note by a half tone, you make it **flat**. An **accidental** is a note that has been made either flat or sharp. Some accidentals share the same note but can be called by either name. For example, the note that is a half step between G and A is called G♯, since it is a half step higher than G, *and* it can also be called A♭, since it is a half step lower than A.

These accidentals fall between some of the other notes and, by definition, each sharp shares a name with a flat. Putting all 12 in order for you (and adding an additional C in order to finish on the same note we started) looks like this:

C	C♯/ D♭	D	D♯/ E♭	E	F	F♯/ G♭	G	G♯/ A♭	A	A♯/ B♭	B	C

Notice that there is no accidental between E and F and also none between B and C. This means that a half step separates B and C as well as E and F. Each of the other nonaccidental notes are a whole step (two half steps) from its nearest neighbor.

The Major Scale

Knowing the notes is the first step to understanding how music works. Knowing the *major scale* is the next. Almost everything that you will ever learn about music is defined by the major scale, so taking a few minutes now to figure it out will help you the rest of your life.

Simply speaking, a scale starts on any given note and then follows a specific sequence of steps, usually a combination of full steps and half steps, until you get back to your starting note.

DEFINITION

Scales are usually given two-part names, like the C major scale, the A harmonic minor scale, or B♭ diminished scale. The first part of the name is a note, which serves as the scale's root and tonal center. The second part is a description (major, pentatonic, Dorian, just to name a few) that is shorthand for the specific pattern of steps and half steps used to create the scale.

There are many different scales, but you probably already know the major scale. Do you remember "Do Re Mi" from *The Sound of Music?* That's the major scale.

Here is the specific pattern of steps and half steps that make a major scale: Start with any note you like; this is the root note. From that starting point, follow this pattern of whole steps (W) and half steps (H) until you reach the root note again:

Root   W   W   H   W   W   W   H (Root again)

Test it out by starting with C. Moving one whole step from C brings you to D, and then one more whole step will put you at E. Next you want a half step, moving you up to F. G would be the next note (one whole step up from F), followed by A (one whole step up from G), and then B (one whole step up from A). Taking one half step up from B brings you back to C again, and that completes the C major scale.

The G major scale starts on G and looks like this:

G   A   B   C   D   E   F♯   G

Notice that F♯, not F, is one whole step up from E. It's also one half step from G, so it does indeed fit the pattern of the major scale.

If you wanted to start with F, then the F major scale would look like this:

F   G   A   B♭   C   D   E   F

The easiest way to get this into your head is simply to write out any of the 12 possible major scales. You can check your answers online at almost any music site by typing "12 major scales" in your favorite search engine.

To make the concept of chords easier, it's helpful to think of scales in a generic form by assigning a number value, or degree, to the note of a scale. Here is the C major scale again, with the generic value listed above the note:

Root	Second	Third	Fourth	Fifth	Sixth	Seventh
C	D	E	F	G	A	B

Creating Chords

Chords are made by combining specific notes together. The harmonies that chords provide can be very simple or have layers of complexity to match that of your lyrics.

There are four primary types of chords: major, minor, augmented, and diminished. Of those four, the major and minor chords occur most often in music. Additionally, you can add extra notes to any of these four primary chords to create more textured sounds.

> **DEFINITION**
>
> Playing two or more different notes at the same time creates a **chord.** There are many different types of chords, but the ones used most frequently in songs are the basic major and minor chords.

Chords are named by their root note. Unless you see a symbol telling you otherwise, you should assume that you're dealing with a major chord.

Two Basic, Two Exotic

The major chord is made up of the root, third, and fifth notes from its major scale. C major, or just "C," is made up of C (the root note), E (the third), and G (the fifth). Using our earlier examples of G and F, you can determine that the G chord is G, B, and D, while the F chord consists of F, A, and C.

To make a minor chord, you start with the major chord and flat the third note, or lower it a half step. A small *m* is used to indicate any minor chord. Cm, therefore, is C, E♭, and G.

Augmented and diminished chords are made by making further changes to the third, fifth, or both. Here's a chart that spells out how to create each of the four primary chords:

Major	Root	Third	Fifth
Minor (m)	Root	Flat third	Fifth
Augmented (aug)	Root	Third	Sharp fifth
Diminished (dim)	Root	Flat third	Flat fifth

If you go to the Book Extras webpage, you can hear an audio example demonstrating each of these four chords. Some people think that major chords sound happy and minors sound sad. Augmented and diminished chords certainly sound unsettled, almost transitory.

Visit us online at www.completeidiots.guide.com/artofsongwriting.

Chords with Accessories

As mentioned, you can create more complicated chords by simply adding more notes, or sometimes removing or substituting notes, to the root, third, and fifth of your four primary chords.

It's important to know here that the musical convention is to name a lot of chords with numbers beyond what seems to be the range of the scale. Remember that all the notes are constantly repeating one after the other, so when you get back to the root note, or the eighth degree, the next note would be the ninth and it would be the same note as the second. Again using the C major scale as an example:

Root	Second	Third	Fourth	Fifth	Sixth	Seventh	Root (Eighth)	Ninth	Tenth	Eleventh
C	D	E	F	G	A	B	C	D	E	F etc.

Here are some embellished chords that you're likely to hear in songs:

"5"	Root	Fifth			
"sus"	Root	Fourth	Fifth		
"6"	Root	Third	Fifth	Sixth	
"7"	Root	Third	Fifth	Flat seventh	
"maj7"	Root	Third	Fifth	Seventh	
"m7"	Root	Flat third	Fifth	Flat seventh	
"add9"	Root	Third	Fifth	Ninth	
"9"	Root	Third	Fifth	Flat seventh	Ninth

Again, you'll hear audio examples of each of these chords on the Book Extras webpage. Listening to these should give you a great idea of what each chord sounds like and the kind of mood it can set for you and your lyrics.

Visit us online at www.completeidiots.guide.com/artofsongwriting.

This chart does not cover every possible chord, but it highlights some of the chords you find in many songs. The "5" chords simply drop out the third from the primary chord. This makes the chord rather ambiguous, sounding neither major nor minor. It's a favorite of rock music and the various rock sub-genres, such as heavy metal and grunge, where "5" chords are called "power chords."

Suspended or "sus" chords replace the third with the fourth, again creating a bit of ambiguity as to a chord being major or minor. You'll find these used in all musical genres.

The various seventh, add9, and ninth chords add even more complexity to the primary chords. While you will hear these chords in a variety of music styles, they tend to pop up more often in blues, jazz, and blues-style rock songs.

Living in Harmony

Music, like life, is constantly moving. Songs don't simply stay on one chord or harmony but change from one to another, creating musical tension and resolution. These changes are typically called chord progressions.

Even though there are literally hundreds of chords, certain ones seems to go better with others. They simply sound good together. In Chapter 13, you'll examine these chord progressions and learn the most common ones used in songs. And you'll also get to hear these progressions on the Book Extras webpage, too.

Visit us online at www.completeidiots.guide.com/artofsongwriting.

For now, let's see how the major scale helps us get a start on which chords are likely to sound good together. And we do that by learning how to make diatonic chords.

Diatonic Chords

The term *diatonic* refers to using notes taken only from one specific scale. So if we use the C major scale as our example, then C, D, E, F, G, A, and B would be our diatonic notes.

To create the diatonic chords for the key of C major, you would begin with each note of the C major scale, using it as a root note, and then take its third and fifth from the C major scale.

Start with C (taking that as your root) and then add E (the third) and G (the fifth); this gives you a C major chord. Moving on to D (and now taking D as your root), you add F (the third from D as you move in the C major scale) and A (the fifth). This is not a D major chord, but a D minor chord.

Going through all the notes, you'd end up with these chords:

Root	Third	Fifth	Chord
C	E	G	C major
D	F	A	D minor
E	G	B	E minor
F	A	C	F major
G	B	D	G major
A	C	E	A minor
B	D	F	B diminished

This pattern of major and minor chords, plus the diminished chord at the end, holds true for the diatonic chords of all major scales. Accordingly, it's a convention to think of diatonic chords generically in terms of their position in the major scale. In the above example, C major would be the one chord, which is the tonal center of the key of C major. Since D is the second note of the C major scale, D minor is the two chord in the key of C major. E minor is the three chord since E is the third note of the C major scale, and so on.

Roman numerals are traditionally used with capital letters denoting major chords and lowercase letters denoting minors or diminished chords, like this:

I	ii	iii	IV	V	vi	vii
C	Dm	Em	F	G	Am	Bdim

Using these generic equivalents allows you to think of chord progressions that can be used in any of the 12 major keys. Take a quick look back at the G major and F major scales mapped out a few pages back. Believe it or not, you now know the diatonic chords for both of those keys. For the key of G major you would have:

I	ii	iii	IV	V	vi	vii
G	Am	Bm	C	D	Em	F♯dim

And in the key of F major the diatonic chords would be:

I	ii	iii	IV	V	vi	vii
F	Gm	Am	B♭	C	Dm	Edim

As you will learn in Chapters 12 and 18, knowing the generic numbering of the diatonic chords can help you to write chord progressions in different keys, which can be very helpful when you've found you (or whoever may be singing your song) can't manage the melody in its original key. For example, suppose you've written a song in the key of C major using just the C, F, and G chords. And also suppose that you've come up with a great melody but it's too low for you to sing. Thinking generically in the key of C, you're using the I (C), IV (F), and V (G) chords for your song. Changing your song to the key of F major, your I, IV, and V chords would be F, B♭, and C. Now when you shift the melody notes from the key of C major to F major, as you just shifted the chords, you'll probably find you can sing the melody a lot easier than before. This process of changing a song from one key to another is known as *transposing*.

Finding "Home"

A key, as mentioned at the start of this chapter, is a tonal center. Think of it as a feeling of "home," if you will. If you play a C chord and then follow it with a G chord, your ears will want to hear that C chord again to give them a sense of completion. This is why the V chord to I chord is considered one of the strongest finishes to a chord progression. It makes you feel that the song has come to a conclusion.

It helps to imagine the harmony of a song as a trip. You have a home base, your I chord, and then you venture among other chords, dropping in for brief visits before stopping back at home and then heading out again. Your diatonic chords will be the places you're mostly likely to visit as those are the closest to your home base. And it's incredibly likely that the V or V7 chord will be the one you visit before ending your trip and coming home to stay.

TUNE TIPS

Following the V chord with the I chord is one of the strongest sounding chord progressions in music, so much so in fact that in music theory it's called a perfect candence (a cadence is the final two or three chords in a musical phrase). But as strong as going from V to I is, playing the seventh chord of the V (which would be written generically as V7) is even stronger. Using the key of C as an example, this would mean playing G7 (which is the V7 chord) and following that with C (the I chord).

Borrowing a Chord or Two

Of course, you aren't limited to using only diatonic chords in songs. If you were, both songs and songwriting would be pretty boring! Occasionally, chords are "borrowed" from other keys, either to make a stronger chord change or simply to make a chord progression more interesting.

Suppose you were writing in the key of C and you knew you wanted to end a phrase on a G chord. You could use a D or D7 chord right before the G, which would give you a strong sense of movement, since D is the V chord in the key of G. (You'll learn more about this in Chapter 12.)

Learning by Listening

Certain types of chords strike people in different ways. When you listen to a song (or to the chord examples on the Book Extras webpage), try to get a sense of how some chords affect you. Does a major chord make you dance and hop about? Do minor chords make you introspective?

Visit us online at www.completeidiots.guide.com/artofsongwriting.

> **TUNE TIPS**
>
> Keep an ear out for chords that grab your attention. Try to make note of the name of the song you're listening to so that you can find out the chords it uses by finding the sheet music or by asking friends who play music. You might also be able to find the sheet music online.

Also get a feel for how chords move you when played one after another or when there is a sudden shift from one type of chord to another. The verses of "Hotel California," for example, have a definite minor feel that temporarily vanishes with the major chords that herald the "Welcome to the Hotel California" at the start of the chorus, only to return again with the minor chord at the end of the second line.

Minor chords don't make all songs sound unhappy, though. And major chords can, in the right context, sound very melancholy, as in R.E.M.'s "Everybody Hurts." You have to remember that chords are simply one part of what gives any song its emotional punch. The melody, rhythm, and lyrics are certainly going to be part of the big picture, too.

As you've learned in this chapter, there are reasons that some chords sound good together. And while it's one thing to use different chords to bring some unexpected spice to your songs, you also have to keep your listeners in mind.

As a songwriter, the more chords you learn, the more sounds you have to play with. This doesn't mean you should toss in every chord you know in a single song. Having a great chord vocabulary gives you the chance to create just the right harmony to fit your melodies and lyrics.

The Least You Need to Know

- There are 12 notes used in Western music.
- Learning the major scale gives you the essential knowledge you need to understand basic music theory.
- The four primary types of chords are major, minor, augmented, and diminished.
- You can create all sorts of chords by adding other notes to any of the four primary chords.
- Diatonic chords are created by using just the notes from a single, specific scale.
- You can work with keys and chords in "generic" terms, allowing you to transpose your song into different keys.

Making Memorable Melodies

In This Chapter

- Understanding how melodies bring lyrics to life
- Matching sounds with notes
- Looking at melodies visually
- Using rhythm melodically
- Finding musical inspiration in old songs

As inspiring or moving as lyrics can be, it's often a song's melody that makes it memorable. You don't walk out of a concert *reciting* lyrics—you sing them! And you rarely find yourself repeating a lyric over and over unless it has a catchy melody.

See whether you can read the following line without singing it in your head:

> *Somewhere over the rainbow…*

You couldn't, could you? It's impossible for anyone not to start singing this phrase. You start out low on "Some-" and then gulp down a bit of air to make the big melodic leap and belt out "where!" Then your voice does a little dip on "over the" before drawing out both syllables of "rainbow."

Words don't become lyrics until you put them to a melody. Without a melody, you don't have a song. Maybe Eva Kern should have told Dorothy Hammerstein, "Your husband certainly did write 'Ol' Man River,' but my husband wrote the part everyone knows!"

Melodies have been getting stuck in people's heads for ages, but only recently has the term "earworm," borrowed from the German *ohrwurm*, become part of our vocabulary. Creating melodies that people remember even after hearing a song only once is both a talent and a skill, and in this chapter you'll learn how to develop the melodies that will turn your songs into earworms.

Singing as Conversation

You've read how your song's lyrics are the message you want to get across, the story you want to tell. Now think about the context in which you're telling that story. Either the song will be playing from a recording or someone (most likely you) will be performing it live. Essentially you'll be having a one-sided conversation with your audience.

This is a vital point to remember because, as you've read in Part 2, your live audience usually gets only one chance to hear your song on any given occasion. Aside from the chorus (should your song happen to have a repeating chorus), your listeners will only hear each line once. And even if it's a recording, few people will keep pressing a replay button just to catch a single phrase they didn't quite get on the first go 'round.

But melodies are repeated and are usually identical from verse to verse, and this repetition works with the lyrics to stick in your listeners' ears. They won't remember every word precisely, but they will remember the gist of the conversation when the melody keeps it fresh in their memory.

The Importance of Breathing

Like a good conversation, a good melody has movement and dynamics. There is a rise and fall to the voice to keep the song interesting. There are long, drawn-out notes and there are pauses where the listener gets a chance to feel the rhythm and digest a phrase or two before going on with the rest of the song.

Of course, you can't sing without breathing. Your melody should resemble a conversation you would enjoy listening to. Few people like to listen to someone drone on and on in a monotone voice, whether singing or speaking.

If you're working on a lyric that has a lot of words, remember to create spaces for both the singer and the listener to breathe. A good melody will do that for you. Think again about "Over the Rainbow" (lyrics by E. Y. Harburg and music by Harold Arlen) and how parts of the melody, like the beginning, are slow and languid, while others ("one day I'll wish upon a star," for instance) are quick and playful. There's a lot of interest created by giving the melody different textures.

Different Approaches for Different Songwriters

Some songwriters create melodies first and then add lyrics later. Others write lyrics first and then work up a melody to go with them. And some start out by putting together chord progressions (which you'll learn about in the next chapter) and then add the melody, sometimes simultaneously with lyrics. There's no right or wrong to any of these methods, and, the more songs you write, the more you'll probably find yourself using *all* of them.

But there is one distinct advantage to writing a melody first, and that's when it comes to singing the song. Lyric writers can unwittingly find themselves falling into a repetitive metric phrase, which can lead to a very monotonous melody. Melodies, by their nature, often have very different metric dynamics than the spoken word and this usually lends itself to creating a more interesting lyric than one might otherwise write.

La, La, La ...

Beginning with a melody or adding a melody to an existing chord progression can also help by shaping the *sound* of a lyrical line. Many songwriters, such as Paul Simon, David Byrne, or Michael Stipe of R.E.M., create melodies by singing "nonsense sounds" ("la, la, la," for instance) or whatever words may pop into their heads.

The objective is to come up with a great melody, but sometimes the sound or rhythm of a particular word goes well with the melody you've created. If you've got a note in your melody that holds for a while, it's the vowel part of the word that's going to be held. Think of the "o" of "ol'" and the "ma" of "man" in "Ol' Man River," for example. If you try to work up a melody in this manner, notice the sounds you like at specific points in the melody. This may give you some hints and directions when you're actually writing lyrics.

SONG STORIES

Paul Simon mentions in interviews that his song "Kodachrome" originally started out as "Going Home," but felt that the title would lead the song to simply rehash clichés. "Kodachrome" came from preserving the same sounds he heard in his melody and gave him a unique subject to write about.

Steps, Skips, and Leaps

Movement is essential to any good melody. Not everyone has a sensational voice, but just about everyone likes to sing. And part of singing is moving from one note to another, sometimes in small steps, if the notes are next-door neighbors, and sometimes in skips or leaps, if the notes are further apart.

Let's go back to "Over the Rainbow" for a moment. The first note (sung with "some") shares the same name as the second note ("where"). If the first note were the low end of a major scale, the second note would be the high end of it. This *interval* between the notes is called an *octave*. That's about as big a jump in melody as most people can comfortably make.

DEFINITION

The distance from any one note to another is called an **interval.** Intervals are named for the generic position of the major scale. For instance, the interval from C to E is a major third. The interval from C to G is a fifth, and the interval from C to C is called an **octave.**

It's also important to remember that you don't necessarily want your melody *constantly* skipping all over the place. Whether you have lyrics to start with or not, some words aren't going to work well if the melody makes them incomprehensible to the listener. So even if you've got the voice to make a melody move like a roller coaster, remember that people are still listening for the lyrics. Keep them as clean and clear as possible.

Melodies as Visual Art

Believe it or not, it's actually possible to *see* whether or not a melody is going to be either fun to listen to or boring. Take a look at these two melody lines. Even if you can't read music, you can still tell which one is going to be monotonous and which one is going to be interesting.

Two melody lines to compare.

Melody A uses only three different notes; Melody B contains seven. All the notes in Melody A have the same rhythmic value. Melody B involves notes of different rhythmic values, giving it both motion, in terms of moving up and down, and space, since some notes will be held longer than others.

Finding the Range

But while movement and space certainly make melodies more interesting and memorable, you also have to keep in mind that someone has to sing the melody. In theory, there are hundreds of musical notes, but the reality is that a singer can hit only so many of them.

Generally speaking, as mentioned earlier, an octave is about the biggest jump most singers can comfortably make. You want to try to keep your melody in a range that doesn't give people fits when they try to sing along.

Later, in Chapter 18, you'll read about ways to come up with even more melody ideas while working with a relatively small range of notes.

The Rhythms of Melodies

When it comes to creating a melody, there are only so many notes to work with, and even fewer when you figure in a shorter range for people to sing it in. This is why rhythm, or breathing, becomes such an important factor. Here are two melody lines that use the exact same notes in the exact same order. You can read them here and listen to them online:

Descending C major scale and "Joy to the World."

Visit us online at www.completeidiots.guide.com/artofsongwriting.

The first melody you may recognize as a descending major scale. This one happens to be the C major scale. It's "do, re, mi" in reverse. But change the rhythm of the notes slightly, as in the second melody, and it's the first line of the Christmas carol "Joy to the World."

Finding a Groove

A good way of finding a lyric's natural rhythm is simply to speak it aloud in a conversational manner. The spoken word has a pulse, as you read in Chapter 9. Even when you speed a phrase up or slow it down, the pulse will usually still be very distinct.

If you're starting with a lyric, you want to reflect its meter in your melody. Suppose your lyric had the line "I can't be-lieve she is go-ing with me." The pattern of stressed syllables in this line is one hard stress followed by two softer stresses.

Using the meter's pattern as a template, you could keep the stressed beats all on the same note and move the melody around on the unstressed ones, like this:

Using a lyric's meter to create a melody.

Visit us online at www.completeidiots.guide.com/artofsongwriting.

Latching on to the pauses or unaccented beats in the pulse can help you find places to make skips in your melody. A great example of this is in the last half of the second verse of Elvis Costello's "Alison," where he sings, "I think somebody better turn out the big light," bouncing between the high octave note and the sixth of the scale.

> **TUNE TIPS**
>
> Elvis Costello might not ever get the songwriting recognition that other artists do, but when it comes to melodies (and lyrics), you definitely can learn a lot from his songs. His albums *My Aim Is True*, *Armed Forces*, and *King of America* are great places to start.

Long Notes, Short Notes

As you're working on melodies and trying either to match a melody to a lyric or come up with a lyric for a melody, remember that the notes of a melody don't have to match up to the syllables of a lyric on a one-to-one basis. You can stretch a single word or syllable of the lyric over a long single note or even a series of shorter notes. Think of the chorus of the Christmas carol "Angels We Have Heard on High," where the first syllable of "Gloria" spins up, down, and around for 14 beats.

Going back to our "I can't believe she is going with me" lyric, here are two possible ways of using different combinations of long and short notes to make the melody even more interesting:

Using long and short notes to create a melody.

 Visit us online at www.completeidiots.guide.com/artofsongwriting.

Hum That Tune

Even though there are only so many notes to work with, people are always coming up with new melodies. The possibilities for combining notes with different rhythms and melodic lines seem fairly endless.

Remember that, first and foremost, your melody has got to be singable. If you can't sing or at least hum it, then it's possible no one else will be able to, either. Most melodies are fairly simple, with rising and falling notes and plenty of places to pause and breathe.

The simplicity of a melody also works for you in that other people are far more likely to be able to remember a melody that they, too, can sing or hum. Some people can sing better than others, so their rendition may be more a "reasonable facsimile" than the actual melody, but if people can sing your song, they'll remember it. This means you've done a great job communicating to your audience.

> **TUNE TIPS**
>
> Humming is actually a great way to create a melody. Whenever you're out walking, your feet usually keep a fairly steady rhythm, so take advantage of that and start humming or whistling away. You might come up with a musical phrase that's really catchy. Be sure you've brought your recorder along or you'll have to hum it all the way home!

But as important as the melody is, it still has to deliver clean, clear lyrical content. Don't let your melody get so complicated that the song's lyrics can't be understood. Both melody and lyric need to work together to make your song the best it can be.

Motifs

Repeated melodic phrases, also known as motifs, are a key ingredient to good melodies. Repetition helps root a song in the listener's ear and keeps him humming the song to himself long after he's heard it.

Going back to Christmas songs, sing "Rudolph the Red-Nosed Reindeer" to yourself. The first line has a distinct melodic wave to it, first going slightly higher, then back to the starting note, then slightly lower before jumping up much higher and then coming back to the original note. The third line ("… and if you ever saw it …") uses different notes, but the rhythm and general shape of the wave are pretty much the same. Likewise, the second and fourth lines mirror each other in rhythm and melodic shape.

High and Low Points

It's incredibly rare for a melody to stick with one note for an entire song. Sitting on a single note can get monotonous fast; even melodies with a very limited range, such as four to six notes, move about quite a bit.

Usually the highest notes of any song tend to be found in its chorus. This isn't always the case, but it is something to think about when you're working on a melody. Often a rising melody goes hand in hand with a song getting stronger and gaining more momentum to carry its listener forward. If your melody starts out as high as you can go, then you may find yourself without any way to make your song more dynamic and climactic.

Don't forget that you can also use low notes to good effect in your melody, like in "Friends in Low Places," by DeWayne Blackwell, Earl Bud Lee, and Garth Brooks, or Johnny Cash's "I Walk the Line." Of course, someone has to sing all the notes of your song, no matter how high or low, so keep that in mind when you're writing.

Using melodies creatively, hitting high and low points, and stretching words out over several notes make songs stick with your audience. They will be singing catchy melodies to themselves even if they don't know all the lyrics, so give them something they will have fun singing.

Singer/songwriter Leslie Ellis, who began her career performing on the Broadway stage and singing major league writers' demos at SONY Music and elsewhere for artists like Celine Dion (she won a Grammy for her vocal work on Celine Dion's "My Heart Will Go On") and Barbra Streisand, says years of singing rangy hit melodies taught her the importance of building dynamics and vocal performance opportunities into your own songs. Leslie offers some thoughts on the advantages being a singer can bring to writing melodies.

A Singer's Perspective on Writing Melodies

I started songwriting because I wanted my own original material to sing as I started performing more in the pop/folk concert genre. Lyrically I followed James Taylor, Joni Mitchell, and Shawn Colvin, but melodically I called on my experiences as a professional singer.

When I started co-writing in California and Nashville, I had a lot to learn about writing lyrics for songs that other artists might record. However, as a singer, what I bring to the sessions is a sense of melody and sing-ability, called *phrasing*. In songwriting, though, you only have a few lines or words to express a thought, and on occasion you need to use more words or syllables than will comfortably fit in the musical phrase. In the studio it has been my job to figure out how to phrase lines in other people's songs, and, thanks to that experience, when writing I can often demonstrate a musical way to make a line work that wouldn't occur to my co-writer.

Making Use of Dynamics

Using the music dynamically to emphasize an emotion in a lyric is also something I learned to do by interpreting other people's songs. I learned to analyze what words are important in a line, so as not to put emphasis on insignificant words. Sometimes it's helpful to just speak the line to see which words the emphasis falls on. This can show you how to write a musical line that will deliver the clearest interpretation of your line.

Technically, demonstrating how a song can build by changing the melody slightly throughout falls under the category of interpretation (as many of my points do), but these melodic components are something I address in the "writing stage" of the song, because that's how I think. Some artists come up with these nuances themselves, but it's always a plus to offer singing options or opportunities by building them into the song.

One way to do this automatically is to add a modulation, a key change into a higher key, to emphasize, say, the final chorus. "My Heart Will Go On," (music by James Horner, lyrics by Will Jennings) sung by Celine Dion, does this in the final chorus.

Creating Dynamics Through Small Changes in Melody

Another way to suggest dynamics is to write a melody and change certain lines melodically toward the climax of the song to pull out the emotion in the lyric. Whether it's a new line on a familiar melody in a verse or a repeating line in a chorus, I think the audience's ear is drawn to the sudden change and listens more carefully. An example of this is "You've Got a Friend," written by Carole King. When James Taylor sings the last chorus, he sings certain lines with a different inflection and melody on "I'll come running, running, running to see you again" and on "All you've got to do is call." These are very key lines that sum up the entire message of the song, and they drive the point home with more strength because they aren't sung in the same way as in the other choruses.

In this case, it was a matter of interpretation on James Taylor's part, but as a writer you can make these decisions from the beginning. If these arrangement elements make the songs more memorable, why not build them into the song in the first place?

Keeping Range and "Lyric-to-Music Ratio" in Mind

Some other things I pay attention to, as a singer writing songs other artists may sing are the song's range and "lyric-to-music ratio." I have a very "rangy" voice, meaning I can sing very high and low notes. Not all singers have this kind of voice. So if I'm writing a song for Carrie Underwood, I don't worry about it. But, if I want the song to be more universal, I try to keep the melody within a certain range of notes that are more easily sung by more artists.

By lyric-to-music ratio, I mean that some songs have lots of words in the lyric and others with fewer words are songs that require more extended notes. I *like* to hold notes—draw them out on certain words—but some artists don't sing like this. So if I'm writing for the artist pool at hand, I try to keep it in between the two extremes.

However, if I know a song will make it to a singer who does typically go for the extended-note type songs, I can make sure that if a note *is* to be held out, the lyric that is associated with that note is made up of vowel sounds that are better for singing on long phrases. Vowel sounds like "eh" are hard to sing but open vowel sounds like "ah" are easy; especially on higher notes.

And finally, I feel the experience of having learned so many songs as a singer has given me an advantage over some of my co-writers in that I have hundreds of melodies and lyrics committed to memory and guiding my understanding of how songs are constructed.

—Leslie Ellis

Learning by Doing

The best possible preparation you can give yourself for writing melodies is to listen to all the melodies you can. A day, or even an hour, rarely goes by that you don't have the opportunity to hear a song. Regardless of what you may think of the song or the lyric, ask yourself whether it has an effective melody. Is this a tune you might find yourself humming later, with no idea where it came from?

You should also try to work out melodies you know on your musical instrument of choice. You don't need to read music to do this—in fact, it's probably better to not use any sheet music to start with so you can work out whether the notes are going higher or lower and just how much they are skipping around. This will do wonders for your ears, not to mention give you a better understanding of how melodies move (or don't move) around.

If you have sheet music lying around, start looking at the melody line with a critical eye. Having a visual sense of melody can help you realize when your own melodies may be a bit boring. Write out your melody lines and look at them. It's one thing to sing something and think you've got a great, interesting melody, but if you write it out and see that you've got only two or three different notes all clustered in the same space, then you'll know better.

Studying the Masters

When you think about it, it's more than slightly amazing that there are so many good melodies out there. There are only so many notes and rhythms, but there seem to be limitless ways to combine them into unique musical phrases.

TUNE TIPS

Obviously you'll want to listen to your favorite songwriters for melodic material to study, but don't make the mistake of missing out on great melodies simply because you don't like a particular artist or even just the lyrics of a song. Not everyone writes great lyrics, just as not everyone writes great melodies. You want to be able to judge melodies objectively in order to gauge how effective they are.

You can find great melodies in all genres of music, from pop to country, from folk to metal. If a singer has a good voice, he or she will want a good melody to showcase it. Even artists that don't seem to have great singing voices manage to come up with great melodies. Bob Dylan's "Lay Lady Lay" is a great example.

Jazz standards, such as "Misty," written by Erroll Garner, or "Autumn Leaves," music by Joseph Kosma, or almost anything by Cole Porter, are still going strong because of their wonderful melodies. You want to listen to music from all eras.

Digging Deeper

If you need further evidence that good melodies last for ages, think about all the songs you know from childhood—not the pop songs on the radio, but the songs that your parents sang to you or songs you may have sung at school or at camp or simply sitting around with your friends. Chances are you can still sing "Twinkle, Twinkle, Little Star," "Pop Goes the Weasel," or "Oh! Susanna," and not think twice about how the song goes.

Folk songs, traditional music, and hymns, especially Christmas carols, have melodies that have stood the test of time. Some of these melodies are actually traced back to even older songs! And when you add phrases from classical music pieces, you've got a rich history of melodies that spans hundreds of years. That's certainly a lot of inspiration!

The Least You Need to Know

- Keep your melody within a reasonable range of notes.
- Looking at the notes of a melody can help as much, if not more, than listening to it.
- Stretching out notes or using several notes for a single syllable of a lyric makes a song more interesting.
- Give your melody movement. Have high points and low points.
- You can find thousands more melodic ideas by listening to old music.

Finding Harmony

In This Chapter

- Creating chord progressions
- Finding many potential progressions with just three chords
- Adding nondiatonic chords to the mix
- Writing chord progressions in minor keys
- Using songs you know as templates

Right after melody, harmony is the second most vital musical component of any song. Songs are identified by their melodies—after all, that's the part of the song that's sung—but it's rare for any song to be sung by a single voice without any musical accompaniment.

That accompaniment—whether it's simple chords on an acoustic guitar, a flurry of notes pouring out of a piano, the bombast of four-man metal band, or the swinging counterpoint of a 42-piece orchestra—makes up a song's harmony.

At this stage of your songwriting career, it's best to think of harmony in terms of chords and chord progressions. After all, you're probably writing music on guitar or piano and don't want to make things too complicated.

Three Chords and the Truth

As you learned in Chapter 10, every key comes with a set of seven diatonic chords. These are the chords you are most likely to encounter in any given song, as they sound very good together coming from the notes of a single major scale.

When you're writing your first song, you may think that seven chords are six too many to choose from! How do you know which ones to play, let alone what order to play them in? And how do you arrange the chords to sound good together in the first place? You can relax, because putting together chord progressions for songs can be as simple or complex as you want it to be.

Even though there are lots of chords to choose from, many songs, probably tens of thousands and more, use just three. There are also a fair number of songs (although nowhere quite as many) that use only two, as well as thousands that use only four. Of course, many use more as well. But it's not the number of chords you use that determines how good your song will sound, it's how those chords, whether 2 or 3 or 27, are used in combination.

y of your song, the tonal center discussed in Chapter 10, comes in. Each key, as you
lete with a set of diatonic chords. Remember again that the I, IV, and V chords are
vi chords are minors; and vii is a diminished chord. And also remember that the
will be the same in *any* major key you use.

You won't see many songs that use the vii chord, because it contains three of the four notes of the
seventh chord of the fifth position (in other words, G7 in the key of C or D7 in the key of G). The V7
chord gets used a lot in songs, so it's a good one to know about.

Here are the six diatonic chords used for the major keys most songs are written in. The I chord is your
key:

I	ii	iii	IV	V	vi
C	Dm	Em	F	G	Am
D	Em	F♯m	G	A	Bm
E	F♯m	G♯m	A	B	C♯m
E♭	Fm	Gm	A♭	B♭	Cm
F	Gm	Am	B♭	C	Dm
G	Am	Bm	C	D	Em
A	Bm	C♯m	D	E	F♯
B♭	Cm	Dm	E♭	F	Gm

These six diatonic chords of each key all sound good when played one after the other in some combination. If you started your song on G, then went to Am, then Bm, then C, and back to G, you'd have the
chord progression I-ii-iii-IV-I, which sounds a lot like the verses of John Denver's "Sunshine on My
Shoulders."

TUNE TIPS

This diatonic chart, plus all the other information on what chords typically are used in songs, is meant
to be a guide rather than a strict set of instructions. Ultimately, a chord progression is all about sounding good. You may find some combinations of chords a bit jarring, but someone else may think they
sound very cool because of that harshness. Don't shy away from experimenting with your own chord
progressions. But also listen critically to whether or not they really work. There's a reason some chord
progressions have been around for hundreds of years: people like to hear them!

Of course, you're not limited to using only diatonic chords in your songs, but they make a convenient
starting place to learn how to combine chords into chord progressions. You can (and are certainly
encouraged to) try mixing and matching chords on your own, listening to how they fit together, and
hearing which progressions you like. You can also use the long history of songs and chords to help you
make decisions on your harmony.

I, IV, V

The I chord is the chord that gives you your tonal center. Most songs will begin on the I chord simply
to establish that tonal center for the audience. Even more songs will end on the I chord in order to give
the song a sense of closure, allowing the listener to feel that he's come back to "home."

Most three-chord songs are made up of the I, IV, and V chords in some combination. Using the key of C as an example, playing two beats of C (the I chord), followed by two beats of F (the IV chord), followed by two beats of G (the V chord), followed by an additional two beats of F gives you a I-IV-V-IV chord progression. You've heard this chord progression in songs like "Wild Thing," "La Bamba," and "Twist and Shout."

In most music that you've heard, the I chord is most often followed by either the IV or V. There are obviously other choices. You will hear the I chord followed by the ii, iii, or vi chord, too, but not quite as often as you'll hear it followed by the IV or V.

Likewise, the IV and V chords tend to be followed by the I chord. Again, there are all sorts of possibilities, so don't worry too much about all this. When you're putting together a chord progression, you just want it to sound good. You want the chord changes to flow smoothly from one to the next. These guidelines are here to give you an idea of what's been working well for several centuries of songs.

ii, iii, vi

The ii chord, more often than not, is followed by the V chord, which in turn is followed by the I. This ii-V-I progression is used frequently in jazz but turns up in most other genres as well.

The iii chord tends to be followed by the vi chord, but it also sounds great followed by the IV or ii chord.

The vi chord is usually followed by the ii or the V chord. Following it with the IV or iii sounds good, too. A lot of songs switch between the I and the vi chord and back again. There is not much difference between these two chords, so it's not the strongest sounding progression, but it certainly works if you're looking for a subtle change.

All Roads Lead to Home

The key for your song gives your listener a big expectation. The ear is ultimately waiting to get back to that I chord in order to have a sense of resolution. You can make all the chord changes you want, but your audience is set on returning to the tonal center.

You want to keep that sense of home in mind when you're coming up with chord progressions. It might be cool to try to write a song with a dozen or more chord changes in it, but all that potential wandering around will lose your listener in the long run. Your job is to bring the listener back home, regardless of how many stops you make along the way.

Strong (and Not-So-Strong) Progressions

Going from the V chord to the I chord gives the listener the strongest sense of musical resolution. If a song is in the key of C, there's a great chance it's going to end with a chord change of G to C or G7 to C.

IV-I and ii-I progressions are good, too, but they don't finish quite as strong as V-I. You'll often hear IV-V-I and, as mentioned earlier, ii-V-I progressions used instead. V-IV-I is also quite common, particularly in country, blues, rock, and pop.

Deceptive Changes

Sometimes you can take advantage of the listeners' expectations to surprise them with an unexpected chord change. If your song uses a IV-V-I progression quite frequently, change the I to vi at one point in the song, particularly to highlight an interesting lyric line.

Making slight alterations in your progression is also a good way to build a song musically from line to line. Say you've got four lines of lyrics in your verse and you want each line to have 16 beats with a chord change every 4 beats. You might start out the first line with a typical I-IV-V-I progression, then in the second line swap it to I-IV-I-V. You could then repeat this new progression for the third line and return to the original one for the fourth line. Or you could instead repeat the first line for the third line and the second line for the fourth line. Or you could come up with something totally different, like I-V-IV-I for the fourth line.

You might even combine all these ideas, including tossing in the vi chord as a bit of sleight of hand, giving you a progression that looks like this:

I	IV	V	I
I	IV	I	V
I	IV	V	vi
I	V	IV	I

In the key of C, this would translate to:

C	F	G	C
C	F	C	G
C	F	G	Am
C	G	F	C

As you can see, you can get a lot of variation using just three or four chords. And the number of different progressions gets bigger when you add more variables, such as changing the number of beats each chord gets.

Setting a Mood

Picking a key not only gives you a set of diatonic chords to start with, it also can help set the mood of your song. Up to this point, you've read only about major keys but you can also write your song in a minor key.

Generally, songs in minor keys tend to sound sad, introspective, or even a bit angry. Even blues songs in minor keys sound a bit bluer than those in major keys. Compare "Before You Accuse Me" or "Sweet Home Chicago" (major key) to "The Thrill Is Gone" or "Riders on the Storm" (both in minor keys), and see which you think sounds more mournful.

Your lyrics will also have a lot to do with how sad or happy your song is, but choosing a chord progression that emphasizes that emotion makes your song stronger. Conversely, you can also use a chord progression that sharply contrasts with your lyric in order to make a memorable musical impression. When angry lyrics get matched with happy major chords, the effect can be quite interesting.

Minor Keys

Every major key has a corresponding, or "relative," minor. To find this, you would simply start your major scale on the sixth note while still using all the notes of your original major scale. For example, you know the C major scale is:

C   D   E   F   G   A   B   C

A, as you see, is the sixth note of the C major scale. To get the A *natural minor* scale, you start with A and use these same notes in order, like this:

A   B   C   D   E   F   G   A

When you rearrange the major scale in this manner, you're also changing the chords that make up the diatonic chords of the key. Your I chord is now A minor, so it would be better to think of it as i, using the lowercase to designate it as minor.

> **DEFINITION**
>
> It's also good to know that there are *three* different minor scales. The **natural minor** scale is formed by starting on the sixth note of any major scale. There are also the **harmonic minor** and **melodic minor** scales, which differ slightly from the natural minor.

Putting together the diatonic chords of the natural minor scale, you see that the i, iv, and v chords are now all minor chords, while the III, VI, and VII are major and the ii is now the diminished chord. Using the key of Am as our example, the diatonic chords play out like this:

i	ii	III	iv	v	VI	VII
Am	Bdim	C	Dm	Em	F	G

Slightly Askew

Because the i, iv, and v diatonic chords in a minor key are minor, some chord progressions that sound strong in major keys, especially those such as v (or v7) to i, don't come across as dynamic. Em to Am, for example, is not a very strong progression. So songwriters writing in a minor key often borrow chords from its major key. The V chord of A major is E, and E or E7 to Am sounds much more assertive. Likewise, it's also a fairly common practice to use a major IV chord in a minor key, as you'll read about in just a few pages.

In some rock songs, particularly in metal, punk, or grunge styles, the 5 chord, which (as you read in Chapter 10) is neither major nor minor, is the predominant chord of a progression. Songs that use only or mostly 5 chords, such as Nirvana's "Smells Like Teen Spirit," often have an ambiguous tonal center and seem very restless and unresolved.

Time and Time Again

Every songwriter wants to be original and come up with something no one else has done before, but that's not easy when it comes to chord progressions. There are only so many chords, and they don't all sound great together. Hundreds of songs, if not more, share the same exact chord progressions. And if you think about chord progressions in a generic sense (as you learned in Chapter 10), then that number multiplies a hundredfold or more. Hundreds of songs use the chord progression C, F, G, F. Thousands more use I, IV, V, IV, which will be different depending on which key you use as your I chord. In the key of A major, that would be A, D, E, D. In E major it would be E, A, B, A.

At some point you will find yourself thinking that your song sounds like another song you've heard. Or someone else may point that out to you. This is normal and you shouldn't worry too much about it. It's copying a melody that you want to be concerned about. If you are worried about your melody being an exact copy of another song you've heard, do your best to track down that song to make certain you have an original on your hands.

Working with the Big Three

As mentioned earlier, you can't even count all the songs that just use the I, IV, and V chords in some combination. A typical blues song, for instance, will start out with 16 beats of the I chord, shift to the IV chord for 8 beats, and then go back to the I chord for 8 more beats. Then it will go to the V chord for 4 beats, followed by 4 beats of the IV chord, and then end with 8 beats of the I chord. This song structure is called a standard 12-bar blues, and it's shared by a lot of early rock songs as well.

You can find all sorts of ways to mix and match the I, IV, and V chords. Remember that you don't always have to start on the I chord. The old standard "Midnight Special" uses IV-I-V-I as its progression throughout the entire song. And "Sweet Home Alabama" uses two beats of V, followed by two beats of IV, followed by four beats of I as its progression.

TUNE TIPS

Adding the vi chord to the I, IV, and V, as you saw in our earlier example, gives you even more choices to work with. A great many songs use the progression I-vi-IV-V, such as '50s and '60s pop songs like "Last Kiss" or "Stand by Me."

Varying and Repeating Progressions in a Song

Some songs, like Neil Young's "Helpless" or Tom Petty and Jeff Lynne's "Free Fallin'," have only one single, short chord progression that repeats over and over. But chord progressions don't have to stay constant throughout an entire song. Often songs will use one set of chords for a line or two and then change to another. "Knockin' on Heaven's Door," by Bob Dylan, uses two similar chord progressions, I-V-ii and I-V-IV, which are played every alternating line. Rick Nelson's "Garden Party" starts out with a couple of I-IV changes before using I-vi-IV-V for its third and fourth lines.

Chord progressions may change from line to line within a verse or chorus of a song, but they don't usually change from one verse to another. The repetition of chord progressions within a song, much like the repetition of lyrics, gives the listener an anchor and also gives the song a musical identity. Take a look at the chord progressions of the verses and chorus of "Human" by the Killers:

Verse:

I-iii-IV-I

V-vi-IV-V

I-iii-IV-vi

IV-IV-V-V

Chorus:

I-iii-IV-I

V-vi-IV-V

I-iii-vi-vi

ii-IV-I-I

You can see that the chord progressions of the verse's first two lines are repeated in the first two lines of the chorus, while the third lines of each are pretty similar. The last line of the verse ends with a V chord, which leads into the I chord of the chorus very nicely. The chorus' last line finishes with the I chord to bring the listener to a satisfying musical resolution.

Adding Some Surprises

While you have a lot of possible combinations for chord progressions using only diatonic chords, tossing in nondiatonic chords can add some flair to your song. If you end a line with the V chord, you could throw in the II chord (the major chord version of the ii) right before the V. For instance, suppose you've written a song in C and the chords of your first two lines look like this:

C   F   G   C

C   F   C   G

You could replace the second C in the second line with D or D7, which would make a slightly stronger sounding progression:

C   F   G   C

C   F   D   G

Another way of incorporating the II chord is using the I-II-IV-I progression. You've heard this striking progression in songs such as the Beatles' "Eight Days a Week" and "You Won't See Me," as well as Pink Floyd's "Brain Damage" from their *Dark Side of the Moon* album.

Another nondiatonic chord that frequently pops up, particularly in rock, country, and pop, is the major chord of the flat-seventh (♭VII). This would be the B♭ major chord if you were in the key of C major. In the key of G major, it would be an F major chord. Many songs make use of the chord progression I-♭VII-IV-I, which in the key of C major would be C-B♭-F-C. If you're familiar with "Taking Care of Business" by Bachman-Turner Overdrive, "Can't You See" by the Marshall Tucker Band, or "Sympathy for the Devil" by the Rolling Stones, then you've definitely heard this chord progression in action.

Minor Progressions

In songs written in minor keys, just as with those in major keys, just about any chord is likely to come up in a progression. You will have songs that stay strictly diatonic and those that will include nondiatonic chords in their progressions, particularly when it comes to the V or IV chord.

For instance, if you were hearing a song in the key of Am, the diatonic chords formed from the A natural minor scale would be:

i	ii	III	iv	v	VI	VII
Am	Bdim	C	Dm	Em	F	G

You're not as likely to run into many songs that only use the i, iv, and v chords as you are to hear songs using major keys, but they certainly do exist. "Black Magic Woman," written by Peter Green, and R.E.M.'s "Losing My Religion" would fall into this category.

Down and Back

A more typical minor-key chord progression would be to start with the i chord, move down the scale to the VII chord, and then to the VI before coming back up again. This i-VII-VI-VII-i progression can be heard in Bob Dylan's "All Along the Watchtower" and "Gimme Shelter" by the Rolling Stones.

Neil Young's "Like a Hurricane" is another example of this descending chord progression. It starts on Am, goes to G, then to F, and then continues on to Em before going back to G and then starting all over again. This would be i-VII-VI-v-VII.

In addition to hearing songs that use the diatonic chords (again, using Am as an example), you can hear many songs that include E major (which is V) instead of Em (v). This is particularly true with the earlier descending chord progression. You will hear i-VII-VI-V in songs like "Runaway" (written by Del Shannon and Max Crook), the Ventures' "Walk Don't Run" (written by Johnny Smith), and many, many other songs.

Minor i–Major IV

You also hear songs in minor keys that use the major IV instead of the minor iv. For example, if you were writing in the key of Am, that would mean using D instead of Dm. You'll hear this i-IV progression used in such songs as Jefferson Airplane's "Somebody to Love" (written by Darby Slick), Santana's "Evil Ways" (written by Clarence "Sonny" Henry), and "Another Brick in the Wall (Part 2)" by Pink Floyd (written by Roger Waters).

Usually when a minor key song uses a major IV chord, the V chord, if used, will also be major. The traditional folksong "The House of the Rising Sun" uses the progression i-III-IV-VI for its first and third lines while using i-III-V in the second and i-V-i for the last line.

Turnarounds

One last trick worth knowing for chords is the *turnaround*. Most verses start with the I chord, and, because going from V to I is one of the strongest possible chord progressions, it's common to stick on a V chord at the end of a chorus, verse, or even a single line in order to lead strongly into the following I chord.

In Bob Dylan's "Don't Think Twice, It's All Right," for example, the chord progressions of the first two lines are as follows:

I   V   vi   vi

IV   IV   I   V

The I chord in the second line comes at the last lyric sung in the line and the V chord is added to create a turnaround, giving the song a stronger transition from this second line to the third, which also starts with a I chord.

Turnarounds can come in many forms. Typically they're a short musical phrase between repeated parts of a song that transition the chord sequence back to the beginning of the next part, which often starts on the I chord of the song. Quite often they're a repetition of the musical intro and they're used extensively in blues and jazz music, but they can be found in many rock, country, and pop songs as well.

DEFINITION

A **turnaround** is a short chord progression or musical phrase (or often both!) at the end of a verse or chorus of a song that prepares the listener for the start of the next verse. It usually does so by ending with a V or V7 chord, which will be followed by the I chord that typically starts the next section of the song.

Learning by Doing

Many songs share the same basic chord progressions. That may initially worry you, but you should instead look at it as an opportunity to hit the ground running when it comes to writing the accompanying chords for your songs. Try playing simple songs you already know, just strumming the chords in your own rhythm on a guitar or playing them on a piano. Play the chords one at a time and listen to them on their own. Without any melody or rhythm to guide your ears and make you think of the song the chords came from, you will develop a sense of how the chords work with each other and hear what makes a good chord progression.

Take a chord progression that you like and make some slight variations to it. Substitute a V7 chord for a V or a vi for a I and listen to how it sounds. Even if you don't use the variation with the song you're working on, you may find a use for it with a different song.

Whenever you hear a song with a very interesting or unusual chord progression, make a note of the song's title and who performs it (and its writer, if you can). Then try to track down the sheet music for the song or find someone who knows how to play it and discover which particular change of chords caught your ear. Try to incorporate that progression into the very next song you write.

John Lennon, for instance, was very fond of using minor iv chords in major songs. "Nowhere Man," as an example, starts out with a I-V-IV-I progression for the first two lines and then finishes out the verse with a ii-iv-I progression. See if it's possible to substitute a minor iv chord for the major IV at any point in your song. Or to throw in the minor iv between the major IV and the I. This progression often works well at the end of a closing line of a verse or chorus.

Beginning a bridge section of a song with either a major IV to minor iv to I progression is very dramatic. So is kicking off a bridge section with a minor iv or even a minor i. Lennon does this to great effect in "Norwegian Wood."

As you'll learn in the next chapter, melody and chords often work hand in hand with each other. Being able to recognize that every note is a piece of many different chords can give you inspiration when it comes to creating chord progressions. In Jerome Kern and Otto Harbach's classic, "Smoke Gets in Your Eyes," and, assuming you're singing it in the key of C, the second verse ends on the C note and the harmony is a C major chord. There's nothing surprising or unusual there, C is the root note of C major, after all. But the bridge then starts out with an A♭ chord, where the C note (which is the third of the A♭ chord) serves as the start of a complete change of key. That's very dramatic and it's one reason the song is so memorable.

Remember it's all about making your song sound its best. As you experiment, you will sometimes find that these more exotic progressions may not necessarily be the best choice for your song. But continue to explore and experiment. Keeping a catchy chord progression fresh in your mind will help you find a place to use it in a future song. And the more musical ideas you stockpile, the more options you'll have the next time you don't know where to go with a song.

The Least You Need to Know

- Songs can have any number of chords, but many have just three or four.
- Most songs stick with diatonic chords, but you can use nondiatonic chords to make your progressions more musically interesting.
- Songs in minor keys often use major V and IV chords.
- Use songs you know as templates for chord progressions of your own songs.
- Experiment with chord progressions and keep notes on songs that have unusual chord changes that you may like to try one day.

Chapter 13

Some Assembly Required

In This Chapter

- Putting melody and chord progressions together
- Harmonizing a melody
- Building a melody from a chord progression
- Discovering tension and resolution
- Using melody notes to embellish chords

Whenever a song idea arrives in your head as a total, complete package—lyrics, melody, and harmony—that's cause for a celebration! Usually, though, song ideas show up in little bits and pieces—a line of lyrics here, a tuneful phrase of a melody there, maybe a chord progression that's been running around in your brain for a while. They're like clues to a mystery or pieces of a jigsaw puzzle that you're going to have to put together into a whole song.

The task of putting together the music portion of a song—the melody and chords—might seem a bit daunting to some beginners, especially if you feel a little shaky with music to start with. You may worry about the music being too plain or ordinary, but you also don't want a melody and accompaniment so complicated that it's not really musical. Plus, you want your songs to be original, unlike any song ever heard before.

You don't have to be a musical genius to create good music. You just have to be able to bring the melodies and harmonies you hear in your head to the outside world. Sometimes this is as easy as singing a simple melody while playing a few chords on a guitar or piano.

Granted, as you gain more and more experience and skill in songwriting, your music may become more complex, as will your lyrics. Fortunately, writing songs is one craft that allows you to learn and develop as an artist even while you are taking your very first steps as a songwriter.

Finding a Starting Point

Just as with a jigsaw puzzle, you have to start someplace. Some people like to begin with the puzzle's border and work inward, but that doesn't usually stop you from finding other matching pieces while putting the edge together.

With songs, you usually start with either the lyrical or musical component. But the music, as you've been reading in the last two chapters, involves two parts—melody and harmony—and your brain may not deliver them at the same time. You may find yourself having to piece together the musical pieces from scratch.

Some people are good at creating both melody and harmony seemingly out of nowhere. They just play and sing and magically conjure up the music for a song. For others, it's often a matter of starting with one component and then adding the other. In other words, you may have a melody that needs a chord progression, or you may have a chord progression without a melody.

When you worked on coming up with lyrics in Part 2, you may have found yourself singing your lines in your head as you wrote them out. And if you did, we hope you took a moment to sing those lines into a recorder—even if it's just your voice mail!—and give yourself a melody that you can now add harmony to. Or you may have created a lyric because you already had a melody in your head. If this is the case, then you've probably got that melodic tune set firmly in your brain.

You should get into the habit of making time to work on melodies in the same way you work on lyrics. If you're taking a walk or driving around, try singing some nonsense syllables ("la-la-la") or humming or whistling to yourself. You'll know a catchy tune when you hear it. Then be sure to record it or keep singing it until you get the chance to record it. A stockpile of melodic phrases can give you material to begin a song as well as help you when you're stuck for ideas in the middle of writing one.

Most writers probably start with a chord progression. In Chapter 12, you learned about making notes of chord progressions you liked or found interesting. Write out a few and then record yourself (or a friend) playing them so you can be free to concentrate on adding a melody to your progression.

Harmonizing a Melody

If you've got a melody in your head, the first task is to record it or write it down. Here's one you can use as an example, which you can hear at the Book Extras webpage.

A sample melody to harmonize.

Visit us online at www.completeidiots.guide.com/artofsongwriting.

The starting note of this melody is C. There are many chords that have a C in their makeup, and you can begin with any of them. For the sake of starting as simple as possible, go with a C major chord and consider C major as your key or tonal center.

> **TUNE TIPS**
>
> You don't have to have the entire melody of your song done in order to begin working on the harmony. Start with small phrases, like the one in the examples in this section. Sometimes the chords you come up with will suggest how the melody might continue through the next part of the song.

You know from your reading of Chapter 12 that the I, IV, and V chords in the key of C major are C, F, and G. Playing around with just those three chords, you might find this progression works nicely:

Adding a chord progression to a sample melody.

 Visit us online at www.completeidiots.guide.com/artofsongwriting.

You can see the melody written out in musical notes with the chords written over the top of the notes. In this example, each chord is getting four beats: first C (the I chord), then G (the V), then back to C, then finishing with F (the IV chord). This means that some of the notes in the melody are *not* notes in the accompanying chord, and that's perfectly okay. In fact, you really don't want to have a one-to-one match up of your melody notes to your harmony. Using notes outside of the harmony creates musical tension that's resolved when the melody again falls on a note that is part of the chord. In this last example, the melody starts on C, which is part of the C chord. It then briefly rises to D (which is not part of the C chord) before hitting C again. That momentary shift causes the melodic tension, which makes the melody more interesting than if it stayed on C for all three notes.

On the other side of the coin, if you were to change chords with each note of the melody in order to keep the melody tension-free, the resulting song would sound so busy that perhaps no one would be able to hear the melody and, consequently, the lyrics. That wouldn't be good.

But you could change the number of beats assigned to some of the chords if you'd like. This next example uses the same three chords, but in a different pattern:

Adding a different progression to a sample melody.

Visit us online at www.completeidiots.guide.com/artofsongwriting.

Here you're still starting out with four beats of C, but then using two beats of F and then two beats of G before repeating this progression. You can hear that, even though the melody is the same, the melody and chords together give the music a little more drive.

Same Exact Melody, Totally Different Key

Playing around with chords and chord progressions can seem very haphazard, but the more you experiment, the more music theory starts taking root in your mind. If you sing the first note of this example, C, and you strummed a C chord, you automatically might start your progression with that C chord. But if you played around a little more, you would probably find that the C note also fits with the F chord. All of the notes in this sample melody are part of the key of F, just as they are all part of the key of C.

So what would happen if you made F major the key or tonal center of this bit of melody? Again, keeping things simple and using just the I, IV, and V chords—which in F would be F, B♭, and C—you might come up with a progression like this:

Changing sample melody to the key of F.

Visit us online at www.completeidiots.guide.com/artofsongwriting.

Instead of the I-V-I-IV of the first example and the I-IV-V of the second, your progression is now I-V-IV and has a different feel altogether.

Really Changing the Mood

How about trying out some minor keys? Here is your sample melody in C minor:

Sample melody in the key of C minor.

Visit us online at www.completeidiots.guide.com/artofsongwriting.

That's quite a bit different, isn't it? And all you did was swap the C-F-C-G in the first example for minor chords, Cm-Gm-Cm-Fm. The difference is even more striking when you throw in a G major instead of Gm:

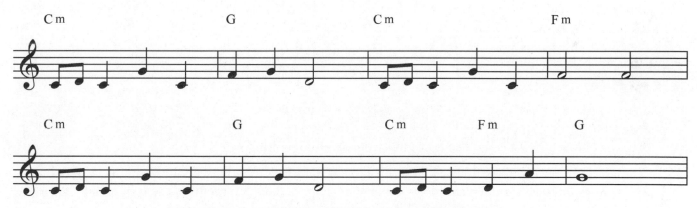

Sample melody in C minor with a G major chord added.

Visit us online at www.completeidiots.guide.com/artofsongwriting.

And here's how it would sound if you used the i-VII-VI-VII progression you learned about in Chapter 12:

Sample melody using the i-VII-VI-VII progression in the key of C minor.

Visit us online at www.completeidiots.guide.com/artofsongwriting.

Finally, take a listen to a possible progression in A minor:

Sample melody in the key of A minor.

Visit us online at www.completeidiots.guide.com/artofsongwriting.

It's hard to believe you're still using the same melody, but that's exactly the point. Both melody and harmony work together to create the mood of your song. And don't forget that the lyric should be an equal partner! All three elements are part of the message you're communicating to your audience.

Progression

Many songs began as little more than a songwriter plinking a few chords out on a piano or noodling around on a guitar. She came up with a chord progression or two that she liked, found a melody to sing over the chord changes, and presto! There's a new song in the world!

Working out a song this way requires a bit of patience, and you should definitely have a recording device of some sort so you don't forget your great melody as soon as you leave the room!

TUNE TIPS

The key and chords you choose definitely affect the mood of your song, but *how* you play a chord progression can also have a big impact on your song's melody. If you're playing some chords in a fast, rocking style, you're likely to come up with a melody with a lot of notes and movement. If you are playing your progression with slow arpeggios (playing chords as single notes, as one might play a harp), your melody might turn out wistful or sad.

It's a good idea as well to have worked out your chord progression in advance so that you have it in front of you when you're playing. To walk you through this process for your first time, we've provided a short, simple chord progression for you (which, like our other examples, you can hear at the Book Extras webpage):

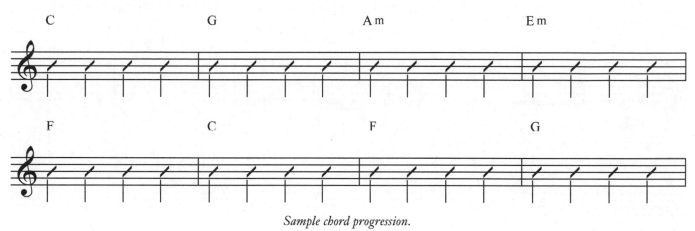

Sample chord progression.

Visit us online at www.completeidiots.guide.com/artofsongwriting.

This progression is in the key of C, with each chord receiving four beats. To make it a little more interesting than a possible I-IV-V progression, there's a mix of major and minor chords.

Adding a Melody

Listen to the progression a few times without even thinking about a melody. Hear the chord changes and soak in the music. Then play it again and try to sing a simple melody along with it.

Your melody can be busy and full of notes, or you can even go with a single note for each chord change, like this:

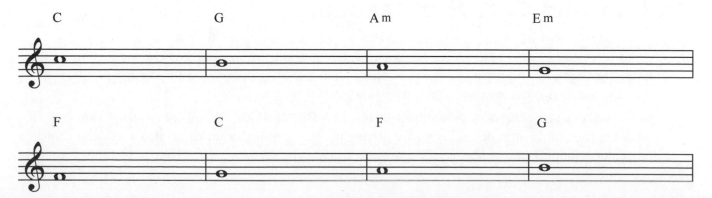

Adding a simple melody to a sample chord progression.

Visit us online at www.completeidiots.guide.com/artofsongwriting.

This line of single notes, descending from C to G and then rising up to B, is about as simple and elegant as you can get. You wouldn't want your entire song to be like this, but having a line or two might work out nicely.

Working the Pauses

Simply by singing, whistling, or humming along with a chord progression, you can come up with a surprising number of different melodies. Again, you want to record every melody you dream up because you never know whether you'll be able to re-create it.

This next example, using the very same chord progression, is quite a bit different from the first one:

A different melody for the sample chord progression.

 Visit us online at www.completeidiots.guide.com/artofsongwriting.

You can hear (and see) that this last melody line has more going on than the first one. You should also hear that, in spite of having a lot more notes, it still finds spaces to breathe. This melody doesn't even begin until the third beat of the accompaniment.

Plus, there are long notes that stretch out over several beats as well as short ones that are less than a beat long. The variation of the length of notes brings a rhythmic pulse to the melody. If you already have lyrics with a good meter, you should approach your song's melody with the same sense of metric pulse.

Melody and Chords in Tandem

You may have noticed that both sample melodies began on C, which might make sense because the chord progression is in the key of C. But you can start a melody on any note you choose. Picking a different starting note will often reshape your melody, much in the same way that using different chords with the same melody creates different moods, as you just learned.

When you're singing along to a chord progression to create a melody, the normal tendency is to start on either the tonal center of the key you're playing in or on a note that makes up that particular chord. Since our example is in the key of C, the notes of the C major chord are very likely to pop into your head first. You can help yourself avoid using the same starting note by deliberately picking a different note from your opening chord. In the following example, the melody begins on G, which is one of the notes in the C chord:

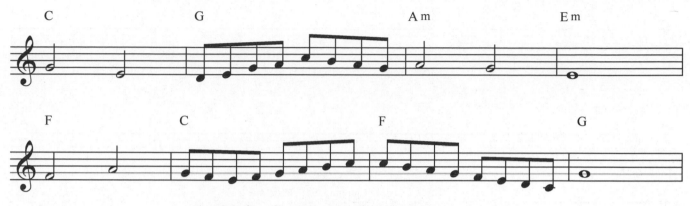

A melody for a C major progression, beginning on the G note.

Visit us online at www.completeidiots.guide.com/artofsongwriting.

Or you can even begin on a note that's not part of the C chord at all, like this:

A melody for a C major progression, beginning on B.

Visit us online at www.completeidiots.guide.com/artofsongwriting.

Tension and Resolution

Just as your ear tends to gravitate toward notes of the starting chord when you're coming up with a melody, it also looks at the notes of all the chords in the progression as safe resting spots. When you reach G, the second chord of this sample progression, you'll probably find yourself hovering around the notes G, B, or D. That's because those three notes make up the G major chord. Likewise, you'll likely find you're partial to the notes A, C, and E, which make up Am, when you get to the Am chord.

Landing on the note of a chord gives *resolution*, a sense of completeness to the music. Your melody and accompaniment are in harmony with each other. But part of the adventure of melody is creating tension by having notes that are not part of your accompanying chord in your melody. These *passing tones* help your melody move around and keep it from being limited to just the notes of the harmony.

You can stress the tension and resolution in your melodies in many ways, some of which are demonstrated in this example:

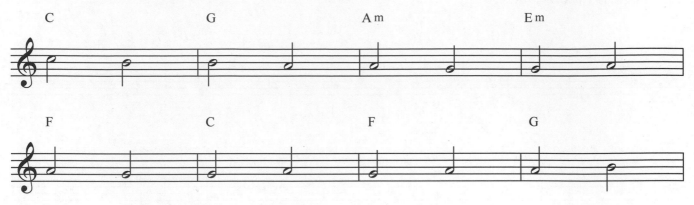

Using passing tones to create tension.

 Visit us online at www.completeidiots.guide.com/artofsongwriting.

You'll notice that this melody is quite similar to the very first melody we used for this sample chord progression. It uses the very same notes, but creates tension either by changing to a note of the next chord while still on the first chord (as it moves from C to B in the third beat) or by staying on a note of the previous chord after the chord has changed (repeating the A note right before the final B note of the melody). These moments of tension, followed by a resolution to a note of the accompanying chord, make the melody much more interesting.

Growing Beyond Simple Major and Minor Chords

Remember that there are more chords than just your basic major and minor chords. In Chapter 10, you learned that many chords are just the basic major and minor chords with added notes. At the beginning of the last example, the melody note of C switched to B while C was still the accompanying chord. Together, the B note in the melody and the C chord in the progression created a Cmaj7 chord.

This is one reason that jazz standards have such interesting melodies as well as more complex chords. Quite often, the melody note combined with a basic chord produces a more exotic sound than you would get if you used only the notes of the basic chord for your melody.

> **TUNE TIPS**
>
> The more chords you know, the more your ears will hear possible melody notes that can add spice to your songs.

And also remember that you can use nondiatonic notes (notes that are not in the key of your song) as part of your melody. The following example tosses in an E♭, D♭, and more:

Using nondiatonic notes in a melody.

 Visit us online at www.completeidiots.guide.com/artofsongwriting.

Learning by Doing (and Doing and Doing)

All this instruction may seem a little overwhelming, but coming up with your song's music really comes down to experimenting and trying out different melodic and harmonic ideas. Even though the process requires a lot of mixing and matching, you can use what you've learned about melodies and chord progressions in the last two chapters to make the process smoother. You might even find coming up with music to be as much fun as writing lyrics, if not more fun. Possibly you'll find it easier, too.

For some, the music aspect of songwriting gets easier with each song. Even though there are only so many notes and so many chords (not to mention only so many that go well together), there are seemingly countless ways of combining notes into melodies. The challenge lies in making certain you don't repeat yourself or accidentally copy someone else's melody note for note.

Likewise, the more times you piece together chord progressions, the more you get a good sense of which chords go well together. And as you learn more chords, you will find even more possible melody lines and harmonies.

As much as possible, you want your song's melody and chords to fit your song's lyrics. Ideally, all three components will complement each other, making the whole song stronger than the sum of its parts. A busy melody can make the lyrics unintelligible; a constantly changing chord progression might muddy up both the melody and lyric.

If you've got a good progression or a good melody that doesn't fit the song you're currently working on, you can always use it for a future song. Just be sure you record all your spare ideas so you can easily find them when you want to.

The Least You Need to Know

- When creating music for your song, you can start with either a melody or a chord progression.
- Experiment with different keys, including minor keys, to find the chord progression you want for your melody.
- Your melody should involve notes other than those in its accompanying chord or chords.
- Use melodic tension and resolution to make your melodies more memorable.
- The experience you gain in creating melodies and chord progressions will make future music making easier.

Rhythm

In This Chapter

- Finding the musical pulse
- Understanding musical meter and typical time signatures
- Using swing rhythms
- Fitting lyrics to time signatures
- Using rhythm in the songwriting process

Songs, musically and lyrically, are about structure and patterns. There are verses, choruses, and bridges, and each section tends to remain structurally the same for the length of the song. The lyrics and the melody of the chorus are usually identical in each repetition of the chorus. The lyrics, too, often have a repeated pattern of rhyme and/or meter that helps the song hook the listener.

Melodies, mirroring the lyric's natural conversational inflection, use notes of varying lengths, giving the music a semblance of breathing and life. Likewise, chord progressions are part of that patterned structure. The accompaniment may use a single repeated chord progression for an entire song, or it may have several different chord progressions, each used for a specific line of a verse or chorus and repeated again the next time that line comes along.

Woven into and underscoring all these parts is a pattern of rhythm. Lyrics and melodies rise and fall between stressed and unstressed syllables. Chords change at specific beats, at specific places in the melody, just like clockwork. Rhythm is the heartbeat of a song that you physically *feel*. It strikes a part of you the lyrics never touch. It makes you sway to a melody and can drive a phrase into your brain like a hammer.

Finding a Pulse

Rhythm is a great songwriting tool, one that can instantly create the right mood and atmosphere for your song. Having an appropriate rhythmic feel is important for both your song's lyrical and musical components, and it can strengthen your music's effect on your audience. Lyrics are the brains, music is the soul, and the rhythm is the heart. The artful use of a rhythm figure to set up or emphasize an important word or phrase, such as the title, can make it unforgettable.

When you hear a song, especially one you like, chances are you tap your foot in time with the music. Sometimes you just can't help yourself. If you're at a show (and if everyone else is doing it, too), you may clap to the beat of an uptempo song or snap your fingers. When you're at a club, you dance to the rhythm of songs being played by the band or DJ. It could be argued that many songs are simply delivery vehicles for their beats.

Getting a sense of a musical pulse is both easy and a bit tricky. Picking up the general overall beat is as easy as tapping your toes. Unless a song is very fast, you typically tap your foot on every beat. It stays steady and even throughout a song. The pulse usually falls at regular intervals or in a regular pattern.

The musical meter or overall beat of songs is usually measured out in sets of four or three. If you look at a piece of sheet music, one of the first things you will see up in the upper-left corner at the beginning of the first line is the song's *time signature*, which is two numbers set one atop the other. The top number, which is almost always either 4 or 3, indicates how many beats make up each measure or bar, the segments the music is divided into.

DEFINITION

In written music, a song's musical meter is noted by a **time signature,** usually a pair of numbers stacked like a fraction. The two most common time signatures are 4/4 (which has four beats per measure) and 3/4 (three beats per measure). The letter "C" (meaning common time) is sometimes used as a substitute time signature for 4/4.

4/4 Timing

The most common timing is 4/4, so much so that it is in fact called common time. How many times have you been at a concert when the drummer will lead into a song by counting, "One, two, three, four" (as in the Beatles' "I Saw Her Standing There") or "Onetwothreefour" (as in every Ramones song)?

Songs in 4/4 timing tend to carry their strong pulses or accented beat every other beat. The stresses can be on the first beat (also called the downbeat) and third, as in **one**, two, **three**, four (think "we will we will rock you") or they could fall on the second and fourth beats (one, **two**, three, **four**).

Having a sense of the pulse you want in your music can help you work out where the lyrics may line up in terms of meter. Having stressed syllables fall on strong beats is a lot easier on the ear than having them land on the weaker beats.

Separating Rhythm from Tempo

It's important to understand the difference between rhythm and tempo. *Rhythm* is the pulse, the repeated pattern of accented and nonaccented beats. *Tempo* is the speed at which the rhythm is played. Tempos are often notated in terms of beats per minute.

DEFINITION

Rhythm, in music, is a uniform or patterned repetition of the pulses caused by strong and weak beats. **Tempo** is the speed or frequency at which these beats occur.

Notes can come in lengths of all sorts, from four beats or more to small fractions of a beat. Just because your song uses a lot of quick notes doesn't mean it's a fast song. It just means that you're cramming a lot of notes into a small space. Many rap songs, or those chock full of lyrics, like "One Week" by Barenaked Ladies, are played at moderate tempos even though it may seem like they're very fast.

Steady as She Goes

Whatever the tempo or beat, keep your rhythmic pulse steady and constant throughout the entire song. True, there are songs that slow down or speed up at specific points—slowing down (retarding) is a classic way of signaling that the end of the song is approaching—but having the tempo continually in flux tends to turn off a lot of listeners. Audiences can be incredibly willing to overlook a bad note or a missed word, but it's almost impossible to ignore a glitch in the rhythm. Again, think about music and dancing. If people are dancing to a song, the easiest way to get them to stop is to make it so they can't find a steady beat to dance to. The good time they might have been having and associating with your music can easily turn to frustration.

Thinking in Threes and More

Obviously, songs can be written in time signatures other than 4/4. The second most common time signature is 3/4 timing, also called waltz time. There are three beats per set and the first beat gets the strong accent more often than not. If you think of songs like "Piano Man" by Billy Joel or Jerry Jeff Walker's "Mr. Bojangles," you can hear the "one-two-three, one-two-three" pulse of 3/4 timing.

Subdividing into Swing Time

Pulses of three can be incorporated into 4/4 timing to create what's called "swing rhythm." (The rhythm of Lennon and McCartney's "Hide Your Love Away" is an example.) Basically, you start with your set of four beats:

1   2   3   4

Then you subdivide each beat into three even segments, called triplets, like this:

1 and a   2 and a   3 and a   4 and a

Finally, you put strong accents on the first triplet of each beat as well as a not-quite-as-strong-but-still-strong accent on the third triplet of each beat, like this:

1   and   **a**   **2**   and   **a**   **3**   and   **a**   **4**   and   **a**

Swing rhythms sound and feel a lot like a heartbeat. You'll hear them in almost all blues and jazz songs as well as in many songs from rock, country, and pop, like Carl Perkins's "Blue Suede Shoes" or Green Day's "Holiday."

Definitely Different

Musical meters of three and four are practically ingrained into your perceptions. When you hear a song like "Take Five," by Dave Brubeck, which is in 5/4 time, or Pink Floyd's "Money," which is mostly in

7/4, it often takes your brain a moment to adjust. Odd meters can be catchy, but songs with different timings require the listener to do a little more work to get into the groove.

Sometimes, though, using rhythm to shake one's audience up a bit can be an effective way to make a song stand out. The verses of the Beatles' "All You Need Is Love" are in 7/4 time and the chorus is in 4/4. And many songs make a quick switch from 4/4 to 2/4 and back to 4/4 again, like Townes Van Zandt's "Pancho and Lefty" or "Know Your Enemy" by Rage Against the Machine. And it's a favorite trick of James Taylor's.

Adapting Rhythm to Lyrics (and Vice Versa)

When you're writing a song, especially as a beginner, keep your rhythms fairly simple and straightforward. Once you gain some confidence, and as your own musical tastes and interests evolve, you'll probably find yourself dabbling in different rhythms.

Sometimes the lyrics or lines that you're working on will dictate whether a song should be in 4/4 or 3/4 time. As you read your lyrics aloud, listen for the meter of the words to hear whether they might already have a strong leaning toward a particular time signature.

But remember that you can tinker with the length of notes in melody. Take a line like this:

"I'd like to say that it's been a fine day"

This might seem to be a prime candidate for 3/4 time. You could easily fit it to a 3/4 time signature like this:

1	2	3	1	2	3	1	2	3	1	2	3
I'd	like	to	say	that	it's	been	a	fine	day	—	—

But you could adapt that same line to 4/4 time by making each stressed note last two beats, like this:

1	2	3	4	1	2	3	4	1	2	3	4	1
	2	3	4									
I'd	—	like	to	say	—	that	it's	been	—	a	fine	day
—		—		—								

Play around with both 4/4 and 3/4 time signatures when you're fiddling with song ideas. And be sure to vary the tempos as well. Being comfortable with these two common musical meters will keep you from using just one over and over again, which will ensure that your songs don't all start to sound the same.

Using Rhythm as a Starting Point

A good way to begin exploring rhythms is to pick one as the musical starting point of a song, the same way you'd start out with either a melody or a chord progression.

Try it in 3/4 time. You first want to get the pulse totally under your skin. Think of yourself as an "oom-pah" band, humming "oom-pah-pah, oom-pah-pah" in your head (or aloud) over and over until it seems second nature. Then take your instrument of choice and play some chords or sing some melody lines to your 3/4 rhythm.

SONG STORIES

According to Paul Simon, "Cecilia" was written by first coming up with the rhythm track, which included (among other things) Paul and Art Garfunkel slapping their thighs and Paul's brother Eddie pounding on a piano bench.

It's tempting to think of 3/4 songs as being mellow and thoughtful, but remember that you can keep a 3/4 pulse going at any tempo you want to. You can write a crying-in-your-beer country waltz or a grunge ballad with a rhythmic feel similar to Pearl Jam's "Elderly Woman Behind the Counter in a Small Town."

Writing from the Bottom Up

Rhythm often goes hand in hand with the bass part of a song. Using bass riffs as starting points in the songwriting process gives you a chance to build a song from the bottom up. Good bass lines often become musical hooks (which you'll be reading about in the next chapter) and can find a home in a listener's ear just as easily as a melody or a line of lyric might. You might even recognize some songs like "My Girl" (Smokey Robinson and Ronald White) or "Come Together" (John Lennon and Paul McCartney) as much by their signature bass lines as by their lyrics or melody or chords.

Working out a chord progression from a bass line is a lot like working one out from a melody, only there will be more emphasis on the root notes of chords. Just as it's good not to change chords with every change of note in a melody, it's even more important to resist switching chords with every new note of a bass line.

Listen to songs with strong bass lines and often you'll hear that they are both melodic and rhythmic, emphasizing both the pulse and the harmonies of a song. It takes practice and a good musical ear to come up with interesting bass lines. If you've got the knack for it, you're bound to create some great ideas for future songs.

Learning by Listening

By this time, you shouldn't be surprised that becoming more aware of rhythm and how it works all starts with listening. But not just listening—listening and identifying what you're hearing. What lyrical rhythmic patterns go with what grooves? What kind of beats and grooves do songs you like have? Are they all different?

Finding Some Grooves

When you hear grooves you like, take them apart musically and figure out what rhythmic parts they're comprised of. As with titles, story ideas, and melodies, have them stockpiled to work with when you need an idea. Working with a groove you don't usually use can give you new melodic and lyrical ideas. You'll notice each genre of music has its own identifiable rhythms. Educate yourself about these as well.

If you have an electronic keyboard, there's a good chance it has some automatic, generic rhythm settings that you can work with in your songwriting. Or get yourself a cheap drum machine or rhythm sampler.

You can also find a lot of different examples of rhythms on the Internet. Typing "rhythm tracks" or "backing tracks" into your favorite search engine should give you links to many downloadable, and often free, rhythm samples. Remember that these are meant to give you ideas and inspiration, not to copy directly into your recordings!

Matching Rhythm to Mood and Message

When a song has prosody, it means the mood or feeling of the music suggests or supports the emotional intent of the lyrics. As you listen to various songs or rhythm samples, try to block out any other instruments and vocals and concentrate just on the drums and percussion. How does the beat make you feel? So happy you want to dance? Slow and heavy as if the weight of the world is on your shoulders? What kind of mood does the rhythm create? What images does it bring to mind? Does it remind you of the summer surf or a romantic dinner?

Listening to a rhythm and writing down how it makes you feel and what images it brings to mind is exactly like the initial steps you took when writing out song lyrics back in Chapter 5. Rhythms can be an excellent tool to start the songwriting process, leading to inspiration for both music and lyrics, as well as setting the mood for melody lines and chord progressions.

Do yourself a favor: don't think of rhythm as secondary to your song's lyrics, melody, or harmony. Treat it as an equal partner and you will constantly find inspiration in the heartbeat of music.

The Least You Need to Know

- Rhythm is the musical heartbeat of your song.
- The most common time signatures are 4/4 and 3/4.
- Swing rhythm is created by dividing a beat into three equal triplets and then accenting the first and third triplet.
- Some songs incorporate changes of time signature into their structure.
- Beginning with a rhythm track can be a great way to start work on a new song.

Chapter 15

Hooking Your Listener

In This Chapter

- Using hooks to catch listeners
- Refining your lyrical hooks
- Adding musical hooks to your songs
- Creating riffs
- Exploring melodic, harmonic, and rhythmic hooks

What is it about some songs that after hearing just a part of them, maybe a few notes of the intro or a bit of the chorus you just automatically want to hear more? And what is it about others that make you sing along when the chorus comes around? Or how can you instantly recognize one of your favorite songs from just the first few notes?

We're talking about "hooks." Like most slang, the term is open to many uses and interpretations, but generally it refers to a musical or lyrical element of a song that makes the listener pay attention to, enjoy, and remember the song. This element hooks you: it sticks in your mind's ear and doesn't let go. One listen and you're hooked.

Hooks can be either musical, lyrical, or both. They can also be nonmusical sounds or spoken words, and they can be the silence of a quick break. "Hook" is quite literally a catch-all term. Some songwriters call a song's title the hook. Others will use the words "hook" and "chorus" interchangeably. Still others will apply the term to a short, melodic musical phrase that is often featured in a song's introduction. Regardless of what you consider a hook, you'd better be able to create or at least recognize one.

That's Some Catch

Hooks can come about in many different ways. You've already read in Part 2 how lyrics can become hooks, particularly song titles and choruses. We hope the title we pick will be one of the elements that make our song stand out and be unforgettable. If it interests the audience enough to listen and the song that follows pays off, the title has functioned as a hook.

Likewise, if the first line of the song compels us to hear what the rest of the song is going to say, it has hooked our attention. And lyrics have many ways of hooking the listener: setting a vivid scene and telling an interesting story with rhyme and alliteration, practicing economy of words and speaking clearly and conversationally, showing instead of telling the thoughts and feelings involved, emphasizing through repetition and building to a satisfying resolution. They make us want to hear the song again.

Where Hooks Fit into the Songwriting Process

Like lyrical hooks, musical hooks can be a melody line that soars high (or dips very low); an angelic harmony that joins in at the chorus; an electric guitar crunching out the opening chords or playing a short, wickedly distorted melodic phrase; a funky bass line; or even a few notes plucked on an acoustic guitar or piano. Even bits of rhythm where everyone in the band is locked tightly into a unison pounding of sound can be a hook.

But you might be wondering just where in the songwriting process you deal with creating hooks? The answer, naturally, is anywhere and everywhere. Sometimes it's a musical hook that jumpstarts the songwriting process. Sometimes hooks develop naturally as you work your way through creating a song. And sometimes they are even added after the fact, as part of arranging and performing or recording a nearly finished song.

How Many Are Enough?

There are no limits to the number of hooks you can use in a song. Some songs have one or two and some are pretty much nothing but hooks. Ultimately it's more about how effective a hook is rather than how many your song has.

A good way to judge both the quality and quantity of your hooks is to ask whether it sounds like it grew naturally out of the song or feels like it's been artificially attached. An effective hook is a seamless part of the song's structure: you can't even begin to imagine the song without it because it's an essential piece of the song's personality. The hook should make the song fun to listen to—you look forward to hearing it. Every music lover knows that feeling!

Another point to keep in mind is that what's catchy to one listener might not even register with another. In other words, what may be a hook to one listener (or songwriter) may not seem like a hook at all to another. And sometimes a musical phrase or a line of lyric may not initially hook you, but later, even days later, this seemingly innocent bit of a song is totally stuck in your head—in a good way, the songwriter hopes, because a listener can also grow so tired of a hook that he or she ends up disliking the song!

Riffs and Fills

Musical hooks tend to be *riffs*, short melodic phrases, usually played in single notes. The notes themselves can be high, like Slash's guitar introduction of Guns N' Roses' "Sweet Child o' Mine," or low, as in the repeated bass notes of the piano line in Carole King's "It's Too Late." And, as you can surmise from these two examples, a riff can have either a lot of notes or just a handful.

Riffs differ from *fills* (or *licks*, as they can be called) in that they are usually repeated at various points of a song, making them ideal hooks. Fills are also short instrumental lines that, as the name implies, fill space in songs. These are more of an improvised nature and are often different each time they occur.

DEFINITION

The terms *riff* and *fill* are sometimes used interchangeably by musicians, but the term **riff** usually refers to an exact musical phrase repeated throughout a song, while a **fill** tends to be an improvised phrase where nothing else is happening. A **lick** is another term, usually used by jazz musicians, for a fill.

Think of the raunchy guitar line that not only starts out Neil Young's "My My Hey Hey" but also occurs like clockwork between the verses. It's a perfect example of a riff serving as a hook. The opening sax line in Gerry Rafferty's "Baker Street" is another.

Riffs can also provide a short musical interlude from one section of a song to the next, like the lilting three note melody in "Harvest Moon," by Neil Young. In addition to using it to start and end the song, Young uses it between the chorus and the following verse and also at the end of the last two lines of each verse.

Where Do They All Come From?

The key elements of a riff-style hook are that it is short, simple, and sing-able. Brevity and simplicity ensure that the riff is just a repeated part of the song—and also that you can play it while performing! And if people can sing, hum, or whistle your riff, then it has the potential of being a good hook.

It really doesn't take much to come up with a riff. Suppose you're working on a song that begins with a strumming of the Em chord, as in this example:

Sample chord strumming.

Visit us online at www.completeidiots.guide.com/artofsongwriting.

This sounds perfectly fine, but there's nothing about it that will really grab the listener's attention. Now add a few individual notes, like this:

Adding a riff to sample chord strumming.

Visit us online at www.completeidiots.guide.com/artofsongwriting.

Now your song has a bit more personality. Anyone hearing you play this will recognize it as your song. You have hooked the listener!

This isn't to say that you want to fill every available space with a riff, but listen for places in your songs where a riff would make sense and add to the musical enjoyment of your audience.

Riffs as Seeds

Anyone who plays (or plays around with) guitar or piano is almost constantly coming up with little bits and phrases of music that may end up as a riff in a song. Some songs actually start out that way, like Pink Floyd's "Shine on You Crazy Diamond," whose melancholy mood comes straight from the haunting four-note phrase of David Gilmour's guitar.

Writing around a riff-based hook can be very easy. Usually the riff will be a melody based on the scale of the key of your song. When the chord changes, you transpose the riff to match the new chord. Or you could also play the original riff with minor variations in order to fit the new chord. Songs like "Day Tripper" by the Beatles or Cream's "Sunshine of Your Love" are good examples of how this is done.

Spreading the Wealth Around

An important but often overlooked aspect of riffs and instrumental hooks is that they can usually be played on any number of instruments. And sometimes the choice of instrument results in creating an even better hook. Think of the recorder in "Ruby Tuesday" or the ocarina solo in the Troggs' version of Chip Taylor's song "Wild Thing" and try to imagine any other instrument fitting the bill.

Songwriters don't have to be song arrangers as well, but having a good idea of how you want your song to come across and which instruments might best suit it will help you be creative when it comes to musical hooks.

Melodic Hooks

Constructing the melody of your song on a short musical pattern that is consistently repeated throughout the song is a common way to establish a hook. A song like "Groovy Kind of Love" (by Toni Wine and Carole Bayer Sager) demonstrates this superbly. Each consecutive phrase of the lyric is sung to the same rhythm figure and a similarly shaped melodic phrase. Listeners often sing along with this song after hearing the first two phrases. Each short lyrical and melodic statement logically leads to the next and follows the one before it. The movement of the music makes so much sense that people feel as if they've always known this song.

These short, repeated melodic statements are called motifs. A motif defines a rhythmic figure and a note pattern the listener quickly identifies with the song. If done right, it's pleasing to the ear and the listener unconsciously expects to hear it again and again as the song proceeds.

Higher and Lower

As mentioned in Chapter 11, pushing a melody line into either the high or low end of one's singing range can create a lasting impression. It's not a technique you'll want to use in every song you write, but if you know your song will be sung by an artist with a great vocal range (or you want to pitch to such an artist), it's definitely one to consider.

Hooking with Harmony

Deep down, just about everyone has a secret Pip inside—as in Gladys Knight and the Pips, her backup singers. Seriously, who doesn't do the "woo woos" whenever "Midnight Train to Georgia" (written by Jim Weatherly) is playing. When the Temptations sing Smokey Robinson's "My Girl," don't you just have to sing the answering "my girl, my girl" parts? What about the background parts on Aretha Franklin's version of Carole King's "Natural Woman"? You can hear how the background singers' parts make the song unforgettable, and they often come right from the writers' original renditions of the songs.

Many songs play directly to a listener's desire to be part of the band by having "sing-along" parts. Usually it's just a simple phrase used in a call-and-response manner, like the "hi-dee-hi-dee-hi-dee-hi!" of "Minnie the Moocher" by Cab Calloway and Irving Mills, or something the singer and audience can sing in unison, as the "oh-oh-oh-oh-oh-oh" chorus of Arcade Fire's "Wake Up."

Progressions as Hooks

You might not think a chord progression can be a hook, but just think about Tom Petty and Jeff Lynne's "Free Fallin'." If you were to pick up a guitar and strum that three-chord sequence, most people would automatically know what song you were playing.

By arranging a song so that one of its chord progressions, even just a short sequence of two or three chords, is played by a single instrument, you place the progression in the spotlight and can often turn it into a musical hook. The two acoustic guitar spots in David Bowie's "Space Oddity" do a good job of this, as does the piano introduction of Journey's "Don't Stop Believing."

Rhythmic Hooks

Creating a hook out of a chord progression often relies on a striking rhythm as much as the chords. The Rolling Stones used just such a moment in "Satisfaction." In addition to a simple but effective guitar riff used in the intro, in each chorus, and in the turnaround, with a contrapuntal, sing-along "hey- hey- hey," they inserted a stop where just a tambourine and the snare drum carry it for two bars. It was one more place where the audience could join in on the hook.

Giving your song a catchy rhythm will always get your listener's attention, particularly if it differs slightly from the typical rock or pop song. You might try infusing a rock song with some Latin rhythms or adding a dash of hip-hop to your pop tune, for example.

And the choices of a particular rhythm instrument can also give your song a memorable hook, like the driving congas of "Sympathy for the Devil" by the Rolling Stones, or even the solo tambourine in the Lemon Pipers' "Green Tambourine." And there are certainly songs that make you play "air cowbell" when you hear them, like War's "Low Rider," Grand Funk's "We're an American Band," and, of course, Blue Oyster Cult's "(Don't Fear) The Reaper."

Stops, Starts, and Dynamics

Some incredibly effective hooks don't involve any music or lyrics at all. Just giving a song a moment of silence, bringing it to a complete halt, and then jumping back in again can work very well as a memorable hook.

Changes of dynamics, the overall volume of your song, like the loud-soft-loud approach of Nirvana's "Smells Like Teen Spirit," can also catch the ears of your listener. This sort of hook works well both with a band and playing solo, and it's easy to incorporate into songs you've already written that may need some attention in the hook department.

Everything Including the Kitchen Sink

If someone asked you whether you knew Tchaikovsky's "1812 Overture," you might have to think about the answer. ("Is that the *Lone Ranger* theme …?") If, instead, they asked about "that classical piece that has cannons firing in it," you'd know exactly what they were talking about. And think about it—that particular hook has been doing its job since 1880!

But songwriters and artists have been coming up with all sorts of hooks for ages. Adding some decidedly nonmusical material isn't new. You could probably write a book about all the songs that use the telephone (or cell phone) or revving cars and motorcycles in some manner. Or you could go with city noises, like the car horns and jackhammer in the Lovin' Spoonful's "Summer in the City" (by Mark Sebastian and Steve Boone).

Remember that even though many of the hooks you've read about in this section are those created in the arranging and recording stage, thinking about them beforehand doesn't hurt. When you get around to making demos of your songs (which you'll read about in Chapter 17), you want them to have great hooks, so make notes and plan ahead even at this stage. The first listeners you have to win over are the people who choose the songs to be sung and recorded.

Learning by Doing

Take a piece of paper and, without thinking too much about it, write down the titles of 5 to 10 of your favorite songs. Then write down the musical or lyrical aspects of each song that automatically occur to you, like "high harmony vocals on the chorus" or "great drums at the beginning." Whether you know it or not, those are the hooks of that song, or at least what's working as a hook for you.

Now take a song that you're working on and write down what sticks out about that song in your head. Better yet, play your song for a friend (or, even better, a group of strangers). After playing it, ask what your listeners remember most about the song. Is it a line of lyrics, a particular chord sequence, even a change of dynamics? There should be at least one thing that hooked your audience's attention.

As you work on a song, add a place in the process to think about and experiment with ways of either adding hooks to it or enhancing the hooks it already has.

As always, listening to songs and trying to pick out the hooks is a great way to develop your own awareness and use of hooks. The same goes for musical motifs. Be on the lookout for those repetitious musical figures and see whether you can use them to make your melodies more memorable. It's also a good idea to compare your observations on song hooks with other people, especially those whose musical opinions you value. They may hear something catchy that you don't find particularly worthy of attention. Likewise, they may not understand why you think a certain musical phrase is a hook because they don't hear it that way. But effective hooks eventually stick with everyone.

Candid and detached discussion on hooks, not to mention most other aspects of songwriting, is educational and can only help you become better at your craft.

The Least You Need to Know

- Hooks grab listeners' attention and make them want to hear your songs.
- Hooks can be lyrical, musical, or both. It's good to have a fair number of them in any song.
- Lyrical hooks can include your song's title, an intriguing first line, clever rhymes, alliteration, made-up words, repeated nonsense syllables, and on and on.
- Musical hooks can be short riffs, catchy choices of instruments, highlighted rhythm or chord patterns, rhythm breaks, or even nonmusical sound effects.
- You want your hooks to be a natural, integral part of the song, such that you can't imagine the song without them.

Getting Better All the Time

As you grow and evolve as a songwriter, you want your art to get better and better. Just writing a song can be easy, but spending a little more time and paying additional attention to fine-tune it can turn your song into something extra special. As a songwriter, you want to learn how rewriting your song can be even more important than writing it in the first place.

It's also important to keep yourself from essentially writing the same song over and over again. In this part, you'll explore ways to approach each of your songs with a fresh viewpoint and keep your music both new and timeless.

Another way to develop your talents in a hurry is to collaborate with another songwriter, or even more than one. Working with a songwriting team may require patience and focus, but it's an excellent way to improve your abilities and expand your network in the music world while creating more songs.

Finally, you'll get tips about creating demos of your songs and putting them to work for you. You'll also discover how the Internet is helping songwriters reach listeners all over the world—without even leaving their home.

The Art of Rewriting

In This Chapter

- The importance of rewriting
- Reexamining your lyrics
- Keeping your listener interested
- Making the music deliver the lyrics
- Avoiding copying someone else's melody

By this point, you should have managed to write either a whole song (maybe several!) or at least just part of one. Between coming up with the lyric ideas and main point of your song, finding the perfect title and opening line, crafting a catchy chorus, and putting it all to music, it's been a fair bit of work. Congratulations on becoming a songwriter!

For most people, however, the job is still far from over. Now it's time to listen to your song as if it's the first time you've ever heard it. Listen with the ears of your audience. Try to find little improvements to make your song even better. And there are almost always some things to find!

Rewriting is a very important part of the songwriting process. Some find it takes even more work because you truly need to put aside your ego and all the time you've already spent. That's not easy. Listening to your song from the viewpoint of someone who's never heard it and has no idea what it's about is very difficult. And if you manage that and discover some things that could be better, then rethinking what you struggled to come up with in the first place can leave you staring helplessly at the page.

Welcome to the club. You wouldn't be human if you didn't think you've written a pretty good song. But you don't get better by settling for "pretty good." The path to greatness requires extra effort and the desire to make your song even better. Quite often, the only difference between a good song and a terrific song is the work that went into it *after* it was "done."

The Craft of Songwriting

They say a craftsman begins by acquiring a basic set of tools and skills and spends the rest of his creative life refining and developing his art. Songwriting is no different. You can count on the fingers of your left hand the number of "hit" songwriters who look back on their first song as their best. Until they have a song or songs that have had some success, serious writers tend to be most excited about their *next* song.

As a fledging songwriter, each new song you write will be a learning experience and a step forward. You will gain more confidence in your abilities to write strong lyrics, come up with interesting and compelling stories, and create catchy melodies, and every new song will benefit from your growth.

Also, each song will represent some refinement of how it was conceived and written. One may originate from a phrase heard on the radio or television and not develop much beyond that. Another may begin as a snatch of melody you started singing while walking down the street and progress through different interpretations to a more viable presentation. And, of course, any material that you can't use in your current song can be recorded and put aside for a song you haven't imagined yet. You will increasingly expect more from yourself as a craftsman of words and music. That's part of the natural evolution of a songwriter. Each new song raises the bar and you expect it to be the best one yet.

Embracing the concept and practice of rewriting will give you a head start on further refining your songwriting process. You'll begin to analyze your songs *hoping* you can find some things to improve that you didn't notice before. It just makes sense to look for anything that could be better before you declare your song finished and present it to an audience. Taking the time to ensure that each song you write is the best it can be can only help make you a better songwriter.

The Reality of the Five-Minute Dream

It doesn't help that you continually hear songwriters talk about great songs that they wrote very quickly, whether it be 5 minutes or 20 minutes. Or reading about how "a song came in a dream and I just woke up and wrote it down." It's not that this doesn't happen, but it's not the norm. The reality is that most songs need to be coaxed into being. How many times have you heard someone at an open mic say, "I just wrote this song—took me maybe 10 minutes," and then after hearing it found yourself wishing maybe he'd taken a bit longer!

It's not that a song can't be done quickly, but aside from the songwriter's bragging rights, who in the audience would know? You'd actually be surprised. Many songs that were written very quickly sound like they were dashed off without a thought. The rhymes, not to mention the lyrics, tend to be obvious and clichéd. What little spark there might be—the unique touch that does make the song shine—is often overpowered by the lack of care for the rest of the piece. It's like tossing a diamond in a landfill.

SONG STORIES

When asked how long it took him to write "The Gambler," songwriter Don Schlitz replied, "It took 23 years, 20 minutes, and 6 weeks: 23 years of living, 20 minutes of walking and making up most of a story, and 6 weeks to figure out how it ended. I thought the song was a throwaway. Jim Rushing told me I should finish it. I figured that would take five more verses! After six weeks of thinking about it, I decided to just write the last verse and let it finish itself."

Just as you'll write every song differently, each song will also take as long to write as it takes. Unless you're under some kind of deadline, there is no time limit. Don't turn writing into a race or you're likely to end up with one of those great song ideas that have little or no development.

The Little Details

As you already know, you usually don't have a lot of words to work with when you're writing song lyrics, so every single one has to count. Rewriting is when you want to check that you've got the precise words you want.

As stories, song lyrics benefit more from active descriptions than passive ones. Why say your song's narrator or character "was" doing something when you can have him actually do it? The more immediate you can make the action, the more actively involved your audience will be.

Also understand that there's a big difference between repetition and redundancy. Songs rely on repetition of lines and phrases to catch and hold the listener's attention. Redundancy is when you use up a line to essentially repeat something you've already said. For instance, suppose you had the lines:

> *Daddy worked hard his whole life through*
> *Every day from nine to five*

The second line, while descriptive, doesn't really add to the narrative of the song. When you talk to people about "working hard your whole life through," chances are that they are already thinking the "nine to five" part. They might even be thinking that nine to five isn't anything out of the ordinary!

Instead, you might try putting in a bit of description:

> *Daddy worked hard his whole life through*
> *Double shifts every day on that assembly line*

Or you might go for a little twist on the "nine to five" to surprise your listener and still drive your point across:

> *Daddy worked hard his whole life through*
> *Out at five and back home after nine*

During the course of rewriting, you want to examine each line to make sure you're not using up valuable lyric space with a line that's pretty much a repeat of another. If you have to say the same thing twice, chances are you could have said it better the first time!

Trust Your Instincts but Know Yourself

Except when you work with a hands-on publisher and/or co-writer, you will be the ultimate judge of when your song could use more work. You may have a good idea of what your finished song should be like, but you also know whether you've given your song your best effort.

If you find yourself tired of writing a particular song, or so stuck that you're spending more time wrestling with it than writing it, put it aside and come back to it later. That could mean later that day or a few days or weeks down the road. Sometimes just taking a break may be exactly what you need to bring it to completion the next time you work on it.

Going Through Your Lyrics

When it comes to rewriting, most of your focus will undoubtedly be on the lyrics. You've already read some ways of working out lyrical rough spots in Chapter 9. Paying special attention to the clarity of your lyrics when they are sung is essential. It's hard to get someone interested in your song if he or she can't hear the lyrics clearly.

Another possible rough spot is the length of your song. Beginning songwriters, like beginning writers of all sorts, often err on both sides of length, but usually they write songs with more verses than a listener can focus on or even wants to listen to. Few if any popular songs can get away with having as many words as a short story. Speaking of focus, all your attention during rewriting should be on making sure your song's message reaches the listeners loud and clear. Is your title catchy and memorable? Is it repeated often enough throughout the song (preferably in the chorus or at least during the verses) so that your audience knows it?

Do all (or most) of your lines of lyrics point the listener directly to your song's message? Have you given enough backstory in the lyrics? Remember that sometimes not knowing the entire story is the attraction of a lyric. Rather than spoon-feeding each detail of a narrative to your listeners, let them work out some of the details on their own. This gives them active involvement in your song and keeps their interest high.

> **TUNE TIPS**
>
> One way to demonstrate whether the title of your song is set up and reinforced well is to play the song for someone, or a group of people, without announcing the title or letting anyone see the lyrics or the label. After the song, ask your listeners what they think the title is. The answers can be quite telling. Often either everyone guesses the title or no one does. Consider using this method to test the clarity of your own song's message and title as well.

The more work you spend rewriting at this stage should help you avoid doing more rewriting when you've gotten to the point of playing your songs in front of people other than friends or family (as you'll be reading about in Chapter 20). It may seem like a lot of effort at first and your initial reaction may be either "Why bother?" or "My song's good enough as it is!" But, if you're honest with yourself, you'll probably find the time and energy you've put into touching up your lyrics has made your song better than it was.

Starting All Over Again

It's amazing the emotional attachment you can develop for the lines you write. But you can occasionally paint yourself into a corner by refusing to edit or totally cut a single line or phrase that you have deemed to be essential to your song. As good as any single line or phrase might be, if it doesn't have to be in the song to get the point across, leave it out!

If you think you've got a good idea but you're just not getting anywhere with it, try keeping a single line or phrase that you really like and try to build the song back up from it. Sometimes taking just a single line of a song may cause you to rethink your lyrical perspective and ultimately give you a better total lyric.

Remember, it's hard to get excited about writing a song that you're not really into writing. And that lack of emotion will likely carry over into whatever lyrics you do manage to write. So if things really aren't working, don't think twice about starting over again, totally from scratch. You'll probably end up with something a lot better than you would have had otherwise.

Tuning Up the Music

Examining the musical parts of your song—the melody, harmony, and rhythms—for the purpose of rewriting is usually a much more subtle process than going over the lyrics.

Sometimes the changes you make will seem very small, replacing one chord with another that sounds very similar but just different enough to make a difference. Say you've written a song that mostly uses the chord E, then A, then back again. This is a nice enough progression and it's used in a lot of songs. But you could make the harmony a bit more interesting by changing the A to Aadd9, which means just adding the B note to the A chord. Because the B note is also part of the E chord, you've created a shared note between the two chords that, when played, gives the chord progression a different mood and feeling than if it were just E and A.

Similarly, if your lyrics were more in the style of a blues song, you could give your E to A progression a blues-y feel by using E7 and A9.

A Part of the Song or Apart from It?

As you read throughout Part 3, you want all the musical parts of your song, whether it's the melody or a riff or even the rhythm, to sound like it's an organic part of the song. You want the music to fit both the lyric and the mood of the song. That doesn't mean that you shouldn't be looking for places where you can put in a bit of a zinger. This could be anything from shifting the melody line up higher in certain places or even just giving the song a total stop, or using any of the musical hooks discussed in Chapter 15.

SONG STORIES

If you're familiar with the old song "Red Roses for a Blue Lady," you probably know the main musical hook is the note sung on the word "blue," which, because it's taken from the minor scale, really puts all the emphasis on "blue."

What makes this even better is that the note in question is called a "blue note"! In music lingo, the term *blue note* refers to three specific notes: the flat third, flat seventh, and flat fifth in relation to the major scale. In "Red Roses for a Blue Lady," the melody note of "blue" falls on the flat third of the key, which literally makes it a blue note.

The rewriting stage is actually a great place to examine just where you might be able to add hooks of any kind. You can also start to tinker with your song's dynamics and give some thought to what type of rhythm and tempo might suit it best.

It's very important to "weight" the title of your song so that more attention is drawn to it than any other phrase or word in the song. The rewrite is a good time to make sure the song ends up with that happening, both lyrically and melodically.

Change of Tempo or Rhythm

Speaking of which, when your song's lyrics are not coming through as cleanly and clearly as you'd like, you might try changing your song's tempo or even the style of rhythm. You might think you can easily adjust that during the demo session, but you're cheating yourself if you don't try to settle that issue while you're still writing the song. When your lyric has a lot of words, the audience might not be able to catch them all if they're being sung at the speed of sound. Slowing the tempo, even very slightly, can make a big difference in how well your lyrics reach your listeners' ears. If that doesn't fix the problem, you may have to rethink the lyric itself.

Rhythmic styles can work wonders when it comes to enhancing the mood of your song. For instance, if you have an ordinary song with playful romantic lyrics, you could try setting it to a tango beat and see whether that gives you a song that your audience will enjoy and remember.

The Teamwork Between Music and Lyrics

When you're exploring ways of fine-tuning your song's music, remember that, above all, the music has to serve the lyrics of the song. And just as you'd cut out a line of lyric that wasn't serving the focus of the song, you should make the same decision about any melody, chord progression, hook, or rhythm that distracts the listener from the story of your song.

A great melody and a great lyric don't necessarily add up to a great song. It's been proven many times over that when the listener has to choose between hearing an especially ear-catching melody and a meaningful lyric, the melody will always win. Make sure the combination of lyric and melody suits both components. Each must complement the other. Make sure the shape and rhythm of the melody don't force you to pronounce words in an unnatural way, putting stress on the unaccented syllable of a word. If there are any problems, don't hesitate to adjust the melody or lyrics to allow the words to flow effortlessly.

It's not the end of the world if you have to start over on the musical aspects of any song if things are not working out. Save any musical ideas that aren't working for possible use in future songs. Record your ideas and revisit them from time to time to hear whether any of them might connect with the lyrics you're working on or have just finished.

Less Is More

When you get to the point where you're thinking your song is done, rewrites and all, give it one last test: go through it all one more time to see whether there's any single thing—a line, a chord, a hook—that can be taken out without changing the overall effect of the song. Does it need the bridge? Is that last verse saying anything new? Is the flashy chord progression at the end of the chorus necessary?

In general, when you find that you can cut something from your song, do it, and then try your song again. If you don't miss it, it didn't belong in the song. You will have made it a stronger piece of music.

Where Have I Heard That Before?

Throughout the entire writing process, you should be listening carefully to your song to make sure you haven't inadvertently copied someone else's song or even a part of it. The melody and lyrics are the parts that require your attention since many songs share the same chord progressions. Your song can have the same title as another song, but avoid that when you can, especially if your song title is the same as a song that's been (or still is) very popular.

SONG STORIES

When the Rolling Stones were working on their 1997 album *Bridges to Babylon,* Keith Richards was playing the song "Anybody Seen My Baby" when his daughter started singing over the chorus the lyrics of "Constant Craving," written by k. d. lang and Ben Mink and released in 1992. Both Richards and Mick Jagger were a bit astonished, as they'd never heard the song before. But, as they realized that their melody was similar enough to be mistaken for "Constant Craving," they gave both lang and Mink songwriting credits on "Anybody Seen My Baby."

When listeners notice a song sounds like another song, at the very least they become momentarily distracted by that realization and miss some of the one that's playing. At worst, they notify the people who wrote the other song and you get sued. Take the time now when rewriting to keep that from happening.

A Rewrite Checklist

To help you with rewriting, the Nashville Songwriters Association International (NSAI) gave us permission to share a checklist that lists the questions professionals in the music industry might ask to evaluate songs for the marketplace.

NSAI, founded in 1967, consists of songwriters from all over the world (both professional and amateur), representing practically all genres of music. Their mission is to "protect the rights and future of the profession of songwriter, and to educate, elevate, and celebrate the songwriter and to act as a unifying force within the music community and the community at large." As such they are constantly giving advice to songwriters concerning almost everything about the profession.

Even if you have no intention of ever pitching one of your songs to a publisher, record company, or artist, you probably will find this checklist very helpful as a guideline for rewriting. It addresses every aspect of your song from theme, title, and opening line to the melody and musical hooks.

And when you think about it, crafting a song that is strong enough to be commercially marketable means that you've created a great song—regardless of whether you pitch it or just sing it to your friends and family. You'll probably find yourself cobbling together your own "rewrite checklist" at some point, so why not use the one from NSAI as a good starting point?

Is Your Song Ready for the Commercial Marketplace?

Once you've written a complete song (words *and* music), you need to decide how commercial it is if you're interested in pitching it. In general, a commercial song has the potential to produce a hit record, motivates people to buy it and request it on the radio, and thus generates income.

The following is a checklist that many professionals in the industry use to evaluate songs:

Theme (underlying idea or concept):

❏   Is the idea one that a lot of people can relate to?

❏   Is it a unique or fresh approach?

❏   Is the idea believable?

❏   Does the song confuse the listener with too many themes or details that don't lead to the hook?

❏   Are the characters interesting and believable?

Lyrics:

❏   Is there a memorable title or hook?

❏   Is there a strong opening line?

❏   Do the words sound old-fashioned or out-of-date?

❏   Are the lyrics something you would hear in a conversation today?

❏   Are the lines concise and does every word count?

❏   Are the rhymes too predictable? (moon/June, true/blue, rain/pain)

Melody:

❏   Is there a strong marriage between melody and lyrics?

❏   Has an appropriate mood been established through the rhythm and tempo?

❏   Is the musical hook memorable?

❏   Is there an interesting melodic change between verse and chorus and/or verse and bridge?

❏   Does the melody build into the chorus?

Overall impact:

❏   Does the song have a beginning, middle, and end?

❏   Are all the verses strong and nonrepetitive?

❏   Is the message powerful?

❏   Does the song generate emotion?

❏   Is the storyline good? (One main point? Well-timed?)

❏   Does the song resolve itself to the listener's satisfaction?

Remember that this checklist is meant to be a helpful guideline. Nothing in the world can guarantee that any song is going to be commercially successful, but it doesn't hurt to have a lot of professional experience and advice to follow.

Know What's Going On!

It should go without saying that, if you want to try your hand at pitching your songs commercially, you should have an idea of what's hot in the current music scene. This is incredibly easy to do online, by checking up on the Billboard charts or seeing the Top Sellers lists on Amazon, iTunes, or any of your favorite music websites.

You also want to keep up with which songs are getting recognized at the various industry award shows, such as the Grammy Awards, the People's Choice Awards, the Country Music Awards, and the MTV Video Awards. Pay attention to all the nominees, not just the winners. Any song that's been nominated in any category had to beat out thousands of others, so it's certainly worth your attention.

And it also doesn't hurt to listen to the winners of any of the major songwriting contests. If you listen with an objective desire to learn, you may find people listening to one of your songs one day!

When Enough Is Enough

It's so easy to get so caught up in the process of rewriting that you forget that your real task is to complete your song! You can end up cutting so much that it doesn't add up to a full minute of music, or adding so much that your song is more like an opera.

Be sure to take frequent breaks in order to reevaluate your song. Remember why you decided to change a line or a bit of music and see if the new ideas work to make the original song better in some way—more focus, less redundancy, better word choice, a more interesting chord or two. If they do, great! If not, then maybe your original choice was the better option. Or maybe you just haven't found it yet!

Sometimes, though, the right word comes through time and getting to know your song better. Some songwriters will joke about their songs continually being "works in progress" and there's more than a bit of truth to that. You will often find the best way to rewrite a song is to just play it often enough to tell you the new words itself! Songs ultimately get written on their own schedule. This isn't to say you shouldn't worry about rewrites: the more you are actively working at improving your song the more you improve as a songwriter. And part of becoming better at your craft comes from knowing when it might be time to just let things stand as they are, at least for a while.

The Least You Need to Know

- Rewriting is an important part of the songwriting process.
- Don't use more words than you need. And don't be shy about cutting out phrases, lines, or even whole verses if they don't add to your song.
- Remember that every lyric line should focus the listener's attention on your song's message or story.
- Experiment with different chords, rhythms, and tempos to see whether they help make your song stronger.
- The music delivers the lyrics, so be certain that the music doesn't make the lyrics unintelligible to the audience.

Turning Your Song into a Demo

In This Chapter

- Using work tapes during the songwriting process
- Deciding why and how to create a demo
- Looking for the right studio and musicians for your demo
- Making the best demo possible
- Using your demos to get feedback and potential work

Music and songs have been a constant part of your life—from radio, albums, CDs, iPods, and MP3 players, from the movies and television programs you watch, from the sound systems in stores and shopping malls, even from your video games and cell phones. It's easy to forget that, in a historical sense, recorded music is a fairly recent development. Only in the last 100 years have we been able to share songs worldwide—and the leaps in technology during the last 20 years have truly given anyone with a computer or even just a cell phone the capability of recording music.

These advances in sound recording, storage, and sharing help make songwriting easier in a lot of ways. When you get an idea for a melody, you can sing it into a phone or an answering machine to retrieve at your leisure. Or you can quickly flip through your playlists to hear a chord progression you think might work on a song you're working on. You can also carry around and listen to the latest bit of music you recorded and work on writing lyrics while you take a walk in the park.

As a songwriter, you want to get in the habit of recording your work. Not only will it be helpful to you as part of the songwriting process, but you will probably have to record your song to have a version of it to give or send to anyone to whom you want to pitch it. Some writers are lucky and skilled enough to be able to play their songs live for artists, producers, and A&R people who are looking for songs for recording projects. Some get their songs cut by pitching live renditions, but most professionals won't listen to a live rendering of a song. They don't want to listen while the writer is there and, even if they like it, they'll want to have a demo they can play for the artist or others.

Work Tapes

Work tapes are recordings made during the songwriting process. These live, unsophisticated renditions merely document what the song sounds like at the time. Think of them as the musical equivalent of a painting sitting on an easel or a sketchpad—you can continually look at it and work on it and improve upon.

You will likely have several work tapes going for any single song. Initially, they may be short recordings of ideas, such as melodies or lyrical phrases or potential musical hooks. As work on the song progresses, you may have work tapes of different ideas you have while the song is taking shape. One may have the lyrics of the second verse swapped with those of the third verse. Another may set the song to an entirely different rhythm, turning it into a pop ballad instead of an acoustic rocker.

> **DEFINITION**
>
> For songwriters, and not counting getting a song recorded (or "cut") on an album, recordings generally fall into two categories: **work tapes** are songs in progress and **demos** are as close to the "finished product" as one can get until the song is cut on an album. Work tapes are used as part of the writing process; demos are usually made when the song is finished and used to "demonstrate" or market the song to publishers, artists, and others.

Ultimately, your song's final work tape will either be a *demo* (short for demonstration) of how you envision the song will be or will serve as a work tape for the musicians that you will have recording the actual demo.

Todd Mack has been writing, performing, recording, and producing music for over 20 years as owner of the Off the Beat 'N' Track recording studio in Sheffield, Massachusetts. Additionally, as the founder of FODfest ("FOD" standing for "Friends of Danny"), an international series of free music concerts honoring the life of his friend and former bandmate, *Wall Street Journal* reporter Daniel Pearl, and as producer and host of his nationally syndicated radio program, Todd spends a great deal of time listening to demos from songwriters and musicians from all over the world. Here are some of Todd's thoughts on demos.

Demos

So you've got a song. You've spent hours reworking it, changing a word here or a note there, pouring your soul into it, and stretching your creative abilities to their limits. Now what do you do? How do you know if it's any good or if anybody else will like it?

A song is like a bird. You have to set it free. And the best way to do that is to share it with others. For some, this isn't easy. Your song may be deeply personal or you may lack the confidence as a writer or performer to let others hear your work. But the only way to know if your song is any good is to play it for others. There are two ways to do that—perform it or record it.

Making a demo of your song is a critical step in assessing how it resonates with others. It is also the best way to analyze your song. The recording process is like a microscope. It allows you to hear your song over and over again, part by part or as a whole, in a way that is much different than how you hear it as you are performing it. But, as writers, we are unique in our perception and interpretation of our work. Simply put, we are too close to it to judge it objectively. Playing it for others is our only chance of hearing it as others do. Their feedback will not only give you insight as to how the rest of the world hears your songs, it will also help you learn about yourself as a writer.

So, if you think about it, a lot rides on that recording. It is important that you put your best foot forward, producing a finished product that is the strongest it can be, even if it is a simple demo consisting of just a guitar or piano and voice. A demo of marginal performance and sonic quality gives your song a disadvantage. You run the risk of it being judged on the quality of the recording rather than the song itself.

In today's digital world, recording has become easier and more accessible than ever. There is a wide range of affordable and even free recording software out there. Hand-held recorders are cheaper than ever. But just because you can record your demo on your own doesn't necessarily mean you should. Get somebody to help you. You don't need a recording engineer; software and hand-held recording units are easy enough to use that just about anybody can help. This does three things for you: First, it affords you the opportunity to concentrate solely on the performance of the song. Second, it is a great first step towards letting others hear your song. And third, it will give you another set of ears to ensure you are giving the best performance of your song you are capable of. Good luck!

—Todd Mack

Reasons for Making a Demo

Demo'ing is essential for several reasons: You need to document your creation. A demo shows what your completed song sounds like. You get to eliminate the distracting mistakes that can happen in live presentations. Depending on your memory and how many songs you write in your lifetime, it can be difficult to remember exactly how each one goes. It's best to make a clear, correct recording of it while it's still fresh in your mind. Next, you need to have a physical copy of your song to register it for copyright at the Library of Congress. Digitally formatted copies (MP3s or CDs) are most often sent in with the other registration information.

Finally, you need a recorded version to copy and send or give to people who you hope will record it. These days, one sends a CD to an office or e-mails an MP3. (Unless the recipient says not to, always include a typed lyric sheet with all your contact info.)

Things to Consider

You're making a demo to show off your song, so when you record it, keep that in mind. Any singing and playing should put the song first and show it at its best. Nothing in your demo should distract the listener from the song. You don't want someone who's auditioning your song to ask you who the guitar player or singer was.

You'll have to learn your own best way to present your songs. Everyone has their unique abilities in the production of demos. Some know how to make fantastic, full-band, multi-track recordings in a home studio that already sound like hit songs on the radio. Some have the money and know who to hire to produce those kinds of demos. And a few are best served by just recording themselves singing and playing their song. If you experiment and pay attention, you'll find out which method suits you best. If your song is a hard rock number, you'll probably want to have drums, bass, and at least electric guitar accompanying a vocalist who can sing in that style. It's said that male artists are not generally receptive to songs pitched with a female vocal.

Don't expect anyone to "hear through" a poorly done demo. It may seem like a joke, but there's a lot of truth to the three biggest lies in the songwriting business:

- "The check's in the mail."

- "We'll fix it in the mix."

- "I can hear through a bad demo."

If you can, be sensitive to the preferences of whom you're most apt to play your demo for. Some people prefer very simple, rough demos, while others expect to hear a virtual hit record with sophisticated instrumental arrangements and A-list players and background singers.

TUNE TIPS

What I've never had any luck with, and would strongly discourage you from ever doing, is writing or demo'ing in the style of one particular artist. Realistically, one has almost no chance of getting a particular artist to cut a particular song. If you spend your time and ideas on a song to fit that one singer, and spend your money demo'ing it to sound like what you think he or she would sound like, and the singer passes on it, it's not pitchable to any other artist. If you do take it to someone else, they'll assume you pitched it to that other artist, got turned down, and now you're coming to them as a second choice. Ouch!

You've written the best song you can write with your idea, so demo it to best represent what the song should be, and then you can pitch it to anyone who would record a song of that or any other genre. That gives you the best chance to get a cut of your song.

If you write for a publishing company, unless you negotiate a different deal, it will probably decide which of your songs get a full-fledged demo and guide you through all of the preceding steps. The company will also usually pay all or at least half of the cost of the demo. Quite often, the publisher will also produce the demo sessions and make most of the creative decisions about the recording and playing. However, I've never known of a writing deal in which the writer wasn't at least afforded the opportunity to make a guitar/voice or piano/voice recording of any of the songs he or she wrote for the company.

From Work Tape to Demo

As mentioned, your final work tape for any given song should be as close to a finished demo as you can do by yourself. It should accurately demonstrate everything you've written into the song: melody, lyrics, and chords, and don't forget the intro, musical licks, signature hooks, turnarounds, modulations (changes of key), and the ending—everything that's integral to the song.

TUNE TIPS

It's good to get as much feedback as you can before you demo your song. Once you've paid for a demo, it's rather discouraging to find out there's something you should have changed.

Depending on your skill at recording, not to mention the equipment you have at your disposal, it might actually be good enough to use as your demo. Do your best to be objective in evaluating yourself and be sure to get as many unbiased opinions from others as you can. It doesn't have to be perfect, but it should be as close to perfect as it can possibly be.

Should you decide to record your demo at a studio, use your final work tape copy (make several copies!) as a guide for anyone involved in the recording process. It will help familiarize the studio staff (producer and recording engineer) with your song or songs, and give the musicians something to practice with before getting to the studio.

Scoping Out a Studio

Depending on where you live and what the facility's like, studio costs can range anywhere from $50 to more than $1,000 an hour. Some may offer packages where you get a discount on the hourly rate if you purchase a block of hours to start with.

If possible, you want to check out the place first and talk to the people you'd be working with. Every studio (and staff) has its own personality, and you want to work in one where you feel very comfortable. Be sure to go over every aspect of the recording process. Think of a studio as a taxi cab: When you walk in, the meter's running! That includes the time it takes to set up microphones, position the drums, take a break for a drink—pretty much everything.

You also want to know that, although you'll devote the most time to the actual recording, you're going to spend a lot more time than you think in the mixing process. Mixing involves setting the levels of the various instruments and voices in relation to each other during the song. Mastering, the process of preparing and transferring the mix to a "master CD" from which your demo copies will be made is another additional expense to plan for.

Go over your budget as well as your schedule with the staff and see where you can arrange the recording to best suit both your artistic desires and your finances.

Putting a Band Together

These days, with the proper equipment, patience, and practice, any single musician can sound like a whole band. Recording software packages, most of which are available for your home computer, allow you to overdub different parts for a song. You can record just your acoustic guitar, for example, and then add a bass guitar or a bit of keyboard—pretty much anything you can play. Plus, you can find software that allows you to use digitally synthesized instrument voices.

But even with all this available musical magic, nothing sounds as natural and immediate as having a band. And it usually takes a band a lot less time to record than to have one person go over each track with several instruments.

You do have to remember that you are the person responsible for putting the demo together. You may have musician friends that you'd like to play on your recording, but you have to be practical first. Not everyone is comfortable in the studio, and you don't want to find out that your friend might be great playing bass when you're at home, but in the studio he needs two hours to record a four-minute song!

Always have a back-up plan, even for playing your own parts. Keep in mind that you want the best demo possible and that may mean using some pros or at least more seasoned musicians. Talk this out with the studio staff before starting your sessions. They can usually recommend good musicians who will do a quick and professional job.

Practice Before You Get There!

Different studios and engineers and producers work in different ways. Typically, though, you'll probably record the rhythm section (bass, drums, and rhythm guitar) in one sitting and then use overdubs to individually record any soloing musicians and vocals.

Be sure everyone in your band has a work tape so he or she can know the song and their parts inside and out. If you haven't figured out what, exactly, you want each instrument to play, then have your band come up with an appropriate part that will fit and compliment your song. Giving your musicians a little creative freedom will usually create a stronger song. They may contribute in ways you didn't dream was possible.

TUNE TIPS

Remember, a demo is not a record. If there's an exciting musical lick or vocal part, use it right away—don't save it for later in the song. Sell your song from the first note of the intro. Don't add instrumentals if they're not necessary, and keep the intro as short as is reasonable. The people you play demos for don't have a lot of patience. Get to the lyric of the song.

If you're going to play or sing on your demo, be sure to practice regularly and often before going to the studio, under as close to the same conditions that you'll be recording under. That will mean singing with a microphone (it's amazing how many people don't practice this way!) or playing guitar with a set of headphones over your ears.

WRITER'S TALK

"Rarely is your first take your best one. Record your song at least three or four times. Pay close attention to how each take varies from one another. Incorporate the components you like of each take into subsequent takes. Choose the take that brings these elements together and best serves the song for your final mix. Ask the person helping you for their input to ensure objectivity."

—Todd Mack

The more you can do to simulate the environment of the recording studio in your own practice time, the more at ease you're likely to be when recording. And being comfortable will lead to having a better performance for your demo.

Mixing and Mastering

If you are putting together a demo of several songs, then you also want to make sure the final mix goes through the additional stage of mastering. Mastering involves adjusting the stereo mix through dynamics and EQ processing in order to get the most audio impact out of each track. Mastering also gives you a consistent overall volume from one song to the next, allowing you to pitch several different songs on one CD without the distraction of louder and softer tracks.

"Make sure the take you choose sounds natural and relaxed, not forced or contrived. Production should be kept to only what is needed for enhancing the song. That tuba part you hear in your head might sound really hip down the road, but odds are in a simple demo recording it will take the listener's attention away from the song.

"Similarly, go easy on the processing and keep the overall sound organic. Caking on the Madison Square Garden–sized reverb might sound cool to you, but it will likely not translate with a simple recording and you run the risk of losing your listener. Lean on the person helping you for input."

—Todd Mack

Now What?

Once you have your demo recorded, you'll want to have some way to duplicate or burn CDs from master copies or computer files. That's easiest to do using your computer with something like iTunes and a CD drive that's a CD burner.

You don't need to have your demo packaged like CDs sold in stores or online, but you do have to create a label of some sort. Along with the title of your song, your name and all your necessary contact info has to be on the CD label and somewhere to protect your copyright you should have notice of ownership of copyright with the copyright symbol, the year, and the owner thereof.

You can get both software and printable CD labels that you put through your printer, peel off, and then stick to your demo CD at many office supply shops. If you truly think you're going to doing a lot of demos, you might want to invest in a printer that will print directly on CDs. Epson makes a good one and the software allows you to print professional-looking CDs.

Carry some CDs around with you whenever you're someplace where you might run into someone in the music industry who can help you out. Additionally, you will probably want to try sending your demos to the A&R reps of various record companies. Do your homework first! Try to find out which companies would be most interested in your song and who their A&R reps might be. Try to get permission before sending the CD; it's rare for people in the music industry to open unsolicited material.

Other people you might consider sending your demo to would be the producer or manager of any artist you think might fit your song.

Using Demos for Feedback on Songs

As you'll read in Chapter 20, demos are a great way for you to get feedback on your songs. Todd Mack offers some more advice on this subject:

"After you've completed your demo, you will need to get it out to as many people as possible. Make CDs to give to friends, colleagues, and people who work in the music industry. Post MP3s on the Internet for the same. Even if you don't have your own website, free sites like MySpace and ReverbNation (and others that you'll read about in Chapter 21) offer user-friendly music players that make it easy for people to check your stuff out.

"Be sure to canvass a wide range of people to get a broad spectrum of opinions. Don't just ask your friends and family, who are likely biased or may not be comfortable being completely direct with you.

Ask for honest feedback from everybody and pay close attention to the critique. Write it down and organize the feedback into a list so that you can make quantitative analysis of what people are saying.

"And be sure to keep the list with you when you sit down to write your next song. You will be amazed at how much you've learned."

The Least You Need to Know

- Make work tapes of your songs at various stages of the songwriting process.
- A demo recording can be used for many purposes, from keeping an accurate record of your songs (for personal or copyright purposes) to promoting your music and songwriting skills.
- Be sure to plan and budget for making a demo. Make the most of your money by making the best demo you can with the best available studio and musicians.
- Practice for recording by using microphones and headphones. It will help you acclimate to being in the recording studio.
- Be sure your demo has all the necessary and pertinent information about both your song and yourself.

Chapter 18

Avoiding Ruts and Blocks

Finding inspiration for songs isn't always something you can turn on and off like a water faucet. As you discovered back in Chapter 4, the world is full of potential song-inspiring ideas, but it won't always seem that way. Some days you might find that you can't come up with a song idea that truly excites and motivates you to write. Just as bad, there will be days when you'll think that everything you're currently writing is just a rehash of other songs you've already written.

The more songs you write, the more you need to replenish and refresh your sources of inspiration for your lyrics—and the more you will want to seek out and explore new ideas for the music of your songs, such as new chord progressions, accompanying harmonies, and different rhythm styles.

Getting Around Writer's Block

"Writer's block" is not so much an inability to write as it is a lack of motivation to write, or the feeling that there's nothing you are inspired to say or write about. Some writers haven't had a lot of trouble with this age-old writer's complaint, but most have experienced times when they felt that they needed to be productive but have seemed to be stymied.

If you find yourself in this situation, here are some of the many remedies you might try. Find something new to listen to, or drag out an old favorite you haven't heard in a while. Whenever one of your favorite writers and artists releases a new album, listen to it and analyze what's being done in each song until you know every word and every note. Something about this method sneaks up on you and, before you know it, motivates you.

Invariably after bingeing on some favorite or new music, you'll find ideas popping out all over the place. You can treat yourself by revisiting an old favorite album or group of records. The Beatles' music does it for a lot of people. So does early Bob Dylan and really early Joni Mitchell.

You can achieve the same kind of results by *not* listening to whatever you've been currently writing and then diving back into it when it all feels new again. If you're very competitive and find yourself harshly criticizing whatever you hear on the radio, try to write the ideas you think the other writers missed. What we need to make clear here, however, is that we do *not* mean to write the same songs you're listening to. Don't write Jackson Browne, Joni Mitchell, Dylan, or Beatle rip-offs. Allow their artistry to inspire you and open new neurological pathways. It should offer new scenery and take you to places where you haven't already said everything you have to say.

Read to Succeed

Reading is another wonderful way to stumble into a new area of awareness. The setting, the unfolding story, the descriptions of characters, and the timing and the twists and turns always offer new ideas. We're not talking about taking a title directly from the text, but notice how you feel as you identify with the main character in certain situations, recognize familiar scenes and feelings, and realize the universality of interactions you thought were unique to you. You may not read a lot, but it doesn't take long for a good book to show you how much you have to say. Try reading something like one of John D. MacDonald's "Travis McGee" novels from time to time.

Also recommended are collections of quotations, once again not to quote them directly, but to start your thinking in unfamiliar patterns. These are treasuries of statements that have been said so well or so uniquely that they've been collected in a book. They're bound to inspire you to say something.

Movies are one of the most common motivators and sources of inspiration for songwriters. For years in Nashville whenever *Gone With the Wind* would play on TV, a few days later the publishing houses would be overrun with new songs with titles like, "Atlanta's Burning," and some use of "Frankly my dear …." The dialogue of romantic comedies is full of great lines to start you thinking about song stories, as are the situations the characters get into and deal with.

Experimenting with Narrators

Here's another trick to use when you can't think of anything you want to say. Turn things around and ask yourself, "What would I like to hear someone say to me?" A little fantasizing can spice up your creative efforts. You can pick anyone out and put words in his or her mouth—let this person speak the very words you'd love to hear him or her say.

Best of all, when you sing those words, no one will know and your audience will assume it was you who thought to say them to the world. You'll be surprised how well this can work. It's rumored that Bob Dylan used to sometimes switch the gender of the people in his songs. It certainly gets you out of the rut of saying the same old things.

The beauty of song narration, as you read in Chapter 6, is that you *can* be anyone you want. Abe Lincoln? D. B. Cooper? How about your own grandfather? Maybe someone from the year 2525? The possibilities are endless, as are the song ideas each new narrator can generate.

Another surprisingly easy way to find your way out of a writing drought is to take a negative song idea, and we all seem to have too many of them, and make it into a positive payoff idea—"The Next Time He'll Think Before He Cheats," for example. Could anything be more satisfying for a woman to sing?

Playing with Song Forms and Genres

Try to write a "form" of song you haven't tried before. Write something without a chorus. Or if you almost always write so-called a-a-b-a songs, write something with a big old chorus. Try to write a song without any rhymes.

Similarly, working in a different musical genre will often affect your lyrical approach, but you can also help matters by putting yourself in the place of a specific artist. If you decide to write a blues song, you're probably going to want it to sound like a song Robert Johnson may have come up with. Maybe somewhere inside you've got a song waiting to be written that Frank Sinatra would have covered.

You can be on the lookout for forms or structures of songs that are off your usual radar and analyze them. Jimmy Webb says he started off trying to write the follow-up to whatever hit he liked on the radio. It's an interesting exercise and it sure seems to have worked for him.

Dodging the "Sound-the-Same Syndrome"

Writers tend to write music they're comfortable playing. It can quickly start to sound the same, but you can use many tricks to get yourself off the merry-go-round.

Same Notes, Different Keys

Do you tend to always write in G or D or E or A, like most of us? Pick an unusual key, one you don't usually sing in, and see what happens. If you pick the right one, you won't be as apt to sing the same notes, intervals, or melodies and instead force yourself to create different melodies. If you play guitar, it can be as easy as placing a *capo* three, four, or five frets up the neck and trying to play the same chord structures you usually use.

 DEFINITION

A **capo** is a clamp that uniformly raises the pitch of all the strings of the guitar one musical half step for each fret up the neck that you position it. If you place a capo on the third fret of your guitar, for example, and play an A major chord, you are actually playing C major, because you've raised each note of the A chord three half steps.

If you use the piano to write songs, then remembering the generic equivalents of chords that you learned back in Chapter 10 will be very helpful. Suppose that you normally play in the key of C and that you tend to use the chords C, F, and G, which are the I, IV, and V chords in that key. Try playing in E♭ instead, where the I, IV, and V chords are E♭, A♭, and B♭. Or play in the key of A using A, D, and E. You'll probably find that you have to come up with different melodies than you have before.

Another approach is to use chords you don't usually use. A V minor chord can jog you into something different. Paul McCartney goes to a I minor all of a sudden in "Penny Lane," and the change in the melody is fantastic.

Play along with songs you don't know and see what chord changes they use. You can bet it will give you some new ideas.

Using Time Signatures and Rhythms for Inspiration

You may also find musical inspiration in trying out different time signatures, particularly if you tend to write every song in 4/4 time. Working from a 3/4 time signature as your starting point will influence both your melody and lyrics in subtle ways that may surprise you. If you've never written a waltz before, you might find that it's a stimulating challenge.

Likewise, playing with tempo and rhythm as a song's starting point can give you an entirely new outlook on writing. In Chapter 14, you read about using drum machines or the preset rhythm patches that come with many electronic keyboards as a way to jumpstart a song. Another idea is to take a song you know and play its chord progression in a completely different musical style and tempo. When you hit on a groove you like, create a new melody, and you've got the music for a new song!

Try a New Tuning

If you use a guitar when you're working, try using a different tuning. It's a sure way to jog yourself out of your usual chord patterns and melodies. Even a drop-D tuning, if you don't usually play that way, will open a whole new world of melodic and rhythmic ideas for you. Your fingers won't be as likely to automatically play in the same patterns or even rhythms. You'll be forced to think and hear things in a new and more creative way.

As you probably know, each of the six strings of your instrument is tuned to a specific note. All the chords you play are formed by shapes based on your guitar being in what's called standard tuning. When you change the tuning of any string, the chord shapes you know are going to produce different sounds than before.

TUNE TIPS

There are also capos that create different tunings. They are made so each string can be capo'ed individually, instead of all at once. You can set up all sorts of tuning combinations so you can keep your guitar in standard tuning but still enjoy playing in alternate tuning!

For example, take the E and A chord progression discussed in "Tuning Up the Music" in Chapter 16. If you were to retune your guitar's G string to F♯, a half-step lower, playing the same chord shapes as E and A would give you Em and Amaj7, which are going to sound a lot different from E and A.

Some songwriters who are guitarists make use of alternate tunings, purposely changing their approach to writing the music for a song. There are many different ways to tune the guitar, and each can create different harmony accompaniments. It's an easy way to find new musical ideas for your songs. You'll have to work a little bit to learn the way they work, but that's the point. You won't be able to stay with your habitual patterns. It sure works well for Joni Mitchell and Keith Richards.

SONG STORIES

If you play more than one instrument, making a switch will make a difference—and possibly inspire your songwriting. Peter Buck, guitarist of R.E.M., bought a mandolin and recorded his attempts at learning to play it. Out of that recording came the main riff and chorus of the band's biggest hit, "Losing My Religion."

Some Tips and Advice from Alex Call

From Alex Call, songwriter ("867-5309/Jenny," "Perfect World," "Little Too Late," and more):

Over the years I have learned as a writer to listen to the little voice inside that says, "This is a good idea; write it right now before it slips away and finds another home." A tiny spark can set me off on a no-parachute flight into a song or even into an entire 350-page book. Once I have a hook or core idea, I don't stop to edit too much on the first pass. I like throwing up a groove feel, a tentative chord progression, and pass quickly over sticky lyrics bits, knowing I'll return to them and make them right later. I use the same technique with my books.

I have always used my home studio as a watercolor easel. I am most definitely not a "legal-pad, silent-room" writer on the initial pass. Many of my best ideas come intuitively. My method is to play and sing; my body produces lyrics faster than I can think of them: first thought, best thought. I will sit later and pound those initial lyrics into submission. There is no being lazy; there are no shortcuts to a good lyric. I tend to do this editing best by myself.

My hits and best songs were largely written solo. The process of co-writing, with the notable exception of writing with a few individuals who allow me the space to function freely, has proven to be often too painful for me. I get that deer-in-the-headlights feeling when I get in a scheduled, forced writing situation, trying to crank out a radio-ready song for what's–his-or-her name, the latest big chartbuster. I'm just not good at it. I hate being polite and I often feel that either I or my co-writer could do the song better if one of us went away.

Sometimes I feel that I'm stuck writing an idea I don't like at all. My skin actually crawls; I get sweaty and want to flee to New Mexico, or at least Bellevue.

I also don't listen too much to the radio. I have no idea what is going on in the charts. When I listen too much, I find myself writing very bad copies of songs I don't like. I read books instead. I get my musical yah-yahs on YouTube: Mongolian music, Kenyan rap, gypsy grooves, old Ray Charles, whatever, as long as it's not some copycat crud that's been payola'd onto the airwaves. When I hear blatant calculation, it makes me quite ill.

I am not a country writer; I write pop-rock with vaguely country modalities. My songs tend to reflect my naively romantic, idealistic view of the world. I greatly admire the Nashville writers who can craft those pointed, expertly honed, emotional or funny, big-payoff lyrics, but I tend to write hooky arena choruses. It's a different bag.

Songs still spring out of my mind and body. I've been playing and writing for 50 years now. Is it hard to find something new? When I seek "new" too hard or when I get caught up in the "industrial" part of the game, yes. When I listen to my inner self, the songs still come.

—Alex Call

Learning by Expanding Your Listening Library

It might seem a bit strange, but often the biggest obstacle to finding more musical inspiration for your own songwriting is *you*. You have developed your own personal musical tastes and you're comfortable with them. You like to listen to songs you like. That's perfectly normal.

But while it's become incredibly easy for anyone to hear music of all styles and genres from all around the world, it's also become very easy to keep one's listening fairly insular, sticking to just a handful of genres or subgenres. The same Internet that offers you Romanian folk music also gives you the choice to listen to only Bob Dylan or Bruce Springsteen or the Grand Ole Opry 24 hours a day. It's hard to get new ideas when your natural tendency is to listen to songs and artists you already know. Unless those artists branch out in new directions, you'll be listening to the same songs for a long time.

The easiest way to discover more possibilities for your own music, as mentioned earlier in this chapter, is to broaden your own listening choices. And sometimes this can be as easy as changing—or not changing—your radio station. If you're the sort who listens to the same station or the same set of CDs in the car, pick one day a week for deliberately listening to something new—a different station, or perhaps some CDs or song suggestions borrowed from friends. Conversely, if you change the channel every few minutes trying to catch a song you know—don't. Just take whatever the radio happens to offer for the duration of the drive.

You can adapt these ideas to your home listening habits as well. If you use an online program such as Pandora, which gives you a personalized song list based on what music you've previously noted that you liked, try expanding the program's parameters a bit. When you hear a song you like during a television program or film, try to find the artist and songwriter. Then add both the artist and songwriter (if they're not one and the same) to your request list.

You're not going to like everything you hear, but understanding what it is about some songs that does or doesn't work for you, is still helpful to you as a songwriter. Learning to avoid potential song mistakes while discovering more and more potential ideas makes listening to new and different material worth your while.

Never Turn Down Going to a Show

One good, albeit obvious, way of getting more music exposure is to go see a show. It doesn't have to be some huge concert in a big stadium—just catching any local band will do. Even going to an open mic simply to listen and not perform will work.

You want to enjoy yourself and have a good time, but the songwriter part of you should be busy making mental notes. How are the songs? Do you like them? More importantly, how do the other people in the audience like and respond to them?

Be sure to listen to the songs for the usual reasons—catchy lyrics, hooks, and the like—but also be on the alert for the unusual. Perhaps the song has a quirky rhythm or a melody or chord progression that you find compelling. You may walk away with a number of ideas to try out on your own songs.

Never Turn Down a Chance to Play

Likewise you should never turn down a chance to play somewhere, whether it's a small coffeehouse or a casual gathering of friends and fellow songwriters who just want to make some music. Playing out offers you the chance to test and get feedback on new songs you're working on. Plus you might get the chance to talk shop and network with your peers. You might even find the opportunity to dabble in a bit of co-writing or collaborations, which you'll read about in the next chapter.

The Least You Need to Know

- Finding new sources of inspiration is a lifelong part of being a songwriter.
- Reading books, newspapers, magazines, or even just quotations can spark your imagination.
- Working with song structures you don't often use, or writing in unfamiliar song styles and genres, might help you overcome songwriter's block.
- Try new keys, time signatures, rhythms, and even guitar tunings to inspire you to write different-sounding songs.
- Never turn down a chance either to see a performance or to play music with others.

Chapter 19

Working Well with Others

In This Chapter

- Reaping the benefits of co-writing
- Finding a songwriting partner
- Understanding the process of collaboration
- Avoiding potential co-writing problems
- Keeping track of your co-writing work

Writing a song is an extremely personal experience. You have to find the nerve and the way to forge your own unique emotions and experiences into a musical message to share with the rest of the world. And, as you've learned, it takes work to make the best song you can, finding that one elusive word or lyrical line that exactly describes a particular feeling, and crafting an unforgettable melody that delivers that word or line to your listeners.

Now imagine sharing that creative effort with another person or two, or even more. Does it seem like writing a song by yourself would be much better and easier than having to work through the process with a partner? Or do you think the extra input would make things easier?

Some of the greatest songs we know are the result of songwriting partnerships and teams. Every generation, every musical genre has its share. You undoubtedly know the songs of Richard Rodgers and Oscar Hammerstein, Jay Learner and Frederick Loewe, Jerry Leiber and Mike Stoller, Burt Bacharach and Hal David, Carole King and Gerry Goffin, Felice and Boudleaux Bryant, John Lennon and Paul McCartney, Mick Jagger and Keith Richards, and Elton John and Bernie Taupin.

And how about Motown's team of Lamont Dozier and Brian Holland and his brother Edward Holland, Jr., who wrote Top 10 songs such as "How Sweet It Is (to Be Loved by You)," "Where Did Our Love Go?", and "You Can't Hurry Love"? The songwriting/production team of Andre Harris and Vidal Davis (who go by "Dre and Vidal") could easily be considered their modern-day R&B counterpart.

Two Heads Can Sometimes Be Better Than One

Collaboration or co-writing can open the door to creative opportunities, adventures, and results beyond what you get when working alone. You need some different skills and it takes some getting used to, but in the right circumstances, most writers find collaboration quite rewarding. Among other things, it's been said to help cure the dreaded writer's block and the pernicious "all my songs sound the same" syndrome, and to re-inspire disheartened writers who usually write alone.

Co-writing most often means being co-published, co-financed, having more people interested in supporting and promoting your efforts. It at least doubles the word of mouth and your chances for a lucky break with the song or songs that come from the collaboration.

Matching Strengths with Needs

The creative advantages of co-writing are best realized when each writer has some understanding of the craft or market that the other does not, so the collaboration balances strengths and shortcomings and turns out to be productive and educational for each one.

The clearest and purest example of this occurs when one writer is strictly a lyricist and the other is a composer. The writing effort is obviously better for both of them. Sometimes in these collaborations the lyric is written to the music, and sometimes the music is inspired by the lyric.

Giving Every Participant a Voice

Most collaborations involve writers who, to varying degrees, compose both words and music. So there must be a greater cooperation between or among the writers and a clear sense of the goals for their collaboration.

The possible configurations of a co-writing situation are many, both in the number of participants and the assets they bring to the table. Those involved can contribute only music, only lyrics, or almost any degree of both, depending on their abilities and the other people involved. Quite often, someone comes in with a hot idea—title, melody, "song needed"—or perhaps a partially written song that needs to be finished or rewritten. Typically one writer will assume the lead, with the other writer or writers offering supporting ideas. The participants need to feel free to suggest almost anything, with minimal self-consciousness, and in turn must be ready to entertain any input and judgment offered by anyone else.

Songwriting being a craft, it usually consists of familiar challenges with which all the participants have developed their own ways of dealing. A balance is always struck between experience and pure creativity, and, in the best of circumstances, all parties instinctively agree on the goal of the work and can build upon each other's thoughts and suggestions to the betterment of the final product.

Working Together

If the collaborators have their own separate roles (words rather than music, for example), usually one will present at least a first draft of his work and the other will use that as a template for creating her part. Some back and forth will follow until both parties are satisfied.

When the contributions overlap, the collaboration requires considerably more diplomatic skill to be productive and have a favorable outcome. A seed idea or several will be presented, comments and suggestions are offered, and everyone expects to contribute and incorporate the best ideas.

Art by committee can be tricky to manage. Every opinion must be respectfully considered, and rarely is everyone's vision of perfection the same. You tend to learn by experience how best to offer suggestions or alternatives and resolve conflicts and impasses. The case study of the song "Soon," which you read in Chapter 8, is a great example of how the songwriter team worked together through the various challenges that the song presented during the collaboration process.

One has to learn to walk many fine lines: making sure the creativity moves forward without commandeering the entire process and making others feel excluded or unheard; offering constructive criticism without hurting a collaborator's feelings; knowing when to insert a "dummy line" and move on rather than struggling to come up with the perfect word or phrase when you're stuck. You should be working with people whose judgment you respect and who may have better understanding of some situations than you do. Ideally, you'll be able to draw on the combined experience, talents, brainpower, and intuition of everyone involved.

Finding Your Partner

Some pairings or groupings of writers work like magic, some don't work at all, and there are many workable levels of compatibility between those two extremes.

Some songwriters meet in school or through friends or just happen to find themselves in the same band. Elton John and Bernie Taupin are supposed to have met by coincidentally answering an advertisement in an English music newspaper that was looking for new songwriters. These days, it's not difficult to find possible co-writers. If you frequent venues where singer-songwriters play, you get a chance to listen for someone whose songs you like or who you think would be a good match for you. Some songwriters' organizations offer lists of writers looking for co-writers; you may be able to access such lists online. Check the bulletin board at the music store and post a "Looking for Co-Writers" card with your info.

Making Contact

Some writers approach bands with hopes of providing an outlet for their own songs and perhaps writing with someone from the band to help develop material for the group. (Deciding up front about the share you'll get from co-written tunes is essential!) If you live in a city where there are publishing companies, you might be able to get a meeting to play your songs and see whether they have writers they'd team you with.

It's a good idea to have some business cards with your contact info identifying yourself as a songwriter. Make it a habit to have professional-looking CD copies of a song or two to hand out to possible collaborators. You could also put the best examples of your music on your website for future co-writers to review.

When you find someone who's interested, meet and try to get to know him or her. Share background info, goals, interests, influences, current favorite songs, and talk about how you like to work and get a feel for what it will be like to write together. This can simply be the first half-hour of your initial writing appointment.

Co-Writing with Artists

One of the best ways to increase your chances of getting a recording artist to cut one of your songs is to co-write with the artist or the record producer. All other things being equal, most artists and producers would rather record a song they had a hand in writing than someone else's, and the advantages for the writer go beyond increasing the chances that the song will be recorded. An artist knows what kind of songs they want to sing and what they want to sing about. You can tailor the melody to fit the singer's voice and tell the story in his or her own words. The producer will have a strong idea of what the song has to offer musically and lyrically as well, and will often be able to guide the song structure to allow for certain production values that either come to light during the writing or were already planned.

It behooves any writer who gets this opportunity to do the research and learn as much as he can about the person he's going to work with. Know what songs and records have been successful for that artist or producer before. Study the characteristics of the artist's best work.

Develop a good idea of your future writing partner's style. Artists in particular have a public persona they present to their world of fans. Start collecting appropriate song ideas, both titles and musical treatments, in case he doesn't have anything he already wants to write.

To make the most of these situations, a writer must be very flexible, knowing when to lead and when to hold back, offering ideas or working to justify the other person's concept, coming up with whatever is needed to complete the song but leaving room for other contributions. This kind of co-writing is not always easy and it takes a special combination of talent, patience, generosity, and diplomacy to be consistently good at it.

As a professional writer you have to be prepared to deal with any level of competence and commitment. Some artists or producers bring less ability or interest than others, and you have to be ready to work smoothly through difficulties and shortcomings without destroying your relationship with the other writer. Most artists and producers who set up these arrangements will be more than up to the task—and you'll probably end up learning something yourself.

If you do get stuck or bogged down, document what you have so far, take a step back, and schedule another time to get together. You can always take whatever the two of you came up with home and work on it for the next time you get together.

Remember, the goal is to end up with something you both like and think is recordable. Just work toward that and chances are you'll get what you want. Some writers have practically made a career of co-writing with "acts," and the practice is so advantageous that, unless you're extremely lucky or one of the top writers around, you'll have to stand in line to get to write with a happening artist or producer.

By the way, all artists (and producers for that matter) start out with very little going for them. If you can recognize someone with potential early in the game, it's a lot easier to get to be friends and co-writers at that point than it is once they're a star. Don't be afraid to start working with people who haven't "made it" yet. Quite often those early relationships blossom into success and last into and beyond the successful years. At the very least you should be able to get some good songs out of it.

TUNE TIPS

Some writers have luck collaborating "long-distance." Writers have worked through the mail and by telephone for quite some time, but the Internet has created new ways to connect and share information. With home-recording advances, it's easy to send MP3 work tapes and demos back and forth. It's even possible to get together and write in real time on audio/visual Internet connections such as Skype and virtual "meeting room" applications and services. So the opportunities to co-write are practically limitless.

Avoiding Co-Writing Problems

Co-writing without first agreeing on the ground rules and the expectations is a notorious way to end up with hurt feelings, strained friendships, and dissolved business relationships. Too many times, disagreements that could have been avoided with a little forethought end up being irresolvable.

Here's a common example: Bruce and John write a song. Bruce takes it to his publisher, who demos the song without consulting John—and then bills John for half the cost. John doesn't like the demo and wouldn't have paid that much for a demo anyway, so he complains to the publisher. The publisher realizes he's not going to be paid, so he forbids Bruce to write with John again. The song never gets pitched anywhere except in the trash, and none of them trust each other to ever work together again.

This kind of misunderstanding happens because the people involved didn't take the time to discuss upfront how they expected to work together once they completed a song.

Here's another scenario that results from not taking a minute to make sure everyone's on the same page: Steve and Tom write together several times and end up with a song from a title and a chorus that Steve brought to the session. Tom comes up with a way to rewrite the chorus that makes it sound like a big hit, and they end up with something they're both really excited about. As they're walking out the door after completing the song, Steve says, "I can't wait to play this for my brother. We never dreamed it would turn out this good." Tom says, "Oh, cool, your brother's interested in your songwriting," and Steve says, "Yeah, we wrote the chorus together so it's partly his song." Suddenly, Tom has gone from half-writer to one-third writer of the song he just made into a great song.

When you've seen enough of this kind of thing, you learn to discuss the situation and ask the right questions before you get too far along. Here are some things you might say or talk about before you're completely invested:

- "I'm used to dividing the songs I co-write equally with who I'm writing with. Is that what you do?"

- "So who's your publisher? We'll each administer our equal share of the publishing, right?"

- "How do you like to demo your songs? What do you usually pay for that? Should we work together on producing the demo?"

- "Do you want to split the fees for copyright registration? Let's remember to get each other's information before we leave today." Write each other's info on your copies of the lyric: legal name, DOB, Social Security Number (if you can get it), publishing company, mailing and e-mail addresses, PRO, and so on.

- As you share song ideas, remember to ask, "Is that all yours?" If the answer is anything but yes, you can decide not to work on that idea or discuss what each writer's share should be.

If the project is to rewrite an existing song or finish an incomplete song and there are already other writers or publishers involved, you can discuss how to handle that. If it seems untenable, you can say you'd rather limit your work to your own ideas.

The point is to know what you're getting into. Don't assume the other person works or thinks the way you do.

Some writers like to use a co-writing agreement that spells out most of the preceding points. Several boilerplate agreements can be found online, and some of the songwriters' organizations have their own contracts for this use.

You might be tempted to think all of this is just the silly "business stuff" you have to get out of the way before you get to the important part. *But it's not silly!* At some point in your career, you'll be sorry if you don't routinely take care of this.

Practical Considerations

Another word or two of caution: When it comes to finding an idea to start with, it's a good practice *not* to present *all* your best ideas to your co-writer. Pick something you think is a good match for this situation and, if your potential partners don't have anything to offer, see what your idea brings. They should offer something if they don't care for that idea.

This is important enough to repeat: Don't throw too many of your good ideas out there, because ideas can't be copyrighted. Only the song you write with that idea will be protected by copyright.

Our memories are surprisingly sticky. Once someone hears your brilliant hook, you can't unring that bell. Even if he or she doesn't pay attention to a title, concept, or story, it can wedge itself into that person's subconscious and work its way to the surface later. It will seldom bear a tag identifying where it came from, so we all assume we just thought of it. Don't give someone else a chance to (accidentally or on purpose) "rediscover" your ideas!

All writers prefer to "trade up" in the collaboration game. We want to write with someone who has more going for them than we do—more experience, more connections, more reputation, and so on. As a result, the lesser writer's only ticket to the game is, quite often, a great idea or title. Even in those circumstances—or especially then—reveal no more of your "hooks" than you absolutely have to.

There are more than a few horror stories about unscrupulous publishers, hit writers, and recording artists who routinely make note of great titles and hooks they hear when reviewing pitched songs and use them for themselves. Most (but not all) big names in the business are loath to borrow a hit idea purposely, but it's extremely difficult for skillful writers and publishers to hear a hit idea that's been poorly written and not think about giving it the rendering it deserves. Your only chance at protecting a great idea is to write the best song that can be written with it. And that still isn't absolute protection.

Put Everything Down on Paper (or Disc)

A helpful way to prevent disputes that sometimes occur when completing or rewriting a song that someone else started is to document what that song looks or sounds like before beginning any combined work on it. If someone has a lyric he or she wants you to help rewrite or finish, make a hard copy of the lyric as it is and have each collaborator sign and date it. If the original you're working from has both words and music, record it as it exists and announce the date and circumstances of the occasion on the recording device you routinely use when you write.

The same advice holds if you're presenting your original to someone else. This can eliminate any later argument about how little or how much and in what way the original was changed. Sometimes people feel that they either didn't get the help they bargained for or they didn't get credit for the improvements they were a part of.

Save Time for Yourself!

If you are capable of and successful at writing by yourself, it's worth reserving an appropriate amount of your writing time, energy, and creativity for that. Co-writing has a way of becoming the default mode, crowding out individual creativity and self-expression. Monitor your time spent and the quality of your results, and don't forget to factor in your pride and personal satisfaction. Make sure you allow time for all your creative needs.

Multi-instrumentalist Todd Cerney moved to Nashville in 1974 to be a guitar player but distinguished himself as a recording engineer, singer, producer, and songwriter. He's written hit songs for artists of all genres: Lynyrd Skynyrd, Bad English, Eddie Money, Cheap Trick, Loverboy, The Four Tops and Aretha Franklin, Phoebe Snow, Levon Helm, Jason and the Scorchers, Little Anthony, Bill Medley, Twiggy, and many others.

Etta James's cut of Todd's "The Blues Is My Business" was on her Grammy-winning CD, *Let it Roll*, and was also featured in the HBO program *The Sopranos*, and Grammy-nominated "I'll Still Be Loving You" by Restless Heart won the ASCAP Country Song of the Year.

Todd used to tell how a fan once told him, "To show you how Southern I am, I used 'I'll Still Be Loving You' at both of my weddings!" Here's Todd's story about writing a song that stayed at #1 for 5 weeks, "Good Morning Beautiful."

Todd Cerney's Story on Co-Writing "Good Morning Beautiful"

I drove down to Music Row to meet Zack Lyle and write for the first time. I'd been around a while, with some major songwriting credits, and he was one of the new guys. So he spent some time beforehand coming up with ideas for us to write. As is often the case, I had already written most of his ideas or titles, or had friends who had. Finally he said he had seen an idea spray-painted on the Demonbeun Street overpass. It was "Good Morning Beautiful."

I told him that was the best title I'd heard in 15 years and said, "Yes, let's do that." He had a little bit of it started and I rephrased the melody—so it fell right out. It probably didn't take an hour. We knew it had to start with the chorus because that's the first thing you would say. That meant we only needed to write one verse and a bridge. Twelve lines total. I've been trying to figure out how to do that again ever since. You get right to the point that way.

We pitched the song around Nashville and had no luck. His plugger gave the song to an unsigned artist named Steve Holy. It was the first song he had ever had pitched to him. He liked it and took it and then got a deal with Curb Records. Fortunately, Steve stuck with the song, because his manager, his producer, and his label didn't really like it and didn't want him to cut it. We even sent him our demo track to put his voice on so he could show them that it was good for him.

They cut the song and enough other material for two entire albums over the next two years—before they put anything out. It was the only song to make it to the CD, *Blue Moon*. The record label put out three singles from that CD over the next three years, then they finally released "Good Morning Beautiful" as a single. It was five years since it had been recorded. Both of Zack's and my publishing companies had been closed for three years at this point. They were just post-office boxes; no phones.

The song went #1 on all three country charts and stayed there for five weeks. It spent 41 weeks on the Billboard chart, wound up being the Billboard Number 10 Song of the Decade and won an ASCAP film award for being in the movie *Angel Eyes*.

So I say, "Keep your eyes on the overpass!"

—Todd Cerney

If you'll take these suggestions and warnings to heart, you can avoid most of the common difficulties collaborators run into, and should have enjoyable, successful, and profitable co-writing sessions and results. Good luck and happy co-writing!

The Least You Need to Know

- Collaborating on or co-writing songs can bring new inspiration to your writing and help sharpen your skills.
- There are many ways of finding potential co-writers, from local music stores and open mic nights to the Internet.
- Establish your partnership's goals as well as your creative and legal guidelines as early as possible.
- Make sure to record material you're co-writing at every stage of the process.
- Set aside time for your own individual work as well as the material you co-write.

Taking Your Songs for a Test Drive

Chapter 20

In This Chapter

- Playing your songs at an open mic
- Visiting songwriting workshops
- Getting helpful feedback
- Taking part in song critiques
- Learning the skill of networking

You've finished a new song. If you're like most writers, you'll want to play it for someone to get his or her reaction. Usually that's someone you're close to, because he or she is probably easier to get a favorable review from to boost your confidence.

Getting feedback, especially constructive feedback, is a big step in the process of fine-tuning your songs as well as your skills as a songwriter. But doing so is a bit of an art itself, requiring patience, skill at turning cryptic comments into constructive ones, and the ability to put your own feelings about a song aside in order to evaluate it objectively.

Ultimately the feedback you get can help you put the finishing touches on your songs. And the next time you play one for someone, perhaps you'll be rewarded by getting the exact reaction you were looking for when you wrote the song in the first place.

Finding Sources of Feedback

If you're like most writers, the first time people hear a new song is live, with just you and a guitar or piano. Having an audience also offers you a chance to get used to presenting the song and to find out whether any of it doesn't feel as strong as you thought, or what parts evoke a positive reaction.

At some point, you're probably going to want to get feedback from people other than your family or friends. If you're not shy about performing, you might try an open mic or visit a songwriting workshop. If you're not comfortable playing and singing in public, then you'll probably want to record a demo of your song (as you read about in Chapter 17) for people to listen to.

If you do go the live route, make sure you're ready. You have to be able to sing and play! You might be going just to have people hear your songs, but if you can't keep a steady rhythm or carry a tune, you'll have a hard time getting the audience to listen. If you're not sure about your own singing abilities, it might be more prudent to have a friend with a good voice sing your songs.

Open Mics

Most small listening rooms have a night or a time they set aside for nonprofessional songwriters and performers to get up and play a few songs, usually three or so per performer. It's a chance to try out your songs and your ability to perform them. Depending on where you live, you may also find open mics in bars, restaurants, cafes, and even bookstores, so look and ask around.

Open mics are usually very low key and the level of competition fairly friendly. There's nothing like performing your song by yourself in front of an audience that may or may not care to make you aware of how powerful your new song is.

TUNE TIPS

Don't think of music—especially songwriting—as a competitive sport. Just why someone prefers one song to another is not only a matter of individual taste, but also a matter of where that person is at that moment in his or her life—or day! A song someone doesn't think twice about today might become a big favorite next week.

More important to you as a songwriter, if you're constantly looking at songs in a competitive manner, you're not as likely to learn objectively or discover a new idea or technique. As you read at the end of Chapter 3, look at every song as a chance to learn. Approach open mics or any opportunity to play your own songs and listen to others' with the idea of making yourself a better songwriter.

Once you're on stage, you also get to see how your song goes over. Stay positive about your work and enjoy playing, but also pay attention to how your song affects your listeners. Try to see when they are right with you while you're singing and also where you lose the audience's attention. Of course, you hope that your song will keep their attention, but you definitely want to be aware of it if it doesn't.

Songwriting Workshops

A songwriting/songwriter's workshop can mean many different configurations of people who want to learn more about songwriting.

Sometimes groups of songwriters regularly meet and, using various study materials, try to help each other in the craft. A leader/organizer usually sets an agenda and coordinates the activities. Regular participants become a support group, sharing, benefiting from, and absorbing each other's various individual insights and strengths and creating an environment of trust and safety in which to ask questions and play things without the pressure of possible embarrassment. You often get to pass out lyric sheets, play your new songs (demos), and get feedback and then follow up in a subsequent meeting with your rewrites.

Depending on who's in the group, the level of understanding and quality of the songs tends to rise over time. Sometimes a music professional mentors the group, and sometimes you'll have other opportunities to have your songs critiqued by a professional.

Songwriter workshops are also organized under the auspices of larger songwriter organizations or people with greater songwriting experience, expertise, and connections to the music business. These are most often paid events that are either stand-alone affairs or part of larger events you sign up for with a famous and/or successful songwriter, publisher, or panel of professionals. They talk about what they do and what you should be doing—and then they listen to demos and, right there in front of God and everybody, tell you what they think of your song. A good bit of wonderful advice is usually imparted at these events, and sometimes one of the aforementioned pros finds a song and (hopefully!) a writer worth becoming involved with.

"Writers In-the-Round"

Again, depending on where you live, you may be able to find songwriters participating in "writers in-the-round" performances, sometimes called "in-the-rounds" or simply "song circles." These are often intimate concerts in small to medium-size venues. Three to six songwriters will take turns performing their original songs, occasionally chatting a bit about a song with both the audience and fellow performers. Sometimes they will also play along with each other's songs.

It's rare for a new songwriter to be invited to a song circle, but if you've been going to open mics and networking in your local music scene, you might be able to get yourself on the bill.

You may also find places that hold open mic–styled songwriters' circles, with the emphasis specifically on the songwriter, as opposed to someone taking the stage to sing a cover tune. The performers usually sit in a circle and take turns performing one of their own original songs for the other members of the circle. Group discussion on each song usually follows and it's a great way to get feedback from your peers.

Online Reception

If you've made a demo of one or more of your songs, whether it is a big production or very simple direct-to-computer recording, you might want to post it online at one of the many song-sharing websites. (You'll read about those in Chapter 21.) Or you may find an online songwriters' group that works like a songwriting workshop, except songs are played online and all feedback is given via Internet discussion.

There are pros and cons to putting songs online, however. Before you do, you might want to think seriously about copyrighting your song (you can read about copyrighting in Chapter 22) to give you and your song some protection. You also will want to do a little research on which sites might give you the chance for feedback. There are literally thousands if not hundreds of thousands of songs on the Internet. You might be a lot better off joining a small but active songwriting community than to just post something on Facebook.

Getting Helpful Feedback

If you're working with publishers or tune pluggers, you'll have the benefit of their critical review. They usually have a good bit of song wisdom from presenting songs day in and day out, face to face, to the market. They are painfully aware of what works and what doesn't with particular producers and artists, and they know what the marketplace in general is looking for. Pay attention to what they tell you and don't argue. Later, try to make sense of what they told you. They may not have said it well or given you a broad enough interpretation, but I promise you, it's well worth thinking about.

Unfortunately, most professionals looking for or auditioning material won't take the time to give you feedback. These days, you hardly ever even get to see or sit down with them. It's too bad, because in the past such professionals used to be quite ready to tell you what was wrong with your song. And once again, whether they were right or wrong, they were telling you exactly what they believed they wanted.

If you have anyone who's been successful in the song biz to talk to, that would be your best chance at getting some quality time and advice. Try to ask for some help without requiring too much time or effort, and don't forget to express your appreciation for whatever he or she has to say.

There are organizations you can mail your song to (along with a fee) for a critique. You take your chances with these outfits. Some are fantastic; some are not. There are also online critiques available at the websites of some songwriter organizations; the Songwriters Guild of America and Nashville Songwriters Association International come to mind. Sometimes if you're a member there is no additional charge. These organizations also sponsor yearly seminars, song camps, or conventions. For a fee, you can participate for a few days of lectures, panel discussions, critiques, and performances by top music business professionals and experts.

As we said before, not all critique givers are created equal. Assume there is at least some truth to what they say and use your developing discretion to glean what you can from their advice. If you keep your ears and mind open, you'll learn a lot.

The Right Mindset for Feedback

Getting feedback about your songs can sometimes be as involved as songwriting itself. Strange as it may seem, you should be certain that such feedback is, indeed, what you're looking for. Many people who say they want feedback or constructive criticism are really looking only for praise and validation. They are too attached and too personally involved to even consider that there might be a way to improve on their work.

This is totally understandable. Writing music is often a very personal and emotionally charged experience. Still, you cannot grow as a songwriter without taking an objective look at what you've created and listening to it with the ears of your audience. If you're writing songs to communicate your ideas and emotions to others, you have to learn to listen to what they say they hear in your music.

Positive Isn't Always Good

Even getting positive responses may not always be helpful until you learn how to tell what positive feedback really means. Most professionals (and sometimes friends) will routinely say something like, "Good tune!" after hearing one of your songs. If that's all they say, you can be assured they're just being polite. In professional situations, the positive response you're looking for is being asked to play the song again, or if they can keep the CD, or when can they get a copy.

Accept compliments gracefully but also try to get your listener to open up. A real dialogue may give you a much better idea of what your listener really thinks.

Another important skill you'll have to develop is the ability to judge the true nature and importance of the reactions, advice, and criticism you get. Ask other professionals and friends for their take on the specific advice you've received. Sometimes they'll agree, sometimes not—and, even more important, you might get a better explanation of something you've heard before that shines a new light on the concept.

At the bottom of all this, you must be able to decide when what you've been told is factual and helpful and when it's not. The safest course is to assume there is something to be learned from what's been said, identify it, and then try to find some way to make yourself believe it.

Putting Objectivity to Work

It's impossible to listen to your own song as if you've never heard it before, but you can find ways to approximate someone else's viewpoint. Recording your work and playing it back the next day so you're just listening gets you part of the way there. Some writers like to listen while they're driving because that offers a slightly different perspective.

You can also assume the role of the person to whom the singer of your song is singing. How would you feel if someone were singing those words to you? Does it make you feel the way you want your listener to feel? Is it possible to misunderstand the situation or the message? You have to learn how to put yourself in that place. Once you find your own methods, your songs will more often turn out the way you want them to.

Learning by Doing

Whether you decide to visit an open mic or a songwriters' workshop or just post material online, do yourself a favor and try to scope out your intended venue first. Not all music venues, both online and in the physical world, are equal when it comes to being friendly or comfortable for newcomers. If you have written a folk ballad that you want to try out, you're not likely to get a good reception for it at an open mic where everyone else is playing hardcore punk.

Also remember that the venues where these open mics and workshops are being held are businesses, usually restaurants, cafes, or bars. Patronize the business and be sure to treat all the staff well. Doing so gives them reason to keep the open mics running.

Critiquing Others to Make Your Own Songs Better

And while you are putting your songs out there, keep in mind that other songwriters are looking for feedback, too. Don't just play your own songs, take in comments and advice, and leave. Listen to the other performers and be sure to give them your thoughts about their music—what you liked, what you thought was clever or catchy.

Likewise, if you join an online songwriting group or post your songs online, be a participating member of the community. Thank people who took the time to listen to your songs and thank them for any feedback they give you, especially if it is helpful. And try to make time to listen to songs from other songwriters and offer constructive, positive comments when you can.

By taking part in any songwriting discussions, you not only get to learn and improve, but you also get to build relationships in the songwriting community. Through time and experience, you will figure out whose advice is helpful in making your songs better. On top of that, you never know when and where you might find a good songwriting collaborator.

Critiquing songs will help you understand that there is more to feedback than "I like it" or "I don't like it." Make a practice of going into the reasons behind your opinions of a song. Always look for positive, constructive ways to express your thoughts and give specific suggestions whenever possible. Not only will other songwriters be glad that you've taken the time to do so, giving well-thought-out critiques will help you find ways to improve your own songs. You'll start to find ways to avoid problem areas in lyrics and music earlier in the writing process because you've become aware of them when helping others.

Putting Everyone to Work for You

Of course, getting all the feedback you can—good, bad, or otherwise—doesn't do much for you if you don't make use of it. When more than two or three people make similar comments about a particular song, pay attention. This is especially true when they comment about not hearing a lyric clearly or not understanding what the lyric was supposed to mean.

You're hoping to have your songs heard and enjoyed by people, and people come from all walks of life. They also have all sorts of opinions. Take good advice to heart when you can. People want to enjoy good music and most will try to help you become a better songwriter. It's up to you to incorporate that advice into your music.

Unfortunately, expert and other advice is not always accurate. It's easy to disregard any adverse opinion or criticism, and far too many songwriters automatically do. But it's not smart. If you look for it, most of the time, you'll find at least a grain of truth in any criticism. One of your hardest jobs is to remain open-minded. The other is to figure out what to believe. Everyone has an opinion, but everyone also has his or her own reasons to say what they say. Some are helpful; some are selfish or misinformed.

One more time: The safest course is to assume there is something to be learned from what's been said, identify it, and then try to find some way to make yourself believe it. If you honestly can't find a way to believe it or find anyone else who agrees with it, put it aside and go forward.

Networking Tips from Doak Turner

Doak Turner, a Nashville songwriter whose song "Talkin' Part" gets regular play on Sirius Radio, also is the creator and owner of "The Nashville Muse," both a newsletter and a comprehensive listing of songwriter appearances and music industry events all over Nashville. Through Doak's networking skills and experiences, he has created "3rd Sunday at 3," a monthly get-together for songwriters to play and network, as well as the annual April "Guitar B-Q," which sees more than 500 songwriters and musicians get together for food, fellowship, and music.

Doak has some excellent advice and tips on networking and he's agreed to share them.

Attitude Is Altitude

You are at songwriting round, open mic, showcase, music conference, music publishing workshop, record release, or other networking event. You attend the event to meet songwriters and other industry professionals, and want to be prepared and leave a great impression on the people you meet.

Leave everything outside the door. If you've had a rough day, been told no by a publisher, agent, or anyone that day—forget about it. Come to the event with a positive attitude and a smile on your face. It's so important!

Before the event, research the host and everyone you know will be in attendance. Google their name and go to websites to learn about the person. After the event, Google anyone you met to learn more about them, too.

Start with an introduction and ask about the other person. Tell them you enjoy their songs if you recognize them as a songwriter or artist, or ask how long they have been in town. *Do not* tell them you're a great songwriter or hand them your CD and ask them to listen to your songs. This is a relationship business, and you need to develop relationships with other people. Take the time to get to know someone, and the right time will come for you to play your songs for that person.

 WRITER'S TALK

It's easy to be nervous at a networking event, and being nervous can lead to trying way too hard to do too much at once. Doak Turner has a great tip about how to avoid this:

"I like to arrive early at an event and get a plate of munchies. Holding a plate in one hand and a drink in the other prevents me from trying to talk to everyone, shake hands, and do the business card exchange."

The key to networking is having a positive attitude. Ask positive questions rather than dwelling on how tough this business is or that you don't understand why your songs are not on the radio. I may ask a question like, "What's happening good for your songwriting (or in your life) these days?" This will get the other person off on a good note and they may want to spend a couple extra minutes talking to you.

Business Cards

When it is time to exchange business cards, be prepared and don't fumble through a pocket full of everyone else's cards trying to find one of yours. One tip is to have your business cards in your left pocket, and everyone else's cards in your right pocket. Always have a pen handy and take notes from your conversations. When you say, "I'll call you next week and set up an appointment," make a note and follow through.

Speaking of business cards, yours should include your name, phone number, address, website, and your e-mail address. And make sure it's all easy to read. Avoid fancy icons such as music notes, unless it's your company logo, and always have your business cards with you at all times. You never know when you will meet someone in the business.

Here's a unique networking use for your business card: When you see someone looking for a piece of paper or fumbling for something to write on, offer your card and a pen and tell the person to use the back of your card to write notes. I got a call one day from a songwriter who had flown back to Los Angeles, telling me that he had six of my cards in his wallet from the previous evening. I asked him if he thought it was a coincidence—"I don't think so!"

WRITER'S TALK

If you're the shy type, Doak has some good advice for you:

"If you are shy or uncomfortable, take it one event at a time and set a goal to meet one, then two, then three or four people at each function. Find a way to ask people about themselves, which will lead to you feeling comfortable at the event.

"If you see others who are shy, perhaps not talking with anyone, go up to them and they will be the easiest to talk to! Ask about them, who invited them, where they are from or what they do, and so on."

What NOT To Do at Networking Events

Do not start a conversation by telling someone everything about you in the first 20 seconds! I was at an event a couple weeks ago and introduced an artist/songwriter to a music industry pro and the artist started off by saying how she knows so and so, and she had won this contest and that contest, and how everyone just loves a song she wrote, how she got a record deal with a new label and it went south and started handing her CD to everyone at the table—without being asked a single question or asking the industry person one question about himself or his company! Then she handed me the CD—with no label on it. Very unprofessional.

I have attended seminars and songwriter rounds and witnessed songwriters almost running up to hit songwriters or artists and handing their CDs and business cards to the pro and asking to write with them. That is not the thing to do, and the pros will do everything they can to avoid that person in the future.

The best thing to do in such a situation is approach the pro and tell them you loved their songs, maybe mention one of your favorites, shake their hand and wish them success. If they have the time, they may ask about you. Tell them what you do in 10 seconds or less and gauge their response.

Whatever happens, tell the artist or songwriter it was great to meet them and you hope to see them again. The next time you see them, re-introduce yourself and remind them they met you at a previous event (do not expect them to remember you or your name). Keep the dialogue short and, again, gauge their response. Remember, wait till they ask about you to start telling them anything about yourself.

If you want to be taken seriously, avoid the photo ops and autographs. You want to be seen as a peer by others in the industry—not as a fan! I see this way too much in Nashville by new songwriters who get to attend events. They ask for autographs and photos with artists and hit songwriters, so they are considered fans and aren't invited to future events.

Find Creative Places to Network

I live in Nashville, and I tell everyone to go to the Acklen Post Office in Hillsboro Village and get a personal P.O. box. About 99 percent of Music Row receives their mail at this location, and this can be a great spontaneous networking location. I've made several contacts, met co-writers, and made one or two appointments just from standing in line at this post office.

If you are in another music city, find out where many of the music people pick up their mail and have your mail sent to that post office. The point is, you need to find creative ways to meet people and build relationships with people in the music business.

Be a Resource in Your Community

Why not start your own weekly newsletter in your songwriting community? Start with your friends—ask them to e-mail their gig schedule to you and compile a weekly gig calendar. Grow your list and build a database and you will be the person everyone in the community wants to know, because you're a resource, and you're connected. They will tell the other people in your music community that you are the person to know, and voila, you're on the road to serious networking.

I know this from experience. Check out www.nashvillemuse.com for a list of songwriting and industry events. You can also get our weekly e-zine publication called *The Nashville Muse*, which is sent to thousands of songwriters and industry pros around the country.

Go out and find your local music community. Attend songwriting workshops (e.g., www.nashvillesongwriters.com) or start your own workshop just by having monthly meetings with the people that play and write songs where you live.

Create an Event

On the third Sunday of every month since March 2002, I host the "3rd Sunday at 3" in my Nashville home. It's an open invitation to songwriters and artists to bring food and beverages to share, network, and play their original songs in four rooms in and outside the house. The 3rd Sunday started as a dinner party when I wanted to share a Sunday dinner with my "songwriting family" and invited a bunch of friends—and that immediately ignited the monthly event.

I found a local restaurant, Bojangles Chicken, to provide food, but I encourage everyone to bring food to share. This builds a community by introducing songwriters and upcoming artists—and sometimes hit songwriters and a well-known artist or two have stopped by for the day. I promote the event through *The Nashville Muse* and also on MySpace sites. Hosting an event like this helps get your name out in the community, not to mention the service you are providing.

Speaking About Your Peers

There's a saying by motivational speaker Zig Ziglar: "In order to get what you want out of life, help others to get what they want in life." This is also true in the music business. If you can help someone, do it! Build your community, get out and attend events, support your fellow songwriters and artists. You will meet the people to help you on your journey through helping others on their journey. I promise you!

Build your friendships with your peers. Don't expect hit songwriters, artists, or music pros to all of a sudden be your best friend just because you showed up. Build relationships, co-write, hang out, and do other things in addition to music. Learn on the journey and make new friends.

Best wishes for your networking and I will see you networking in Nashville!

—Doak Turner

The Least You Need to Know

- Open mics and songwriting workshops are good ways to try out your songs before an audience.
- You want to evaluate objectively the feedback you get on your songs. Use constructive criticisms to make your songs better.
- Try to participate in giving feedback to other musicians' songs when you can.
- Use the helpful feedback you get to strengthen your songwriting skills.
- Networking with other songwriters and musicians helps you connect with those who can help you grow as a songwriter and perhaps further your opportunities.

The Digital Age

In This Chapter

- Ways to use the Internet
- Potential problems to songwriters
- Online tools to help you
- Creation of your own website
- The world of social networking

Music and songs have been a huge part of people's lives since they started beating sticks on stones and chanting about that day's hunt for food. But it's fairly safe to say that people today probably have more ready access to more music than at any other point in history.

Thanks to the rapid and seemingly nonstop advances in digital technology, you can carry thousands of songs—tens of thousands, actually—with you on a device hardly bigger than a business card. You can record music or your musical ideas for possible songs on your cell phone and listen to them at your leisure. There are software programs—some free and some reasonably priced, considering all that they can do—that make writing and formatting music a breeze and will even transcribe it from an audio file.

Linking this all together, of course, is the Internet, which is doing more to change the face of music and the music business than the electric guitar ever dreamed of. It's not the single solution to all the questions a songwriter may have, but the Internet offers you a lot of options at many phases of song-writing, from how you might decide to record, arrange, promote, and market your songs to finding valuable feedback and help with your writing.

It's a Small World

These days, anyone with a computer can hear songs posted on the Internet by people from all over the planet. With a good connection and the right URL, a businessperson sitting at home in Singapore can listen to the Grand Ole Opry from Nashville, a student in Prague can enjoy a Beethoven symphony broadcast from Tokyo or dance to the latest hip-hop beats from Los Angeles. An Arcade Fire concert in Madison Square Garden can be seen in Moscow or the home-recorded demos of a fledgling songwriter in South Africa can be heard by another songwriter in South Dakota.

It's possible to share your songs with people from all over the world. You can make contact with possible songwriting partners and get feedback on tunes you're working on, not to mention create and nurture a fan base. To enable someone to hear your songs on the Internet, you have to get them online. There are many ways of going about this. You can create your own personal website where people can learn all about you and your music or you can create your own personal account at one or more of the many social networking sites or websites, some of which are specifically set up for musicians to share their music.

The Good Side

For songwriters, this brave new digital world is a blessing and a curse. On the plus side, there is the facility of computers, especially with laptop mobility, word processing, file storage and retrieval, wireless Internet access to information, online rhyming dictionaries, thesauruses, instant multitrack digital recording, e-mail, and so on. Through the Internet, you can register your songs quickly, easily, and even less expensively with the Library of Congress; index your songs with your PRO ("PRO" stands for "Performing Rights Organization" and you'll read about them in Chapter 23); interact with other writers; and do most of your song business instantaneously, without leaving your house or office. You can co-write with people in other parts of the world through e-mail or use apps such as Skype and be able to work in real time, seeing and hearing the other writer. The Internet allows you to join songwriters' organizations almost anywhere in the world and enjoy their wealth of benefits, advice, and information.

At the professional level, but strictly with permission, you can make pitches to various record label A&R departments, producers, managers, and artists via e-mail and other online contrivances. Opportunities to make such pitches are usually the result of personal contact or tip sheets and mostly done in MP3 format. But once again, this requires permission from the intended recipient. These and many other conveniences offered by computers make them almost indispensable to today's songwriters at all levels.

The Flip Side

Unfortunately, the downside of having computers in our songwriting lives can all but outweigh the myriad advantages. More extensive discussion about protecting your ideas and music—what strategies you should use, what can happen, what the piracy sites have done to the record business and therefore the songwriting business, and so on—is essential for you to understand the stakes clearly before you do anything online.

Short of not releasing any of your work to the public, there is currently no way to protect it from being stolen or misused. You can refrain from posting it on the Internet, but once anyone else has a copy, however it was obtained, he or she can share it with the rest of the world for free.

The laws are on your side, but they're generally unenforced and all but unenforceable. Even with a proper copyright, your songs can and will be used without your permission or even knowledge. Except for the rarity of people knowing and obeying the law and being moral enough not to steal, copy, or sell your work, there's nothing to stop them.

The music industry is still trying to work out reasonable and secure ways for people to share music while still protecting the creators' rights and giving the songwriters and artists their fair share of the proceeds for the art they created. Eventually, one hopes, things will be fairly settled for all involved—songwriters, performers, recording engineers, and anyone else who helped create the song or ethical consumers and users of art, literature, and music. But it is going to take time before that happens, so beware!

Tools You Can Use

When it comes to songwriting, you'll find all sorts of help on the Internet simply by typing in a topic on your favorite search engine. Need a rhyme? Search "rhyming dictionary" and you'll find dozens, if not more. Some sites combine general reference materials and lyrical resources—you can often find dictionaries, rhyming dictionaries, and thesauruses all in one convenient place.

On the music side, you'll also find all sorts of assistance. There are websites that chart typical chord progressions and others where you can hear the chords you're thinking about using for a song. And you can search out rhythm tracks to use as ideas for your own writing.

Additionally, you can probably record your demos directly to your computer using a microphone for your voice and instrument or a direct hookup from your instrument to the computer. Numerous free recording software packages, such as Audacity, allow you to mix, overdub, and make a lot of the effects that you might achieve in a recording studio available right there at your desk.

A Place of Your Own

Before making a decision on just what kind of Internet presence you want to have, you should ask yourself some questions as to what exactly you're hoping to get for your time and energy. Do you want people to be able to hear your music? Do you want them to know every time you post a new song online? Do you want your listeners to be able to leave comments and feedback about your music? Do you want to post information concerning your shows? And just how much time do you want to spend online?

Putting together your own webpage takes a bit of work. You need to find a webhost and then create your website. Ideally, you should try to use your real name (or business name) as your domain name, but that may not always be possible, so it's good to have other ideas for domain names that are both easily remembered and easily identified with you. For instance, if your name is John Smith, it's very likely that www.johnsmith.com is taken. But www.johnsmithsongwriter.com or, even better, www.johnsmithsongsmith.com might not be.

Setting up your own website can be an adventure in itself! Fortunately, all sorts of guides and reference materials are available for you, from classes at your local community center or community college to books such as *The Complete Idiot's Guide to Creating a Website* (Alpha Books, 2008) by Paul McFedries.

TUNE TIPS

Depending on just how much time you're planning to spend online, you may find it best to go with more of a blog than a full-fledged website. A blog is a website where you can quickly post anything from short notices to long articles. There are many blog software programs available for free on the Internet and they usually require a lot less work from you in terms of maintaining your site. WordPress (www.wordpress.com) is one of the many free blog software programs you can find online. It's free and very easy to use.

Take your time setting up your webpage and be sure to proofread it numerous times before going public. Think of it as your little porch on the world where everyone can stop by any time. You definitely want you and your songs to make a good first impression.

Setting Up Shop in Someone Else's Shop

If you don't want to spend the time and energy putting together your own webpage but still want to have a place online where you can post your music and elicit feedback, you can become a member of one of the many social media sites. You're undoubtedly familiar with Facebook and MySpace, but you might also be interested in sites like Merge FM, ReverbNation, SoundClick, and SoundCloud, which specialize in music and songs.

On sites like these, you get your own personal page where you can post your songs and get feedback. Some, such as SoundClick, also offer you the opportunity to sell your songs for downloading.

If you're on Facebook, MySpace, or another generalized site, you might want to consider opening a second home page strictly for you as a songwriter. This allows you to have a calendar and comment section devoted specifically to your songwriting.

Joining any of these organizations is usually free. But many websites that focus on music will offer "member services," usually for an ongoing monthly fee. These can range from getting a personalized page of your own (as opposed to the generic page everyone gets) to tracking all sorts of statistics on your songs, from how many hits and downloads you get to where in the world your online traffic is coming from.

Social Networking

Whether you want to meet other songwriters online or develop a fan base, social networking sites are one of the fastest ways to promote whatever you're doing and get your name around. Keeping up with and communicating with people on these networks is fast, easy, and free! Using your name for your site's URL, and posting an accurate photo, will make it easy for people to find your site. You can give them just the personal info you want them to know. If you're a performing songwriter, you can publicize upcoming engagements and post pictures and reviews of recent gigs. If there are people doing what you want to do, you can try to "friend" them and see how they go about it.

Twitter

In addition to employing the typical social networking sites, you might also consider using Twitter to maintain contact with your fans and business associates. You can think of Twitter as a virtual bulletin board where you can post very short notes (just up to 140 characters at a time). So if you've just landed a radio interview for this very afternoon, you have a way of letting folks know about it! Twitter is for up-to-the-minute communication and response.

One Connection for Everything

More and more people are getting online every day, and trying to keep up with everyone can take more work than you really want to put into it. After all, that's time that you could spend writing your next great song!

Whenever possible, try to use online subscription services, such as RSS feeds for your blog that will alert anyone who's on your subscription list of any new updates as they occur. Nowadays it's also possible for your friends to get these updates on their mobile services, so try to get your friends to subscribe to your blog or social network pages.

On Stage All the Time

Regardless of whether you create your own webpage or blog, go the social network route, or both, keep in mind that whatever you post on the Internet is always going to be a reflection on you. And you never know who's going to read it. Unless you want to court trouble and possibly lose fans and friends, stay away from religion, politics, and so on. Whenever you state an opinion, someone is going to disagree with you. If you can respect that and move on, you'll be fine.

It's difficult to be liked by everyone all the time, so just do the best you can and settle for that. Thank everybody for visiting your site and try to be smiling in all the pictures.

Being Social

Having a blog or being part of a social network, just like performing a song, is a two-way street. Just because you've created a website or joined Facebook doesn't mean people are automatically going to find you. You usually have to go out and let people know that you've arrived on the Internet.

You must visit other people's sites, comment on their "goings-on," and electronically rub elbows if you expect them to keep up with your posts and victories.

TUNE TIPS

Be sure to have your Internet addresses, the URL of your webpage, blog, or social network (or *all* of them!) printed up on any material that you hand out—business cards, bio sheets, even CDs. People like to have a way to find out more about you and your songs.

Keep your website or social network page up to date. Not every new item has to be earthshaking news. Simply being social and reminding people, "Hey, I'm here!" is part of keeping up your end of the social contract.

Being Careful

Likewise, you want to be careful about joining or signing up for contests. Song contests are popular and fun, but can also be expensive and sometimes even dangerous.

Be very careful who you give your songs and information to when signing up for offers and competitions. Read carefully what you're agreeing to before you commit. You could be giving the rights to your song(s) away without realizing it. You can check out Internet offers and claims on several reputable online sites such as www.snopes.com, and it's worth making sure they're legit before you get your hopes up or agree to participate. The many songwriter organizations, such as the Songwriters Guild, also keep up with the major legitimate contests, and they can be a place to clear them as well.

It's best not to enter too many songs, maybe one or two at most. Don't spend a lot of money for any contest. Some of these "opportunities" are phishing scams, just trying to steal your private information. All of them make a very nice profit for whoever is running them, and, no matter how good your song is, you have only a slight chance of winning anything. However, people *do* win, and if it's a real deal, it could be you and your song. Keep a copy of the official details and whatever application you send in with your tunes, and good luck.

Keeping Current

To say that the Internet is constantly changing is a huge understatement. Likewise, new technology in communications is constantly being developed. Even though it may seem like they've been around forever, Facebook's only been around for seven years at the time of this writing and Twitter for five. In the time it takes you to read this chapter, there will probably be dozens if not hundreds of new and improved ways to connect with other songwriters, potential publishers, and possible fans.

It's tempting to say that all these new ideas really have nothing to do with songwriting, but the truth is that the Internet offers you a lot in terms of both your actual songwriting and your ability to connect your songs with an audience. The good thing is that you don't have to be an expert to make use of it. Simply being aware of the many things it can do for you is a great start.

The Least You Need to Know

- The Internet can help you as a songwriter in many ways.
- Currently, there are no ways to absolutely protect your songs online.
- It's in your best interest to set up your own webpage or blog or, at the very least, to join a social network website.
- Through social networking, it's possible to promote your music as well as your performances.
- Try to update your website, blog, or social network page on a regular basis. Participate in the social process.

Going Pro

Moving from casual songwriter to someone making money or maybe even making a living by writing songs is a huge step. In addition to knowing and really refining your craft, you also need to understand the business side of the music business.

In this part, you'll get the rundown on how your songs make money, how copyrights work, and how royalties are earned. You'll also be introduced to the many people you will want on your team as a professional songwriter.

Copyrights

In This Chapter

- What copyright can do for you
- What copyright doesn't protect
- How and where to file a copyright
- How to create and maintain your personal archives
- How to stay current with copyright law

Once you've written a song, it's up to you to protect both your song and yourself. That's where copyright comes in.

Not all that long ago, many people would mail themselves a copy of their newly written song via registered mail and keep this unopened packet, complete with postmark, as a record of when the song was written. This "poor man's copyright" is not given the same validity by the courts as a Certificate of Registration from the Copyright Office. As they say, the law is generally what the judge says it is. You would have an expensive, uphill battle even trying to get a judge to consider hearing the evidence of your postmark—and you'd probably lose. The accepted proof is the date on the Certificate of Registration, so don't even think about trying to get by with anything less these days.

Besides, you can now take advantage of technology to file your copyrights online, not to mention copyright your songs in a batch rather than one by one. Thus, the Internet makes it very easy to have the law on your side. And when it comes to your music, you certainly want to protect it as best you can.

What Is Copyright?

Copyright is a form of legal protection grounded in the U.S. Constitution for original works of authorship fixed in a tangible medium of expression. Copyright covers both published and unpublished works.

What Copyright Does

Copyright comes into effect the instant you create a unique expression of an idea. For our purposes, it means that, when you write a new song, you have the exclusive right to say who can make copies, publish copies, create other versions, and make recordings of that song. It also allows you some control over who can perform your work in public. When you sign, sell, or assign a song to a publishing company, you're giving the company your copyright.

What Does Copyright Protect?

According to the U.S. Copyright Office:

> *Copyright is a form of intellectual property law and it protects original works of authorship including literary, dramatic, musical, and artistic works, such as poetry, novels, movies, songs, computer software, and architecture. Copyright does not protect facts, ideas, systems, or methods of operation, although it may protect the way these things are expressed.*

What Does Copyright Not Protect?

Copyright protects your particular "expression of an idea" from being copied without your permission. It does not protect the idea itself. For instance, if you write a song with a unique melody about a silver dog, you can claim copyright for *that song* as your own words sung on your own series of notes. For the life of your copyright, no one else will be able to use those words on those notes without your permission. Owning the copyright does not mean that you own the sole right to songs about silver dogs, only the exact song that you wrote.

Registration with the Copyright Office (the Library of Congress)

Though your work is protected by copyright as soon as you create it and "fix it to a tangible medium of expression," it's possible you will be called upon to prove exactly what you created and as of what date it existed in order to uphold your rights. The standard for proving the particulars of your copyright is to have registered it with the U.S. Copyright Office. If two parties go to court in an infringement dispute and one has a certificate of registration and the other doesn't, guess who will win the argument?

The registering process, which should be a matter of course for any serious songwriter upon completing a song or group of songs, involves filling out a form and sending it along with a recording or lead sheet of the song, and a small fee, to the U.S. Copyright Office (which is part of the Library of Congress) for it to file. The Copyright Office sends you a document with a serial number that says it received the songs or group of songs from you on the specified date. You make note of the serial number, then file that document where you can find it, in case you ever have to prove when you registered your work and what it sounded like.

TUNE TIPS

Even if you are more of a casual songwriter, you still want to protect your music. Copyright your songs in a group to save yourself money and paperwork. Depending on your output, registering your new songs once a year or even once every six months could work.

It's even easier and cheaper to register these days because you can do it online, send an MP3 of your work, and pay a slightly reduced fee (for electronic filing) by credit card. For more information, visit www.copyright.gov/.

TUNE TIPS

One often hears from people who claim to "know" that what constitutes infringement is a certain number of identical bars of music. This is *not* true. In fact, copyright infringement is enforceable if you can prove (a) that the infringing work is "substantially similar" to your copyrighted work and that the infringer in all likelihood was aware of or had heard your work, or (b) that someone has used your protected work without your permission.

Your Personal Archive

One of the most important things that too few songwriters think of is to establish a record of your songs and what you've done with them. Someday you'll need a copy of the lyrics of one of your songs or a copy of a demo of one of your songs to send to someone; or you'll want to remember that joke about the music biz you were going to make into a song, when exactly you wrote a particular song, when you signed with a publisher, which of your songs are owned by which publisher, what the provisions of that publishing contract were, who you wrote a particular song with, whether you ever registered it with the Copyright Office, or the address and Social Security number of a co-writer you haven't seen or heard from in years … the list is endless.

And unless you're different from almost every other songwriter, you'll have trouble locating the information you need. Here's your chance to do yourself the biggest favor possible: organize and preserve all the records of your songwriting life.

Getting It All Together

It's a big job, and it's almost impossible to keep track of everything, but your only hope of finding information or materials when you need them later is to establish a system of storing it and stick to it. There are two essential parts of this ongoing task.

First, you have to obtain the information in the first place. This includes all official papers or copies thereof. Even if you have an attorney or someone who handles your business, get copies of everything for your personal records: everything you sign or that's signed on your behalf, everything that's filed that has to do with your songwriting or music business endeavors, even the actual scribbling and notes you make when you're working (ideally all with a date and other relevant information on them, including who you were working on each idea with). It's easy to forget such information and sometimes it's impossible to search your memory or unorganized records and figure things out. Don't forget you also need all your work tapes, writer's renditions, demos, and cuts in a playable form with all pertinent information tagged on them as well.

Second, you have to organize and update your information so you can find it when you need it and, in the case of recordings, you still need to be able to play them. Some people use paper files for papers, organized in sections of a file drawer or in different drawers, or computer records, which have to be backed up so they don't disappear.

Sound recordings are more of a problem, since audio technology changes. Some formats used in the past are not permanent (tapes eventually disintegrate) and players go out of style and are hard to replace. Good reel-to-reel and cassette players are hard to get these days, and digital audiotape (DAT) players are almost impossible to find.

Keeping Up with the Latest Laws

Along with technology, the laws governing copyrights and other regulations occasionally change, often requiring action on your part to protect your work. Make sure you stay up to date on what's going on legislatively and in business practice so you won't miss an opportunity or get left behind.

For instance, far too many copyright holders are not aware of the changes that occurred due to the 1976 Copyright Act. As of this writing, years after the fact, few songwriters are aware of how long their current copyrights will last or what the current statutory mechanical rate is. Most don't know they may soon be able to reclaim some or all of the copyrights they signed away to publishers, nor what that process entails.

Many other issues that change from time to time can easily go unnoticed unless you make it a point to stay informed. It can make a huge difference to anyone in the songwriting business. There are song-writer's organizations, newsletters, and websites that will keep you informed. You'll find many of them, such as the Songwriters Guild of America, the Nashville Songwriters Association International website, as well as the three PROs (ASCAP, BMI, and SESAC) and the U.S. Copyright Office listed, along with their websites, in Appendix B of this book. Check out who they are and get hooked up so you'll know what's going on.

The Least You Need to Know

- Copyright gives you the exclusive right to say who can make and publish copies or make recordings of your songs.
- Make a routine of copyrighting your songs on a regular basis. You can even file online.
- Be sure to keep a thorough file on all of your songs.
- Organize your personal archive so that you can readily access any important papers or other information when you need it.
- It's smart to keep up with all the latest changes in copyright laws.

The Business of the Music Business

In This Chapter

- The importance of knowing the business
- The ways that songs make money
- Mechanical royalties and performance royalties
- Other ways songs earn their keep
- Finding music professionals to help you

It is amazing how many people who work in the music business and hope to become professionals (and in some cases already are) have almost no idea of how the business really functions, what the terminology they use daily actually means, or how to keep their business affairs in order.

Please don't be one of them. Information is everywhere these days. There are books, websites, professional organizations, and seminars, all of which have at least some correct information. The stakes are too high to just assume you know the answers or that what you've heard is true. You owe it to yourself to know the rules of the game you're trying to win.

If you're lucky enough to get one or more of your songs recorded by an artist or used in a motion picture, television show, advertisement, or theatrical production, you'll need to be ready to deal with the "business" part of the music business.

How Songs Make Money

The particulars of how songwriters get paid are somewhat complicated, and from time to time the rules and regulations change, so be ready to study and keep current. Here's a description of how the business works when you're a professional songwriter. We've talked about how to write songs, so let's assume you're actively doing that. And for the purposes of this discussion let's say one of your songs has been recorded on an artist's CD.

We're going to call the person or entity that takes care of the business and endeavors to exploit your songs a *publisher*. The publisher's job can include guiding your creative efforts, connecting you with other songwriting projects and co-writers, helping with demos, registering songs for copyright with the Library of Congress, indexing your songs with the performing rights organization with whom you're affiliated, trying to find commercial uses for your songs, licensing those uses, collecting the income from those licenses, accounting to you and paying your share of the earnings, and sometimes even paying you in advance against the money it hopes to collect on your behalf in the future.

However, unless you have an exclusive writer's agreement with a publisher, you are *self-published*, and all those duties are yours. If you're going to be your own publisher, you should seriously consider making a deal with a professional copyright administrator, as there is a lot more to being an effective publisher than choosing a name for your company. We'll discuss that option later in this chapter.

Basically, you should be paid whenever a copy of your song is sold or when it is played in a place or on a device that's profiting from playing music. The money due from copies sold is referred to as *mechanical royalties*, and the proceeds from your song being played somewhere are called *performance royalties*. Your publisher collects the mechanical royalties and pays you your share, usually half of the amount received, biannually or quarterly with an accounting statement.

The *statutory rate* is set by Congress based on the Consumer Price Index and is supposed to be the minimum price per copy sold that a record company agrees to pay the publisher as a mechanical license fee for reproducing your song. In truth the statutory rate functions as a guide, and often, for various reasons, the publisher must agree to a lesser rate. The current statutory rate is $.091 per copy. Many publishers contract with the Harry Fox Agency to do their licensing and collection of royalties.

The standard way the royalties for mechanicals are divided is half for the publisher(s) and half for the writer(s). Publishers account to their writers.

Whichever performing rights organization you're affiliated with collects your performance royalties and sends a statement and a check with the writer's share to you and the publisher's share to the publisher(s). A lot of arithmetic goes into figuring what percent goes to each writer involved and each publisher.

Performing Rights Organizations

The three performing rights organizations (PROs) in the United States are the American Society of Composers, Authors, and Publishers (ASCAP); Broadcast Music Incorporated (BMI); and the Society of European Stage Authors and Composers (SESAC, Inc.). Each has its own system of doing business, and very few people in the world fully understand any of them. A writer (who must show that he or she has or soon will have performance money to be collected) can be represented by only one of the PROs at a time, and they compete with each other to attract members. There are, in fact, pluses and minuses to being with any of them, but a good rule of thumb is to meet with each and see which one seems like it will best fit your needs.

Each organization has personnel in its membership department whose job it is to take care of the members' concerns. It's also their job to sign new members, and they *are* usually longtime and well-connected music biz veterans who have a lot of contacts and connections and tend to know how things get done. Since the PROs deal directly with every publisher and collectively with every money making writer, they can help you get in to see just about anybody in the business. Don't hesitate to ask them for help with anything in your career. Though all three PROs actively promote the careers of their members, SESAC has been notably helpful to its writers in pursuing recording deals.

Most of the money you make from the PROs is for radio airplay, so if your song is chosen to be pushed to the radio stations by the record label as a single, you will get some money about six to nine months later with your performing rights statement.

Other Sources of Revenue

Songs used in advertising, motion pictures, television, video games, music-sharing websites, and ring-tones are licensed and the fees are collected by your publisher or copyright administrator. The license fees for these uses of your music are negotiated on a per-deal basis. The publisher has to be aware of the current rates and fees to be able to do a creditable job.

There are companies and individuals who specialize in finding, licensing, and "placing" songs in films and television. They are music supervisors, publishers, licensing agents, and music libraries. Some are actively looking for music to represent and some are not. A search online will give you a list of companies that produce and license music. You can try to find one to work with, but be warned, the competition is fierce. Some people have had luck with TAXI as a way to get through the door. You can also get lucky with a direct submission if you can find out where to send it. If you're able to contact someone and they're willing to listen to your music, do not send demos or MP3s. They want to hear professionally produced music of the highest technical quality. You also must be prepared to sign away all publishing and sync rights, and the rights to the master recording. And make sure your PRO affiliation is in order, because that's where a large part of any money you'll get will come from.

There are two types of songs for advertising. First there are ad music and jingle houses that specialize in music for ads. If you want to work in that industry, you have to find out who the companies in your area of operation are, get an appointment, and go in and audition your music and skills. The work you do for them will be "for hire," and they will own whatever you write forever. You'll be paid a one-time set amount for your work no matter how successful it is. The other music that gets used in ads is, of course, songs that have been hits. Usually in those cases an advertiser will make a deal with your publisher to use your song and the fee will be as much as your publisher can get. These are usually big-money deals, and the people who do the ad don't get any rights to the song other than to use it in their ad.

Songs licensed for ringtones are also generally songs that have been hits. Your publisher licenses and collects for those and it's not extremely lucrative.

Learning by Doing

This will give you an idea of how much terminology and procedure you need to learn to be an informed songwriter or operate your own publishing company.

Print a copy of the SGA single-song contract available on the opening page of the Songwriters Guild of America website, www.songwritersguild.com or copy it from the forms in back of the book, *This Business of Music.* You'll find both of these sources listed in Appendix B.

You can make up a title for the song that got cut or use the title of a song you've written. To sign your song to your own publishing company (make up a name unless you already have one), read the contract and try to fill in all the information it asks for. For a royalty rate, put in the current statutory rate for a three-minute song, which we mentioned earlier is $.091.

How many of the terms in the contract do you actually know the meaning of? Don't be discouraged if you don't always know what the contract is referring to or can't figure out what to put in the blanks. The point of this is mostly to let you have this experience before you're presented with it for real. There are many more technical points about song contracts than we can explain in this book, but there are books and websites that offer accurate explanations of almost everything you need to know. The Songwriters Guild offers a detailed written explanation of what the various sections of its contract concerns and helps you decide what to put in the blanks. Take advantage of those resources and get ready for when it's for real.

When you get the song entirely signed to your company (or have done as much as you can), try to calculate how much money you'll make on that song if the CD it's on sells a million copies at statutory rate. There's no way to accurately predict what will be earned from performing rights, so don't worry about that.

Remember, we're assuming that you're the publisher and the only writer so all the money is going to be yours. 1,000,000 × $.091 = $91,000. But what if this was a song you signed to that other publisher we mentioned? Then half of the money goes to that publisher and you would get $45,500 as the writer. But wait! More often than not, at least one other writer is on the song as well, so we have to divide the money in half again; now your earnings before taxes are $22,750.

It's sobering to look at the facts isn't it? How many writers get to have a million-selling cut? How many years in the business does it take to be that successful? Most writers can't live on the royalties they make. If you'd never done the math and you had a million-selling hit, think how surprised you'd be at how little you make on mechanicals.

Fortunately there are also performing rights royalties, which, although they're impossible to accurately predict, can be more than the mechanical royalties. Here, too, there are some common disappointments that you can avoid. The performance money is earned on the basis of how many times the song is played over the airwaves, cable, and in venues. If your song is released as a single and it climbs moderately high on the charts, it will earn you quite a bit of money in addition to what you were paid for the copies sold. A #1 song can earn as much as $200,000 or $300,000 for the writer(s) as well as the publisher(s) in performance royalties. However, if your song was just an album cut and wasn't played much on the radio, you will probably hardly earn anything from performances. This confounds a lot of writers whose songs are on top-selling CDs who can't understand why they didn't get a big PRO check as well. Also, remember the writer's take of the money will still be divided by the number of writers on that song.

So if you want to know what to expect, it's imperative to understand as much about the business as you can from the start.

You Can't Do It All by Yourself

Even when you know the music business, songwriters obviously need people. You've spent a great deal of this book focusing on your listeners. After all, they're a big part of why you write in the first place. But as a professional songwriter, you are your own business. Accordingly, you're going to need people to help you with the many details of managing your business—especially if you want to be able to spend your time writing songs!

Depending on how involved and successful you become in the music business, you will probably want to hire the services of some of the following people.

Agents

Agents commonly represent performers. If you're a recording artist, a performing songwriter, or someone who writes theatrical works or movie music, you'll probably need to find an agent to book jobs for you. But it's very difficult to attract one to your cause when you need them the most. Because the most lucrative work is booked solely through agents, it's very difficult to get them interested in you if you're a newcomer

An agent gets you work. He or she is the person between you and the people who hire you. An agent gets a percentage of the money you earn doing the work he or she gets for you. If you have an exclusive arrangement with an agent, when someone wants you to work for him, you put him in touch with your agent.

> **TUNE TIPS**
>
> Although the best way of finding any professional help, such as an agent, music lawyer, or accountant, is through personal referrals, you likely don't know anyone who already uses the services of such people! Fortunately you will find many organizations, such as the Songwriters Guild and others, listed in Appendix B that will be happy to give you referrals. Don't hesitate to send them any questions you might have.

Agents are only motivated to get involved with people who are sure to earn them enough money to pay for the time they spend booking them. If you already have a career, they'll judge your viability by what you've been able to do so far. If you're a performing songwriter who is signed with a record label, they'll be more apt to work with you because they know the record label is going to help get you out performing so you'll sell records.

Managers

A manager, like an agent, is more commonly employed by recording artists, performers, and people whose careers are more complicated and diverse than those of us whose business consists of writing songs and occasionally recording demos. Unlike agents, managers do not directly get work for their artists. They work between the artist and the agent, helping the artist decide which jobs to go after and accept. They advise their clients about all phases of their professional lives and are paid a percentage of all professional monies earned personally by their artists.

There are managers who work with high-profile songwriters, but the nature of their business relationships is beyond the scope of this book. So if you should decide to become a performer who also writes songs, then you probably want to look into getting yourself a manager.

Publishers

If you're strictly a songwriter, most of what an agent would do is handled by your publisher. The publisher will probably sign you to an agreement/contract of some sort. Depending on what you agree to, the publisher makes money by owning some percentage of the copyrights you create under that contract. The publishing company collects the money for the licenses it grants usually through the licensing and collecting company, such as the Harry Fox Agency. The publisher accounts to you and pays you your share. The publisher's job is to do all the business of protecting and exploiting your copyrights, create opportunities for you to create copyrights, and advise you about and promote your career as a songwriter. In most cases, the publisher does not collect your share of performance royalties.

Music publishers are everywhere. Some smaller, effective publishers are more open than the major publishing houses to recognizing potential talent and developing new writers. Ask the other writers in your area who they work with and try to find a way in the door.

The larger ones have mostly become part of the corporate structure of larger entertainment groups and seem to be merging with each other so often that it's hard to keep up with where they are. For the most part, the big-time American music business companies have their offices in at least one of the three big music centers in the United States: New York, New York; Nashville, Tennessee; or Los Angeles, California.

Writers can still sometimes get an appointment at a publishing house to play songs for someone and perhaps stir up some interest and maybe even a working relationship. But most songwriters, other than those who are well-known or corporate commodities, begin working with publishing companies by writing with one or more writers signed there. If you write a song with someone who has a publishing deal, or if a publisher becomes interested in one of your tunes (that you publish), you might be able to end up with a co-publishing deal on that song.

If you're asked to sign a co-publishing agreement with a major publisher, the company will assume that you'll let it administer the copyright, which means you own your half of the copyright, but you don't get to make any of the decisions regarding licensing, editing, usages, and so on, of your half of the copyright. The publisher will collect the mechanical royalties—those are the royalties for sales of physical copies (like CDs) of your song—and issue you a statement and a check when one is due. Your publishing share of the performance monies will come straight to you from the PRO. You'll have no control over the copyright; you'll just own your half. Before you sign anything, take it to your music biz lawyer!

If you can get two publishers to agree to co-administration of the copyright instead, you'll each make all the decisions as equals without the right to interfere with what the other publisher has agreed to. So if one publisher agrees to license the tune to a record label, the other has to go along unless that license would somehow devalue the worth of the copyright. The money is collected directly by each publisher for itself. It gets more complicated, but you get the picture.

I think one of the biggest "AH HA!" moments I had in the music business was when I asked myself this question: "Are my songs good enough to make someone keep his job?"

When you write a great song, you make your publisher look like a genius for signing you. So he gets to keep his job. The artist and producer also get to keep their gigs, as does the A&R person at the record company.

Once I realized this little fact, my songs got stronger! They couldn't just be good—they had to keep people employed!

—Liz Hengber, songwriter of "For My Broken Heart," "It's Your Call," "And Still," "Forever Love" (all #1 hits for Reba McEntire) and many more.

Other Music Business Professionals

In addition to agents, managers, and publishers, consider obtaining the services of one or more of the following people should you decide to get seriously into the business of music.

Attorneys

The music business has its own set of unique practices, characteristics, and laws, which makes it absolutely necessary for songwriters to have an expert in music business law to advise and represent them before they sign or agree to anything. Your family attorney is not a suitable substitute.

Once again, if you have friends in the business, ask what attorneys they recommend or know of. If you can't get a referral from someone you trust, an Internet search for "music business attorney (your town)" will supply you with names of candidates and you can make appointments and find out more about them face to face.

Accountants

Most people earning money in the entertainment field find it necessary to have an accountant or even a certified public accountant (CPA) to help with financial records and tax issues. As we said about attorneys, the music business has its own ways of doing things and its own kind of trouble you can get into. Look for someone who has a lot of experience or, even better, who specializes in dealing with music clients.

Copyright Administrators

If instead of signing with a publisher you decide to be self-published, you'll probably want some help with those responsibilities. We've already talked about aligning yourself with a music attorney so you'll have help with the legal matters of setting up a business and running it and a CPA to organize your money, banking, bookkeeping, and tax filings. You might also want to consider a copyright administrator, someone to handle the licensing and copyright registration of your songs.

A copyright administrator also collects the license fees (mechanical royalties), deducts his or her percentage (administration fee), and gives you a check for the rest. Some also insist on monitoring your publishing company's performing rights statements and money from which they also deduct their percentage. There are individual administrators who work with just a few publishing companies and there are large, well-staffed administration companies who work for many companies. A few offer tune pitching as well.

Tune Pluggers

A small number of copyright administrators will also pitch tunes for you, but most of the time you need to do that yourself or hire a song or tune plugger. As the name implies, this is someone who tries to get recording artists and other users of original music to record or use your songs. Usually they want a periodic retainer (weekly, monthly, and so on) plus additional payments based on if the song gets cut, if it makes it onto the released CD, if it's a single, if it reaches a certain chart position, and so on, or a percentage of the publishing earnings or even a percentage of the publishing if they are successful in getting something cut.

As with other professionals, ask people you know for recommendations and what experience they've had with those you know are in the business. Song pluggers usually work on a nonexclusive basis, meaning they pitch several writers' tunes. Almost all of them will promise to give you a report of who they pitched which of your songs to and what the results were. Too often, however, you won't know exactly what they're doing for the money you're paying them.

There are great song pluggers, terrible ones, and everything in between. Considering the cost, lack of accountability, and low percentage of success, the most reasonable way to work with a plugger might be to offer them a percentage of the publishing ownership if they get the tune cut by a major artist—period!

Business Manager

Another type of professional advisor works with somewhat bigger moneymakers, taking the place of several of the other professionals we've mentioned. A business manager specializes in broader financial guidance, often taking care of accounting, taxes, investments, budgets, and everything that has to do with the money coming in and going out. This professional usually is paid a small, single-digit percentage of any of your money that he or she has anything to do with.

Creative People

On the creative side of things are other people who can make a huge difference in your professional life. You will probably demo songs you've written on a regular basis. In this era of digital recording, many people can afford professional-quality recording equipment for their office or home and enjoy the process of producing and sometimes performing their own demos. Some are skilled and talented enough musicians and singers to make the top-quality recordings that you need to be taken seriously in the business.

Other songwriters, however, do not possess those skills, don't care to take on that responsibility, or only occasionally need the kind of professional product that can be captured only on state-of-the-art equipment. For these writers, especially, it's good to develop a relationship with a studio and engineer with whom you like to work.

As a matter of fact, if you don't intend to sing all your own demos or play all the instruments, find singers and players you like and get to know them, so that when you do need a state-of-the-art product, you won't have to develop those relationships on the fly.

The Least You Need to Know

- It falls on you to understand how the music industry works.
- Songs earn mechanical royalties for copies sold and performance royalties for being played.
- Your songs can earn money from being used in movies, television shows, advertisements, video games, and ringtones, among other things.
- Mechanical royalties are paid to writers through their publisher (which is you if you're self-published).
- Performance royalties are paid directly to writer members and publisher members by one of the three major performing rights organizations: ASCAP, BMI, and SESAC.

New Horizons

In This Chapter

- Constantly using the techniques you've learned
- Being an around-the-clock songwriter
- Keeping your focus
- Remembering it's all about the emotions
- Wishing you well on your songwriting endeavors

Songwriters don't always know how to answer the question, "Why do you write songs?" There are the usual responses, ranging from "I've got something to say," to, "It's a living!" But in truth, it's almost like you were born to create music. If you weren't writing songs, you'd be expressing yourself in some other artistic fashion. Because the music is in you, you find yourself constantly coming up with little melodies or catchy lines that are meant to be sung. And anything that's meant to be sung is meant to be heard.

Throughout this book, we hope you've learned a lot about how to take your ideas, both lyrical and musical, and craft them into songs. You've examined how to focus your messages and stories into great opening lines and memorable choruses. You've discovered how choosing the right narrator for your song can make its story more intimate and immediate. And you've been shown how to use imagery and other poetic tools to shape your lyrics so that they make a lasting impression on your listeners.

Likewise, you've explored the musical aspect of songwriting, delving into melodies, harmonies, and rhythms and how each contributes to making your songs stand out. And you've also discovered how the step of rewriting is essential in making each song its best. You've got all the tools you need to take your natural talents and bring the songs in you out to a waiting world.

Putting What You've Learned to Good Use

Typically songwriters begin with very little idea of what their craft is really about. Armed with the vaguest notion of what constitutes a "good song," we decide to try our hand at making up something to sing. Fortunately, we're all unconsciously trained by the songs we've heard all our lives. You may have given little or no thought to how the words were picked and put together, nor wondered why the melody moved the way it did in the songs you liked. But those songs are what you use to pattern and compare your early songwriting efforts.

So you began writing and you became aware of patterns—rhyme schemes that are typical, or unusual ones that catch a listener's ear, chord progressions that seem to pop up over and over again, the rise and fall of the melody at certain points of a song. And as you became more aware of the elements that make up a song, you moved firmly into the "student" phase of the art, reading how-to books, going to lectures, attending panel discussions. And now you've almost completed this book and all it has to say on the documentable details of songwriting.

These are all helpful tools and they certainly teach you the terminology, standards, and "rules" of songwriting, as well as insights that others who have walked the path before you can share. From time to time, it will be a godsend to be able to consult your books and notes, to remind yourself of a truth or a lesson that has slipped away.

Double-Checking Your Focus

You've learned what to focus on, what to emphasize, and how to make sure your song has accomplished what you set out to do. You know it's best to start with a title or at least a main idea so you know where you're going. Every line in your song has to point directly to that one main point, with no wasted words.

The language generally has to be conversational, make perfect sense, and be easily understandable. The lyric should float effortlessly on the melody; the melody has to be sing-able and memorable. The first line must catch the listener's attention and pique his or her curiosity; the story has to be about something the listener cares about and pay off to the listener's satisfaction. And, after hearing the song once, the listener must unquestionably know the title.

TUNE TIPS

It's interesting to note how many successful hit songwriters played and sang in cover bands in their formative years. Having to learn and perform the words and music to the best songs is a powerful way for a young songwriter to learn structure and craft. Make it your practice to learn to play and sing your favorite songs, even if it's just for your own amusement. It is one of the best learning tools, and it's free.

Reading Is Not Doing

Let's say you've read an entire manual on how to swim. It's given you all the rudimentary and technical information about how to choose a safe place to start learning, what to do when you get into the water, how to move your arms and legs, how to breathe without inhaling water, what the names of all the strokes are, and what the necessary safety warnings are.

But you still don't know how to swim. You'll only learn that—and never forget what you've learned—by getting in the water and trying to make it to the other side of the pool. What people tell us and what we read can't compare with the understanding we absorb trying to stay afloat in an ongoing, real-life situation. This is where we absorb into our very fiber the lessons we're not even aware we're learning.

Suppose you think you need a better word in a particular line in a song you're working on. You and your co-writer have been through the logical alternatives and haven't come up with anything that works. It looks like the word doesn't exist.

So, just for grins, you think about how you want the line to feel and start singing anything that comes into your mind, even words you don't think will work. All of a sudden, you accidentally sing something that says exactly what you wanted to say and more! What you learned in that instant about the process of songwriting is something no book and nobody else could have taught you.

You can't explain the feeling that something wasn't right, nor what happened to let you finally discover what made the line work. But you'll know that feeling the next time it comes up.

We learn thousands of little lessons like this almost every time we write, and we don't usually even take note of them. But we'll use and draw on them automatically without even thinking about it.

This is where the fine-tuning of your songwriting process will come from. All the conventions and forms you've learned are a great foundation, but the difference between an informed songwriter and a consummate professional craftsman is the understanding that you'll unconsciously develop through songwriting experience.

The Endless Ladder

There's a common bit of self-defeating insanity that people in any career can get caught up in, and this book wouldn't cover all the bases if we didn't try to head this off. When we first start writing songs, we think how great it would be to actually finish one. So we work and struggle and finally complete a song—only to realize that the cool thing is to have written a song that people like and say is really good. So we work to achieve that goal, and finally our friends say how good our new song is—maybe even as good as another friend's song that was signed by a publisher. And suddenly it's all about getting a publisher to sign one of our songs.

This seems almost impossible, but we roll up our sleeves and work and study how-to books and attend seminars and critique sessions. We even experience one of those moments when someone is moved by one of our new songs, indicating that we really connected with them. We've even had a few chances to play for a publisher, and all of a sudden in a pitch session one of them says, "I'll take that one to listen to again." We just know we will have made it once we become a published writer—and then that day comes when the receptionist at the publishing company where we've been camping out says, "I've got a contract for you to sign."

Woo-hoo! A published song! So we sign three copies of a Single Song Agreement (usually without reading anything beyond the title of the song we're signing over)—and then at lunch the next day, another writer we've been working with announces that a well-known recording artist just placed a *hold* on one of his songs. Suddenly, getting a song published feels like nothing! Having a song on hold is clearly the goal to strive for.

DEFINITION

When an artist, producer, or A&R person puts a song on **hold** and the publisher agrees, it means the artist is planning to cut the song and the publisher will not pitch the song to anyone else. It's not a secure arrangement, however, because the artist doesn't always cut the song, and the publisher may have already pitched the song to other artists or may continue to play it for other artists after telling them it's on hold.

And so it goes, on and on, up the endless ladder. As we continue, looking only at the next rung and not valuing the achievements that lifted us to the level we're at now, negativity sets in. We're always thinking if we could only get to the *next level*, we would really be somewhere.

This is a game that's designed to make you doubt yourself, become frustrated, and quit trying. There's an equally ruinous version of it in which writers try to copy another successful songwriter's style. Hall of Fame songwriter Sonny Throckmorton, three-time ASCAP Songwriter of the Year, refers to this as "chasing the rabbit."

A Healthier Perspective

There's a much healthier, positive way to look at your developmental journey, to look at what you *have* achieved instead of what remains beyond your reach.

Completing a song is better than not completing a song. Receiving compliments on your song is better than just completing a song. A publisher wanting a copy of your song is better than just your friends saying it's good. A publisher wanting to publish your song is better than a publisher just wanting to hear it again. Having your song put on hold is more meaningful than having a publisher sign your song.

Getting your song recorded is better than getting it put on hold. Finding out that your song is definitely going to be on the CD is better than it just getting recorded. Your song being chosen for the single is better than just having it on the CD.

Hearing your song on the radio is better than having it chosen to be the single. Having it reach the charts is better than just hearing it on the radio. Your song going to #1 is better than having it just make the charts. Your song being #1 for two weeks in a row ….

It's the same reality, but there's value to every step. Instead of embarking on an unending quest of mirages that turn to nothing when you reach them, you celebrate a series of achievements. Give yourself credit for each improvement; each step up the ladder reveals more of the big picture. Revel in where you are and how far you've come!

You Are and Always Will Be a Songwriter

It's easy to say that once you finish that first song, you can consider yourself a songwriter. But the truth is that you have probably always had it in you to be one. You just needed some help and encouragement to make your song a reality.

Even though this is the last chapter of this book, it's really the start of a wonderful chapter of your life. As you read in Chapter 4, songwriters are songwriters around the clock, 24 hours a day, 7 days a week. Or eight days a week, as a couple of songwriters might say! You'll start looking at just about every part of life, yours and others', as potential song material. You'll hear song titles in everyday conversations; see them in the books, magazines, and newspapers; and find ideas pretty much any time, whether you're awake or dreaming.

And you'll keep tinkering with the songs you're writing. You'll try out different lines to hear which ones give your lyrics the clearest, most concise delivery, and experiment with different rhythms, chords, and instrumentation, not to mention all the many musical genres you can incorporate into your songwriting. One of the greatest things about being a songwriter is that you truly have limitless musical roads to travel. You should never find yourself bored; each song will present its own challenges to be mastered in their own unique ways.

Don't Forget the Feeling!

You'll also start listening to songs with a new ear, analyzing structures and chord progressions, evaluating melodies and how well the lyrics fit with them.

But be careful! You may spend so much time mentally grading songs that you forget the whole point of songwriting: to communicate ideas and feelings. While you're busy analyzing and evaluating songs, be sure to remember that the appeal of any tune is ultimately in how it makes you, as a listener, *feel*.

You may not particularly like a lot about a specific song, but if it makes you happy or want to dance or clap, then why deny that it's effective in its own way? Always look for why a song works, or, if it doesn't happen to work for you, why it works for other people. Concentrating on the positive aspects of music will always make your own writing better.

As mentioned way back in the introduction, we've been fortunate to get many songwriters to contribute stories and tips to *The Complete Idiot's Guide to the Art of Songwriting*. When we got this one from Wood Newton, who's written some great songs such as "Bobbie Sue" (performed by the Oak Ridge Boys), "What I Didn't Do" (a big hit for Steve Wariner), and "Twenty Years Ago" (performed by Kenny Rogers), it seemed to be a very appropriate way to wish you the best of success in your own songwriting.

A Final Word from Songwriter Wood Newton

If you care about songwriting enough that you bought this book, and read this much, then don't worry, you're one of us. People have different goals regarding songwriting. I've heard people say they just want to get one published or hear one they wrote on the radio. It seldom happens for those who are just giving it a fling.

If your goal is to become a professional, then the first thing it takes is commitment—a commitment of time, money, energy, ego, and life. The same rules of success that it takes to make it in any profession apply here. A positive attitude and the ability to let the rejection go are essential.

The term "emotional baggage" is a good one. Music is about emotions, and you need that sensibility to write great songs. If you let the negative emotions keep building up in you, then you become your own worst enemy. Rejection, envy, anger, and pessimism can kill the creative spirit unless you redirect it and use it, or let it go. Those who stay the course have those same feelings, and they can hurt just as much and even more, but the way to overcome it is to focus on the positive. Success is only a three-minute song away.

Here are some positives I like to focus on; some even call them blessings. The act of making music, the singing and playing, is so good for us that it's used in all kinds of therapeutic ways. It is a part of most religions, and to some it is a religion. The process of writing is so different each time, and making something you feel compelled to share with others is a great reward in and of itself.

The music community is made up of so many talented people, and I appreciate not only those who write and perform, but those in all the businesses that help to make it a profession, as well as the audiences (of which I am also a part), those who buy it, and applaud it. They're all as important as those who make it.

There, I feel better already. I think I'll write another one, or two, or a thousand. Here's wishing your dreams come true.

—Wood Newton

Even if (especially if) your dream is simply to write a song to play to your family or friends and hear them say they like it, we wish you the best of success with your songwriting. Who knows? Perhaps one day we'll all have the honor and the pleasure of hearing your music.

WRITER'S TALK

"Believe in yourself, 'cause if you don't, nobody else will." This is the message Larry Henley, writer of "Wind Beneath My Wings" has for his fellow songwriters. It's also the theme of his song "You'll Cast a Mighty Long Shadow."

The Least You Need to Know

- Use all the ideas, techniques, and tools you've discovered to make your songs better.
- Remember that book learning doesn't compare to actually doing the work.
- Constantly listen to the music all around you and let it lead you to other new ideas.
- Don't forget that songwriting is all about communicating ideas and emotions.
- Enjoy every step of being a songwriter and appreciate everything you achieve. Your songs will be better for it.

12-bar blues   A standard blues format involving specific chord changes over the course of 12 measures.

A&R   Artists and repertoire, the department of a record company that handles the signing of new artists as well as the choosing of song material for them.

accent   To apply extra stress to a note or chord, *if on guitar*, by striking it harder with the pick.

accidental   A sharp sign, flat sign, or natural sign.

acoustic guitar   A nonelectric guitar with steel strings.

agent   An individual who represents a performing songwriter, serving as the intermediary between the artist and those who would hire him or her.

alternate tuning   Tuning of the strings of the guitar to notes other than those of standard tuning.

anticipation   playing or sounding the target note or chord before the beat, usually coming in a half a beat earlier.

arpeggio   A chord played one note (usually on separate strings) at a time, usually in an ascending and/or descending order.

ASCAP   The American Society of Authors, Composers, and Publishers, one of three organizations responsible for collecting and distributing performing rights royalties for songwriters and publishers.

augmented chord   One of the four basic chord types, made up of the root, major third, and augmented fifth degrees of the major scale.

bar   Also called a *measure*; a distinct measurement of beats dictated by the time signature. In written music, the end of a bar is indicated by a vertical line running through the staff or bass guitar tablature lines.

blue notes   Notes common to the blues style of music which are sung or played to sound in pitch somewhere between the minor and major 3rd, between a flatted and a major 5th, and between a flatted and major 7th of a major scale.

BMI   Broadcast Music, Inc., one of three organizations responsible for collecting and distributing performing rights royalties for songwriters and publishers.

bridge   A section of a song that's usually different from the verses and chorus both in melody and chord progression. Lyrically, the bridge often contains a twist or a surprise that strengthens or sheds new light on the final verse and chorus.

capo   A clamplike device attached to the neck and fingerboard to raise equally the pitch of all six strings.

chord   Three or more different notes played together at the same time.

chord progression   A sequence of chords played in a song or in a phrase of a song. Chord progressions make up the harmony of songs.

chorus   The part of a song that usually repeats at various points. Usually, it's the section most listeners remember well enough to sing along with.

co-publishing   A joint ownership of the publishing rights of a song.

co-writer   Someone who shares in the writing, credit, and subsequent earnings of a song.

common time   The symbol "C" used as a time signature; another name for 4/4 time.

copyright   A catch-all term for all the exclusive rights granted by statute to creators for the protection of their original written works. The laws are quite specific and include the right to say who can copy or use (perform, record, or publish) that work.

diatonic   The notes used in a given major scale or the chords derived from the triads of that scale.

diminished chord   One of the four basic chord types, made up of the root, minor third, and diminished fifth degrees of the major scale.

drop-D tuning   An alternate tuning in which the low E string is tuned down a whole step to D.

dynamics   Changes in volume or tempo while playing a song.

economic picking   To play guitar with a pick, using downstrokes on the lowest three strings and upstrokes on the three highest strings.

fill   A short musical phrase that fills a space in the music. Similar to riffs, except that riffs are usually repeated and fills are usually improvised and different each time.

flat   An accidental sign indicating lowering a note a half step.

genre   A specific style of song or music, such as rock, country, blues, jazz, folk, and so on. Many musical genres are also broken into subgenres, such as punk rock, alternative country, thrash metal, and so on.

harmony   Two or more notes played simultaneously.

Harry Fox Agency   An organization that specializes in the licensing, collecting, and distributing of mechanical royalties for publishers.

hook   Any lyrical or musical aspect of a song that catches and holds the listener's attention.

interval   The distance, in terms of steps and half steps, of one note from another.

key   The tonal center of a piece of music.

key signature   The number of flats or sharps (if any) used in a song, which indicates the key the song is in.

lyrics   The words of a song.

major chord   One of the four basic chord types, made up of the root, major third, and perfect fifth degrees of the major scale.

major scale   The basic building block of music theory. This scale begins on any note, which is its root note (see *root note*), and uses the following sequence:

> root   whole step   whole step   half step   whole step   whole step   whole step   half step (the root again)

manager   A person or business who, for a fee, advises performers (including performing songwriters) about and helps direct their entertainment careers.

measure   Also called a *bar*; a distinct measurement of beats, which is dictated by the time signature; the end of a measure is indicated by a vertical line running through the staff or bass guitar tablature lines.

mechanical royalties   The earnings made from the sales of copies of songs on CDs and other audio formats.

melody   The musical part of a song that is sung (or hummed or whistled). A song's lyrics are sung to the notes of its melody.

minor chord   One of the four basic chord types, made up of the root, minor third, and perfect fifth degrees of the major scale.

MP3   Digital sound format used for storing and playing audio files on a computer or other MP3 playing device.

note   A musical tone of a specific pitch.

octave   An interval of eight named notes from the root note, always bearing the same name as the root note.

prosody   The matching of lyrics and music in a song.

riff   A short musical phrase, often repeated during the course of a song as a possible hook.

root note   The note named by a chord; C is the root note of the C major chord. It's also the root note of the C minor chord. The root note is also the starting note of the scale of any given key. For example, the root note of the A major scale is A.

SESAC   Society of European Stage Authors and Composers, one of three organizations responsible for collecting and distributing song royalties for songwriters.

sharp   An accidental sign indicating raising a note a half step.

standard tuning   The way that the strings of a guitar are usually tuned. From low to high, standard tuning is E, A, D, G, B, and E.

step   The difference, between two notes, of two frets on the neck of the guitar.

straight eighths   Eighth notes that are played as even eighth notes, that is, dividing the beat perfectly in half.

swing rhythm   A rhythm created by playing eighth notes in the manner of playing the first and last of a set of triplets. Swing rhythms are used in most blues and jazz songs and can be found as well in many other musical genres.

syncopation   Rhythm in which notes fall on the offbeats.

tempo   The speed of a song, usually indicated in beats per measure (BPM).

time signature   In written music, specification of how many beats each measure receives (the upper number of the fraction) and which type of note is designated as a single beat (the lower number). It is usually indicated by a fraction at the start of a piece of music.

transposing   Changing the notes (and chords) of a song from one key to another.

triplet   Three notes of one beat's duration.

tune plugger   Also called a song plugger; someone who pitches a songwriter's material to artists, producers, and others who might potentially record a songwriter's material.

verse   The part of a song's lyrics that usually tells the song's story.

Reading and Resources

Songwriting is a very personal experience, but that doesn't mean you have to do everything yourself! At the very least, you have hundreds of years of songs to use as guides and inspiration. And having a lot of the music of the last hundred years available through recordings, whether on disc, other digital format, or vinyl, certainly helps!

Recommended Books

Being able to study how other songwriters perfected their art through the songs themselves is always going to be your primary source of learning. But you are also lucky enough to have a lot more sources from which to learn. Sometimes it seems that there are more books about songwriting than there are songs!

There are a plethora of books and websites about songwriting, but to get you started, here are some books and websites we think you'll find particularly helpful as you grow and evolve as a songwriter.

The most authoritative book on the music business is *This Business of Music* (Billboard Books, 10th Edition, June 2007), by Sidney Shemel and M. William Krasilovsky. If you plan to be in the music business, you should own and read this book. In the latest edition, Krasilovsky is joined by John M. Gross and Jonathon Feinstein, both of whom, like the late Sidney Shemel and Krasilovsky himself, are experienced music attorneys with a great deal of hands-on experience in the corporate music world.

For more on the music business itself, try *The Musician's Handbook: A Practical Guide to Understanding the Music Business* (Billboard Books, Revised Edition, April 2008), by Bobby Borg. Although it's geared toward performers (Bobby spent more than 25 years as a drummer for many bands), it has a lot of good information for songwriters as well. And Bobby's writing is both informative and engaging.

The Craft of Lyric Writing (Writer's Digest Books, October 1984), by Sheila Davis, is a must-read for anyone who wants to write song lyrics. If you're serious about songwriting, you should own this book. You may have to shop around to find a copy, but it will be worth it as you'll refer to it often.

Always Magic in the Air: The Bomp and Brilliance of the Brill Building Era (Penguin Books, September 2006), by Ken Emerson, details the songwriting careers of seven teams of writers who created many of the hit songs of the '50s and '60s. You'll read fascinating accounts of the songwriting teams of Burt Bacharach and Hal David, Jeff Barry and Ellie Greenwich, Carole King and Gerry Goffin, Jerry Leiber and Mike Stoller, Barry Mann and Cynthia Weil, Doc Pomus and Mort Shuman, and Neil Sedaka and Howard Greenfield.

Makin' Stuff Up: Secrets of Song-Craft and Survival in the Music-Biz (Alfred Publishing, February 2010), by Rand Bishop, is a very entertaining and educational guide through the songwriting process, as well as a fun and down-to-earth narrative of the music business. This is well written and highly recommended.

You've read some good advice from Pat and Pete Luboff in this book. They've been teaching songwriting since 1979 and you definitely will find even more great tips from them in their own book, *101 Songwriting Wrongs and How to Right Them: How to Craft and Sell Your Songs* (Writer's Digest Books, 2nd Edition, 2007). Also be sure to check out their website at www.writesongs.com for news on their latest workshops and songwriters events.

Your First Cut: A Step-by-Step Guide to Getting There (Publishing LLC, November 2002), by Jerry Vandiver and Gracie Hollombe, is a book, or workbook if you prefer, designed to guide and encourage the aspiring songwriter toward achieving the goal of acquiring his or her first cut. You can also visit the authors' website at www.YourFirstCut.com.

The Berklee School of Music has published many of their guides and exercise books, such as Pat Pattison's *Songwriting: Essential Guide to Lyric Form and Structure: Tools and Techniques for Writing Better Lyrics* (Berklee Press, 1991) and *Songwriting: Essential Guide to Rhyming: A Step-by-Step Guide to Better Rhyming and Lyrics* (Berklee Press, 1991), and Jack Perricone's *Melody in Songwriting: Tools and Techniques for Writing Hit Songs* (Berklee Press, 2000). Don't be put off by the long titles! These books, like this one, spend much more time on the crafting of music than you'll find in most songwriting books. They're definitely worth your time and attention.

If you're looking for more help on the music side of songwriting, you might want to start with Michael Miller's *The Complete Idiot's Guide to Music Theory* (Alpha Books, 2002) as well as his *The Complete Idiot's Guide to Music Composition* (Alpha Books, 2005). Both books work well together at explaining both the basics of music and the intricacies of melody and harmony.

And it's always great to get your advice directly from the songwriters themselves. Be sure to check out Paul Zollo's *Songwriters on Songwriting* (DaCapo Press, Fourth Edition, 2003). With over 50 interviews with songwriters you will immediately recognize (as well as a number you won't), this book will show you a lot about how each songwriter approaches his or her craft.

And this book will likely lead you directly to Jimmy Webb's *Tune Smith: Inside the Art of Songwriting* (Hyperion, 1999), which gives you an incredibly detailed and insightful look through the eyes of this legendary songwriter.

Organizations

Thanks to technology, many of the resources and organizations a songwriter might need can be found with just a click of the mouse. Here are a few you might find handy:

American Society of Composers, Authors, and Publishers
www.ascap.com
ASCAP is one of the three performing rights organizations (PROs), which are organizations that license music for performances and collect and distribute those performance royalties directly to their publisher and writer members. ASCAP is owned and operated by songwriters and composers.

Broadcast Music, Inc.
www.bmi.com
BMI, likewise, is another PRO. It is owned by the broadcasters.

SESAC
www.sesac.com
SESAC is the smallest of the three PROs. Founded in 1930, the name was originally an acronym for the Society of European Stage Authors and Composers, but the original name was dropped and technically "SESAC" no longer serves as an acronym. Unlike ASCAP and BMI, SESAC is a private business and selects its membership.

Harry Fox Agency
www.harryfox.com/
Established in 1927 by the National Music Publisher's Association (NMPA), the Harry Fox Agency is an organization that for a fee handles licensing of copyrights and collection of the mechanical royalties for those licenses for publishers.

Library of Congress Copyright Office
www.copyright.gov
This is where you go to copyright your songs to ensure protection to the fullest extent of the law. You can also read up on the latest copyright laws as well as search through copyright records.

Nashville Songwriters Association International
nashvillesongwriters.com
NSAI is a 501(c) 6 not-for-profit trade association that offers a variety of services to professional and aspiring songwriters, including efforts as a legislative advocacy group on behalf of songwriters' right to be paid, to be taxed fairly, to be recognized, and to protect the future of the profession of songwriting. NSAI teaches writers the "craft" of writing, offers mail-in song critiques for a fee, and teaches writers about the music industry—how it works and how to position oneself and songs within the industry for the greatest possibility of achieving success.

National Association of Composers, USA
www.music-usa.org/nacusa
NACUSA is a nonprofit organization devoted to the promotion and performance of American concert hall music.

National Music Publishers Association
www.nmpa.org/home/index.asp
The largest music publishing trade association in the United States, the NMPA serves to protect, promote, and advance the interest of music publishers. They also own and operate the Harry Fox Agency.

Recording Industry Association of America
www.riaa.com
The RIAA's mission is to protect the intellectual property of songwriters, artists, and music labels. It also certifies recordings as gold, platinum, and so on.

Rightsflow

rightsflow.com

Rightsflow is a provider of a mechanical licensing and royalty payment technology platform for online music services, record companies, distributors, and artists. As new methods of consuming music keep emerging, Rightsflow is working to solve the complex issues of copyright compliance and royalty payment from online sources.

Songwriters Guild of America

www.songwritersguild.com

Originally formed in 1931 as the Songwriters Protective Association (SPA) by three of the leading songwriters of that time (Edgar Leslie, George Meyer, and Billy Rose), the Songwriters Guild is a major advocate for songwriters' rights. The only organization exclusively for songwriters and their heirs, the SGA constantly works to ensure the protection of professional songwriters' earnings through legal and legislative initiatives and also serves the community at large with outreach programs to further educate songwriters and the American public in the art of songwriting and basic music skills. The SGA offers its members catalog administration, a royalty collection plan, estate planning, contract review, and a "single-song contract" that is the best available to songwriters.

SoundExchange

www.soundexchange.com

SoundExchange is a nonprofit performance-rights organization that collects statutory royalties from satellite radio, Internet radio, cable TV music channels, and similar platforms for streaming sound recordings. The Copyright Royalty Board, which is appointed by The U.S. Library of Congress, has entrusted SoundExchange as the sole entity in the United States to collect and distribute these digital performance royalties.

Networking and All-Around Help

www.MusicStartsHere.org

A virtual one-stop resource center for all things musical (who, what, when, where, why, and how) in Nashville, Tennessee.

NashvilleMuse.com

Music biz event listings (for Nashville, Tennessee), interviews, articles, and professional advice by Doak Turner. One of the best networking guides ever!

www.SongU.com

SongU.com provides online multilevel songwriting courses developed by award-winning songwriters, including song feedback, mentoring, one-on-one song coaching, co-writing, unscreened pitching opportunities, and more.

As a special offer, all readers of this book can receive a $20 discount on their first quarter at SongU.com. Visit www.SongU.com, click on the "Join" link at the top, and use promotional code CASEYKELLY when signing up as a new member.

The Songwriter's Network

www.thesongnet.org

SongNet is an online network of songwriters, musicians, artists, and industry professionals who support each other through various seminars, showcases, and other events.

Songwriter's Resource Network

www.songwritersresourcenetwork.com

SRN is an online resource network providing educational and networking opportunities to help songwriters.

TAXI

www.taxi.com

Think of TAXI as an independent online A&R department, designed to help songwriters (as well as artists) get access to people in the music business. They also can be a window to film and TV music placement.

Tracks and Fields

www.tracksandfields.com

Tracks and Fields connects musicians, producers, and the music industry to work on new projects. Artists from all over the world find the right people to write, produce, or remix music and collaborate online through dedicated tools.

Lyric Help

You can find more help than you imagine at www.rhymezone.com. There's a search engine that will find rhymes (organized by syllables, yet!), near-rhymes, words that sound similar, synonyms, and more.

Places Where You Can Share Your Music Online

There are many social networks on the Internet that specialize in bringing a songwriter or an artist's music to the general online public. They all offer similar services, but they also can differ in presentation and outreach. Check to see which might be best for your music. Here are a few to start with.

Merge FM

merge.fm

ReverbNation

www.reverbnation.com

SoundClick

www.soundclick.com

SoundCloud

soundcloud.com

Places Where You Sell Your Music Online

Bandcamp
bandcamp.com
Bandcamp is a commerce platform that lets artists sell their music and merchandise directly to their fans.

CDBaby
www.cdbaby.com
CDBaby is a digital music distributor that will sell your music on its own site as well as iTunes and Amazon MP3. They will also contract to duplicate members CDs.

TuneCore
www.tunecore.com
TuneCore is another digital music distribution site that, for a fee, places your music in online stores and subscription sites such as iTunes, Amazon MP3, emusic, and more.

Contracts and Paperwork

When you're doing business on your own, sometimes just having the right paperwork can be a hassle. The Internet does have a number of websites where you can download free contracts (just type "free downloadable music contracts" in your search engine), as well as many places where you can get contracts for a fee. The best single-song contract for songwriters is the one by the Songwriters Guild of America. Unless you've researched a contract "blank" fully and carefully, there's no way of knowing whether it's going to serve your purposes or not. The Library of Congress and the Copyright Office websites are the places to get copyright information and forms.

The book *This Business of Music* has most of the contracts you could ever need and if the edition you own is the latest, you'll be fairly safe referring to it as a reliable reference.

NOTE: Before you sign a contract offered by anyone else, or while selecting which forms you're going to use, it's best to have the advice of a music attorney.

Index